DIVIDING LINES

DIVIDING
LINES

How Transportation
Infrastructure Reinforces
Racial Inequality

DEBORAH N. ARCHER

 W. W. NORTON & COMPANY

Independent Publishers Since 1923

For information about permission to reproduce selections from this book, write to
Permissions, W. W. Norton & Company, Inc., 500 Fifth Avenue, New York, NY 10110

For information about special discounts for bulk purchases, please contact
W. W. Norton Special Sales at specialsales@wwnorton.com or 800-233-4830

Manufacturing by Lakeside Book Company
Book design by Chris Welch
Production manager: Lauren Abbate

Library of Congress Cataloging-in-Publication Data is available.

ISBN 978-1-324-09213-1

W. W. Norton & Company, Inc., 500 Fifth Avenue, New York, NY 10110
www.wwnorton.com

W. W. Norton & Company Ltd., 15 Carlisle Street, London W1D 3BS

10 9 8 7 6 5 4 3 2 1

The legacy of Jim Crow transportation is still with us. Even today, some of our transportation policies and practices destroy stable neighborhoods, isolate and segregate our citizens in deteriorating neighborhoods, and fail to provide access to jobs and economic growth centers.

—THE LATE CONGRESSMAN JOHN LEWIS

To my parents,

for believing in me before I believed in myself

Contents

Opposite: *The Black Bottom neighborhood in Detroit, Michigan, before and after the interstate.*

Introduction

The Other Side of the Tracks

We thought we were moving on up, leaving the relentless grind of the inner city for the land of opportunity: the suburbs. My family was finally going to live the American dream. Or so we thought.

I started life on the wrong side of the physical and metaphorical tracks in Hartford, Connecticut. It was not an easy place to grow up. My family experienced all the challenges that come with being trapped in a low-income neighborhood. I watched my parents marshal every resource they could to navigate a system built for them to fail. I watched them fight every day to provide their children the future they dreamed for us. They wanted us to thrive and to enjoy the kinds of opportunities that were never available to them. My father worked two jobs in different factories. My mother worked twelve-hour shifts, starting at 6:00 a.m. and ending at 6:00 p.m. Both had immigrated from Jamaica and graduated from segregated public high schools in Hartford.

Some of my earliest childhood memories include being bundled up every evening and driven to my grandparents' house in a Hartford suburb. My father would take me there during the short break between his jobs so that I would not have to wake up with the sun when my mother headed off to work. When he had a little extra money, we would stop by McDonald's for a treat on our way to my grandparents' house; to this day, I have a fondness for Filet-O-Fish sandwiches. Public transportation was not an option for shuttling me back and forth between Hartford and South Windsor. It was not easy for poor or struggling people to get out to the suburbs. And there were not enough hours in the day for my father to go back and forth between his jobs, our Hartford home, and my grandparents if he had to rely on the public transportation system, with its limited schedules and reach. So, my parents scraped together what they could to buy a used car and joined the many others driving daily on the streets and highways of greater Hartford.

We ultimately made our way out of our rough Hartford neighborhood. When I was in kindergarten, we moved from a multifamily home on Sterling Street to a tree-lined suburban community of modest one-family homes. The goal was to give my brother and me a chance for a better life by moving to a safer neighborhood with better schools. I was excited about the move because I wanted to ride my bike just like the kids on TV did—for long stretches with the wind blowing in my face. Between the dangerous people who often hung out on our block, the bumpy sidewalks, and the cars racing past our home and in and out of driveways, my parents had deemed Sterling Street unsafe for bike riding. So, I had been confined to riding up and down our own, very short driveway.

We were one of the first Black families to move into the suburban neighborhood, a fact that initially boosted my parents' feelings of pride in what they had accomplished. Moving gave us a sense of what opportunity looks like, and it brought us close enough to take advantage of it. I do not believe that I would be where I am today if my family had not managed to leave Hartford for the suburbs. But traversing the boundaries that separate communities of disadvantage from communities of opportunity is difficult, and too few families find a way to make the journey.

Place mattered deeply in my life, as it does for all of us. We often talk about "good neighborhoods" and "bad neighborhoods" as though they are natural and inevitable. But those distinctions do not happen organically. Our laws, policies, and practices make neighborhoods "good" or "bad," often by placing barriers between them. In moving us from a "bad" neighborhood to a "good" one, my parents faced substantial economic challenges. They also faced racial discrimination, both obvious and more subtle. They cannot count the number of homeowners and real estate agents who, without explanation, refused to even show them houses during their search. Sometimes they faced threats and intimidation. I vividly remember the day when we woke up to find "KKK" had been spray-painted on our house and car. It rocked my world—I was afraid to be in our home, to play in our yard, and to ride my bike through the neighborhood. My parents considered selling our house and moving us back to Hartford. That is how we normally think about exclusion and segregation: they refuse to sell you the house, they redline you out of resources and support, you cannot get a mortgage, or they try to scare you into leaving. Such barriers have been breathtakingly effective in this country for a very long time.

Yet for many people and communities, the boundaries are also physical. The phrase "the other side of the tracks" is often used to evoke a metaphorical distinction between communities. We often miss that across the United States there are physical "tracks"—actual railroad tracks as well as highways, roads, and the like—that serve as lines of demarcation, sorting and dividing communities. Depending on which side you live on, the "other side" might represent safety, good health, and access to opportunity. Or it could embody all the social and economic ills of racial segregation and concentrated poverty. These tracks do more than simply reflect preexisting racial and economic divisions in our society; they *create* and *reinforce* those divisions. Crafted across generations, these lines persist to this day, reflecting the marriage of racially discriminatory housing policies and the power of transportation infrastructure to divide, exclude, and destroy.

Where you live matters. Connecticut is a wealthy, politically progressive state that is also intensely segregated by race and class. It can thus stand in for much of American society. Racial segregation divides Connecticut between communities of opportunity and communities excluded from that opportunity; between communities where families are a part of the American Dream, and communities where that dream is perpetually denied.

My Hartford neighbors had limited access to healthy foods and effective health care. Good jobs—those that paid a living wage and offered retirement and health benefits and a pathway to the middle class—were hard to come by. Neighborhood kids attended racially and economically segregated schools. The air we breathed was often poisoned by factories, car exhaust, and more. We did not have access to the opportunities, capital, or networks that have been shown time and again to be essential for success.

Injustice and inequality were built into the very fabric of our neighbor-hood. The streets, highways, and sidewalks we traveled every day were fiendishly effective in keeping some people down while allowing others to thrive. My Hartford neighborhood was walled off by highways and encir-cled by major roads and railway tracks. Public transportation, as my father knew well, was limited and did not allow easy access to jobs and housing in the suburbs.

Two major highways run through Hartford, and they fundamentally transformed the city when they were built. Interstate 91 cut Hartford off from the Connecticut River, creating a concrete barrier along the eastern edge of the city and separating it from the surrounding, white suburbs. The construction of Interstate 84 destroyed hundreds of homes and razed historic buildings. The highway's eight lanes isolated the predominantly Black North End from the rest of the city.

These two highways intersected in the heart of downtown Hartford. They consumed the city's central business district, inhibited economic growth, and became a permanent barrier to pedestrian routes between the separated communities. The highways were layered on top of decades of redlining, discriminatory lending practices, and exclusionary zoning that had already helped deny the predominantly Black and Latino residents of Hartford access to the wealthy white suburbs and the opportunities there. The highways quite literally cemented racial exclusion.

Today, racial segregation and concentrated poverty in Connecticut endure. The highways, railroads, and roads that crisscross the region are like permanent scars. And each geographic barrier reinforces the harmful impact of the others. More than two-thirds of Connecticut's residents of color live in only 15 of its 169 municipalities. In Hartford, approximately one out of every three people lives in poverty, and many residents lack access to grocery stores, health care, and high-quality schools. And those people living in poverty are disproportionately, overwhelmingly, Black and Latino. The lines that separate us—the barriers between communities where opportunities are rampant and those where oppression is the norm—can often be traced to highways, railroads, roads, and other transportation fea-tures that seemingly made permanent the centuries of unequal treatment.

———

THE NATION'S TRANSPORTATION SYSTEM IS A MATERIAL MANIFESTATION of the structural racial inequality built into the foundations of this country. And as with the legal and social barriers that separate us, these physical barriers are not the unfortunate by-products of well-meaning bureaucrats who did not understand the impact of their choices. It is not a coincidence that the transportation infrastructure decisions of the twentieth century buttressed the racist decisions that came before them. Often, one set of choices was as deliberate as the other.

In many ways, these physical barriers are more effective than purely legal barriers, because as hard as it is to change a racist law or discriminatory social norm, it can be even harder to tear down a highway or reroute a subway line. As civil rights advocates forced changes to the law in the early and middle decades of the twentieth century, city planners could no longer rely on racial zoning laws, housing covenants, racial terror, and other tools of segregation to keep Black people "in their place." They needed barriers that were more durable, barriers that could not simply be overruled by a court or a legislature.

There is an irony here. Roads, highways, and public transportation investments have been instrumental in connecting far-flung communities to one another. The American economic engine, and the wealth and opportunity it has provided for generations, would not be possible without them. For many Americans, the open road is synonymous with freedom. But this nation's transportation infrastructure was never intended to provide those opportunities to everyone.

Sometimes, highways and roads were built with the express purpose of keeping people apart, to eviscerate communities that did not have the power to defend themselves. All infrastructure projects—such as a waste transfer station or an affordable housing development—bring associated costs. And public officials make choices that shape whether those costs are borne fairly and equally by all communities under their purview. From this fact arises the problem of NIMBY—or "Not in my backyard." All communities may reap the benefits of an infrastructure project, but few want to bear the burdens.

In the twentieth century, many city officials used transportation infrastructure to enforce white supremacy. It proved a powerful tool to ensure that some people and communities would benefit from economic investment while others would be starved for economic opportunity. Some would have views of the skyline, waterfront, or parks, while others had front row seats to traffic racing along the overpass. Which side you were on was far too often determined by race.

Many predominantly Black neighborhoods were systematically sequestered because they lacked the power to effectively fight back, or because they were perceived as having *too much* power. Sugar Hill in Los Angeles is one of many examples. Named after the legendary neighborhood in Harlem, Sugar Hill was the heart of cosmopolitan life for many affluent Black people in Los Angeles. They fought for their right to live in this community and won that right after white residents of the neighborhood unsuccessfully sued to enforce racially restrictive covenants. But their victory was short-lived. In the early 1960s, Sugar Hill was bisected by the new Santa Monica Freeway, with the government seizing homes through eminent domain and providing inadequate compensation. Government officials used the goal of "slum removal" as a pretext for their anti-Black agenda. At the time, it was reported that the freeway was routed through Sugar Hill in order to save the predominantly white fraternity and sorority row area around the University of Southern California.

The story told in this book is not about Connecticut or Sugar Hill, or about the South. It is a story about America. Racial oppression in this country is about place, on multiple levels. White supremacy depends on Black people knowing "their place" in the social hierarchy and staying there. It demands that Black people know and adhere to the constraints that it puts on their lives, and it enforces those limits, often brutally, when Black people resist. There is a famous photograph of an effigy strung up by the Ku Klux Klan in Miami, Florida, in 1940 with a sign pinned to its chest: "This Nigger Voted." The message was clear: Dare to stray from your preassigned role and face the consequences. But one of the most effective means that white supremacy has of ensuring that Black people know their place socially is to keep them in their place *physically*. What better way to let people know that their lives are limited—that they can never be who they want to be—than by penning them in, constraining their movement, determining where they can and cannot live, or work, or walk, or rest, or play.

In his writing, W. E. B. Du Bois often focused on what he called the color line, the role that race and racism play in dividing America. He understood the deep and reinforcing connections between race and space. In his 1903 classic *The Souls of Black Folk*, DuBois wrote that "usually in cities each street has its distinctive color, and only now and then do the colors meet in close proximity." Indeed, across the country there are streets more known for how they divide people by race rather than for how they connect. These are the physical manifestations of the color line. Such roads are ubiquitous, and yet we barely notice them.

In researching and writing this book, I wanted to understand how the nation's transportation system helped extend and create the exclusion of predominantly Black communities that may seem natural today. Of course, it is anything but. Defenders of the status quo often say that segregation is a product of millions of personal choices—that poor people made bad decisions, that Black people prefer to live near other Black people and white people prefer to live near other white people. Even when they acknowledge the prevalence of discrimination, they blame it on the actions of individual bad apples, shrugging their shoulders and bemoaning how difficult it is to change people's hearts and minds. In this view, segregation is inevitable, and no amount of government intervention can make a difference.

In fact, government has made all the difference. But as I show, we must expand our understanding of government-sponsored racism beyond racial covenants and redlining, which have been studied and written about in some of the most important books of our era. It is not just the invisible lines created by local, state, and federal law that divide us. It is also the physical, literal lines running through and around our communities—lines that may seem innocuous, or merely practical or necessary, but that are part of the architecture of systemic racism.

One of the primary contentions of this book is that transportation infrastructure is white supremacy by another means. After the outlawing of racial zoning laws and racial covenants by the Supreme Court's 1917 decision in *Buchanan v. Warley* and the 1948 decision in *Shelley v. Kraemer*, respectively, the forces opposed to integration and equality turned to other tactics. Those efforts kicked into high gear when the court signaled the fall of segregation in *Brown v. Board of Education*, decided in 1954. In the chapters that follow, I explore the role that transportation infrastructure and policy have played in racial segregation, isolation, and exclusion. The book is historical, reaching back to the early twentieth century, but it is also about patterns still evident today.

My focus is largely on Black communities. Although many groups have been harmed by highways and the like, and have stories to tell about the resulting devastation, Black people have had a unique experience. This fact stems from multiple causes: the distinctive historical relationship between Black people and transportation; the intentional racial discrimination that has driven transportation infrastructure development in Black communities; the layering of transportation infrastructure on top of decades of discriminatory housing laws, policies, and practices; and the stark second-class status of Black Americans that persists in American life to this day.

Set aside transportation: Black Americans have always had a fraught relationship with simple *mobility*. In a free society, the ability to move about unencumbered is fundamental. Facilitating and protecting that ability is one of the government's central functions. After all, what does it mean to be free if one cannot go where one chooses? The freedom to travel to buy what you need and sell what you make; the freedom to spend time with family and friends, to explore other places, and come home when you are done; and the freedom to gather with others in your community and make decisions together, to worship together, to celebrate together, and to protest together—and to do these things without interference or harassment—are at the heart of full citizenship.

While the freedom to move about with safety, autonomy, and dignity is taken for granted by many Americans, Black people in the United States have never fully enjoyed that right. The story of Black America begins with Africans being forcibly removed from their homes, taken across the ocean against their will, and having every aspect of their lives be under a "master's" control. From the moment Black people were forced to step foot in colonial America or the United States, they have had to overcome the barriers to their mobility that sustained their enslavement. In the antebellum South, Black mobility was criminal. Movement without permission posed an existential threat to white property rights and the established legal and social order, and confining Black people to plantations was key to the institution of slavery. Restricting Black movement was a core task of the slavers and the lawmakers they elected. Black people were confined to what historian Elizabeth Stordeur Pryor called "Black geographies": the spaces that reinforced their subjugation and servitude.

Although these obstacles were part of the condition and existence of slavery, new ones were created after Emancipation as Black people sought to move out of the spaces that had imprisoned them. Mobility means freedom. Therefore, under any form of racist order, Black mobility is suspicious and dangerous and must be curtailed with every available tool. The war on Black mobility that sustained enslavement would persist and shape the racial hierarchy that followed Emancipation.

That racial hierarchy was enforced through systems of economic oppression, such as sharecropping, that tied the formerly enslaved and their descendants to white-owned land while robbing them of the economic benefits of their labor. It was also supported by the criminal legal system, which worked to extract labor from Black people while keeping them physically confined. A new legal and social system arose to restrain Black people physically in order to constrain them socially and economically.

Highway developers and road builders have been essential contributors to this racial hierarchy. A central thread throughout this sorry history has been governments' willingness to use public goods—such as roads, highways, and public transportation that Black people have helped build and pay for—to further the private aims of white people. Government officials and private white citizens repeatedly worked together to keep Black people from exercising their freedom to travel. White people were empowered to police Black mobility for their own social and financial gain through racially discriminatory laws and via the support—sometimes tacit but often explicit—of public officials who gave public effect to private discrimination. In many respects, it was a symbiotic relationship: a partnership between government and white people. Black people were most affected but had little or no agency.

A great deal of the transportation infrastructure in this country was built to control Black mobility—physical, social, economic, and otherwise. This becomes manifest when we move from broad regional and national trends to the experience of specific communities.

THE OFFICIALS WHO BUILT THE INTERSTATE HIGHWAY SYSTEM, OUR ROADS and community grids, and our public transportation systems were often motivated explicitly by racism and placed little value on Black lives, Black families, and Black communities. Alfred Johnson, executive director of the American Association of State Highway Officials at the time the Interstate Highway Act was passed, recalled that "some city officials expressed the view in the mid-1950s that the urban Interstates would give them a good opportunity to get rid of the local 'niggertown.'" Their wish was granted.

The effects of "spatial racism"—the ways that racist policies and beliefs are enforced by the organization of physical space and who has access to that space—can be seen clearly in the Black Bottom neighborhood in Detroit, Michigan. Black Bottom was a thriving majority-Black community in downtown Detroit with a nationally renowned music scene. It was also home to Black luminaries such as the legendary boxer Joe Lewis, Detroit's first Black mayor Coleman Young, and Ralph Bunche, the first Black person to receive the Nobel Peace Prize. It was a middle-class community that Mayor Young once described as "a wonderfully versatile and self-contained society." Black Bottom began as an enclave for Eastern European Jews. In the early twentieth century, the population of Black Bottom began to shift from immigrant to migrant as Black people fleeing the brutality of the Jim Crow South as part of the Great Migration found economic opportunity in the city's auto factories. Black people were prohibited from living in other parts of Detroit by racially restrictive covenants, so the migrants settled in Black Bottom.

By the 1950s, Black Bottom was the center of Detroit's Black economic and social life. Yet, in the late 1950s and early 1960s, Black Bottom and neighboring Paradise Valley were demolished to make way for I-375,

Route 10, and other infrastructure projects. Tens of thousands of residents were exiled and forced to choose between high-rent properties they could not afford on the one hand, and high-rise public housing projects in deeply segregated and underserved neighborhoods on the other. Although city officials promised that new affordable housing would be built to replace the housing lost in Black Bottom, the resulting developments were neither affordable nor open to Black residents. Instead, many of the people who called Black Bottom home were given only thirty days to find a new residence. Black Bottom was destroyed by overlapping and compounding transportation infrastructure projects. Black history, homes, community, and wealth were destroyed along with it. Today there are plans to replace I-375 with surface-level boulevards and reconnect communities that were separated or eliminated. While this project would serve as a form of recompense, it can never bring back all that was lost.

Across the country, one can find traces of many communities like Black Bottom—that is to say, communities that simply do not exist anymore. Many other predominantly Black neighborhoods still exist but continue, like Hartford, to bear deep scars.

Those scars are not the result of highways alone. Choices made with regard to roads, street grids, sidewalks, and public transportation have and continue to have a deleterious effect on Black communities across the country. This book tells those stories, too. The chapters are organized along a loose chronology but also around different modes of transportation that have played a part in separating us. You may be surprised to learn about the significance of a sidewalk, or the lengths to which a mostly white community might go to prevent a new bus stop from being installed nearby to help the Black people already working in that community.

IF ONE OF THE PRIMARY CONTENTIONS OF THIS BOOK IS THAT TRANSPORTA-tion policy has been a painfully effective tool of white supremacy, especially as advances in civil rights laws made other strategies of white supremacy less effective, another is that the racialization of transportation infrastructure has revealed both the power and limits of those civil rights laws. These are the laws we see as among the greatest achievements of the civil rights movement, laws sometimes referred to as constituting a "second Reconstruction." Yet the nefarious genius in using highways, roads, public transportation, and pedestrian infrastructure to cement racial inequality was the belief, on the part of planners, that the exclusionary impact of transportation infrastructure would both outlast existing laws that facilitated racial exclusion and skirt possible future laws promoting integration. These predictions have proven to be largely correct.

The most famous was the Civil Rights Act of 1964, which broadly prohibited racial discrimination in areas ranging from employment to public accommodations and outlawed racial bias in programs that received federal funding. Another was the Fair Housing Act of 1968, which banned racial discrimination in the sale, rental, or provision of housing. Highway development was not central to these laws, which were adopted after most of the interstate highway system had already been constructed. But these laws could have been used to shape *subsequent* transportation choices. Unfortunately, the courts have robbed them of much of their potential to do so. Courts have largely interpreted these laws to apply only to discriminatory decisions *after* those decisions have been made. They place the burden of proof and enforcement on members of the community rather than on government agencies that typically have the resources and expertise to police those decisions more effectively. And the laws are applied against a legal backdrop that focuses on intentional racial discrimination by individual "bad actors" while ignoring systemic and structural inequality and decades of accumulated harm. Transportation infrastructure provides a unique vantage point into the limits of these laws—limits which are often obscured in other realms of American life.

Similarly, by the 1960s, rising concerns about the destructive impact of the interstate highway system led Congress to adopt targeted legislation to curtail some of the worst practices of state highway departments. These laws protected parks, historic districts, and other environmentally sensitive places and, significantly, required limited relocation assistance for people displaced by construction. However, curbing racial bias and advancing racial equity were not the main motivations behind these laws. Although these statutes required state departments to demonstrate more careful and coordinated planning, they fell far short of requiring racial equity. And they still do to this day.

I HAVE SPENT MY PROFESSIONAL LIFE AS A CIVIL RIGHTS LAWYER TRYING to force this country to live up to its promises. I have focused on advancing voting rights, opposing employment discrimination and the denial of economic opportunity, and promoting school integration and educational opportunity. Transportation justice had not been a part of my docket until 2019, when I was asked to help support activists in Syracuse, New York, who were attempting to ensure that racial justice was a central consideration as the state embarked on a project to rebuild Interstate 81. It was through this work that I began to truly understand the effects of transportation infrastructure—including on the shape of my own childhood in Hartford and its suburbs. Through this work I witnessed the labor of organizers who have stood with these communities over decades, fighting for their survival and prosperity; and through this work I have come to grasp the limits of our nation's civil rights laws' effects in defending those communities. Since 2019, I have been honored to join communities across the country as they fight for equity in transportation infrastructure.

Transportation is far more than a means of moving people back and forth. Transportation systems shape who is allowed to feel that they belong. They determine who enjoys access to the many opportunities that this country offers, who gets to live with safety and dignity, and conversely, who gets locked out and left behind. Transportation infrastructure is the infrastructure of equitable education. It is the infrastructure of good health and economic opportunity.

Transportation infrastructure is also basic to a vibrant democracy. You cannot tell the story of America's second Reconstruction without mentioning the 1954 Montgomery Bus Boycott, the Freedom Riders who tested the right to interstate travel, or the protesters who took to the streets across the Deep South, marching for the right to vote. Indeed, Dr. Martin Luther King Jr. and Rev. Ralph Abernathy, two of the founders of the Southern Christian Leadership Conference, originally wanted to name the organization the Southern Leadership Conference on Transportation and Nonviolent

Integration. Black freedom fighters have long fought for the right to equita-
bly use transportation, and they have long used transportation infrastructure as a platform to make their demands heard. They still do.

In 2020, protesters demanding an end to racialized police violence
after the murder of George Floyd took to the very highways and roads that
once destroyed their communities and continue to separate residents from
opportunity. They marched along one of the tools of their oppression to
demand justice. When Interstate 94 was built in St. Paul, Minnesota, in
the 1960s, it was routed directly through the Black, middle-class neighborhood of Rondo, which was St. Paul's largest Black community. I-94
destroyed more than three hundred businesses and the homes of about
six hundred families. It deepened racial segregation and inequality in the
region. In June 2020, thousands of protesters occupied I-94 in St. Paul.
In September of that year, protesters demanding justice for Breonna Taylor, a twenty-six-year-old emergency medical technician who was killed
by police as she slept in her Kentucky home, again marched on I-94. Just
four years earlier, in July 2016, people grieving after the killing of Philando
Castile—a thirty-two-year-old school cafeteria worker shot by a St. Paul
police officer in front of his girlfriend and her four-year-old daughter—had
shut down portions of I-94.

Across the country in 2020, Black people and other advocates protesting Floyd's murder and the broader web of anti-Black racism did the same.
In Little Rock, Arkansas, protesters marched down I-630, a highway that
had displaced large segments of Little Rock's established Black community and helped cut the city in two. In Memphis, Tennessee, protesters
took to I-40, a highway that had eliminated hundreds of Black homes and
Black businesses. And, in Cincinnati, Ohio, protesters stood on I-75, which
decades earlier had flattened the predominantly Black West End neighborhood. It was no coincidence that people were using highways to tell the
world to stop, listen, and understand.

ACHIEVING TRANSPORTATION JUSTICE WILL NOT BE EASY. BUT THERE ARE
reasons for hope. Nothing, not even a road, is truly permanent. Segments
of the interstate highway system built in the 1950s and 1960s are either

past or approaching the end of their useful lives. Many such segments are surrounded by predominantly Black communities that are still fighting to overcome the harm caused by the highways when they were originally built. In 2021, President Joe Biden and members of his administration promised to ensure that new infrastructure projects funded with federal dollars would explicitly adopt the goal of promoting racial equity in transportation and work to redress the harms of past projects. The Biden administration's commitment to a new approach to highway development was the culmination of decades of advocacy by communities who repeatedly find themselves facing the wrecking ball. Since the 1960s, the so-called "highway revolts" have brought together environmentalists, preservationists, and supporters of public transportation in an off-and-on alliance with racial justice advocates to change the future of our transportation infrastructure.

However, despite this ostensible progress, the new approach shows just how much it will take to overcome the past. Even with new protections in place, Black communities are still sometimes viewed as the path of least resistance. Also, it takes time for complex new infrastructure projects to get off the ground. There is the risk that a different set of lawmakers at the federal level could undo the work of the Biden administration; the possibility that government officials will once again achieve progress for some on the backs of others remains acute. How do we break the link between transportation and racial inequality? The final chapter of this book suggests how we might begin to do so.

A shift in national policy, including reimagining how we use transportation and infrastructure to serve and support communities of color, is a critical step in reversing the historical exclusion of Black Americans. I hope this book provides deeper understanding of how we got here and shines a light on how we can move forward.

Chapter 1

Killing Two Birds with One Stone

Dwight D. Eisenhower interstate highway system sign.

The law that would transform the country had a quiet start. Just two years after the United States Supreme Court's decision in *Brown v. Board of Education of Topeka, Kansas*, and just two months after over one hundred United States senators and representatives signed the Southern Manifesto pledging to defend racial segregation by all available legal means, Congress passed the Federal-Aid Highway Act of 1956, often referred to as the Interstate Highway Act. During the final days of debate around the law, President Dwight Eisenhower had been in Walter Reed Army Hospital recovering from an intestinal ailment. On June 29, 1956, at Walter Reed, and without ceremony or fanfare, President Eisenhower signed the law that would become the defining achievement of his administration.

The seeds for the Interstate Highway Act were planted long before 1956. In 1919, then Lieutenant Colonel Eisenhower was assigned as an observer to the First Transcontinental Motor Convoy, a road test for military vehicles intended to identify the challenges of moving troops from coast to coast. The Convoy traveled 3,200 miles from Washington, DC, to San Francisco. Eisenhower was appalled at what the convoy encountered: unpaved paths, narrow roadways, and aged bridges. Eisenhower would go on to become one of the architects of the defeat of Nazi Germany during World War II. General Eisenhower took note of the autobahns, the vast highway system that the Allied armies used to travel in Germany. One of Eisenhower's top priorities upon becoming president was to secure legislation for an interstate highway system that would rival Germany's.

The legislation came together in the shadow of another watershed event: *Brown v. Board of Education*. On May 17, 1954, the United States Supreme Court unanimously overturned its ruling in *Plessy v. Ferguson*, the legal foundation for Jim Crow. On June 7, 1892, Homer Plessy purchased a first-class ticket from New Orleans to Covington, Louisiana. Plessy was one-eighth Black. Other than his great-grandmother, his relatives were white, and he had very fair skin. But he was Black under Louisiana law. He took a seat in the white car and refused to move to the area of the train designated for Black people when ordered by a conductor. He was arrested and convicted of violating Lousiana's Separate Car Act. The case made its way to the Supreme Court. On May 18, 1896, in a seven-to-one decision, the court ruled that laws mandating separate accommodations on public transportation did not violate the Constitution. Justice Henry Billings Brown, writing on behalf of the court, found "the underlying fallacy of the plaintiff's argument to consist in the assumption that the enforced separation of the two races stamps the colored race with a badge of inferiority." "If this be so," Justice Brown wrote, "it is not by reason of anything found in the act, but solely because the colored race chooses to put that construction upon it." The "separate but equal" doctrine that resulted from Homer Plessy's unsuccessful attempt to challenge racial segregation in public transportation went on to infect all aspects of public life in America.

After the ruling in *Plessy*, railroad operators from Maryland to Florida were required to provide separate cars for white passengers and passengers of color. *Plessy* not only provided legal and moral cover for racial segregation on trains and buses, but in all public accommodations. In *Plessy*'s wake, Jim Crow laws flourished, across the South and in many other parts of the country, too. Communities created segregated spaces for white people and Black people at pools and theaters, in restaurants and schools, restrooms and hospitals, cemeteries and courtrooms. The decision helped to solidify Jim Crow and usher in a world in which white people and Black people lived separately, learned separately, traveled separately, and socialized separately.

In Georgia, Jim Crow laws mandated that no Black person could be buried in a cemetery reserved for white people and that no Black barbers could style the hair of white women or girls. It was not enough to keep Black and white people on separate sports teams: Georgia passed a law making it "unlawful for any amateur white baseball team to play baseball on any vacant lot or baseball diamond within two blocks of a playground devoted to the Negro race." "Separate but equal" dictated, at the same time, that it was also "unlawful for any amateur colored baseball team to play baseball in any vacant lot or baseball diamond within two blocks of any playground devoted to the white race."

Of course, segregation extended to more serious pursuits than sports and haircuts. In Alabama, it was unlawful to require white nurses to provide care to Black male patients or to even work in a hospital where Black men were cared for. In Mississippi, hospitals were required to have separate entrances for white and Black patients and visitors. Indeed, across the South, many Black patients died or were denied care because nearby hospitals only treated white people or because there were no "Negro beds" available. Equality may have been nominally part of such laws, but in practice, it was never the actual result.

Plessy, and the Jim Crow regime it legitimized, not only set the rules and parameters of daily life throughout the South; they dictated the framework that advocates for racial equality used in the early days of the modern civil rights movement in the 1940s. *Plessy* defined constitutional equality in a way that led civil rights advocates to accept the separate and engage in a constant fight for the equal. Much post-*Plessy* litigation attempted to take *Plessy* seriously. Advocates did not yet challenge the decision head-on; instead, they demanded that Black communities actually receive the same quality of services as white communities. So rather than challenge separate hospitals, civil rights advocates fought for equal hospital facilities, equipment, and staff. Rather than challenge separate libraries and recreational facilities, civil rights advocates fought for more and up-to-date books, and better and safer buildings.

Brown, too, had a ripple effect and ultimately triggered a seismic shift in the country's racially segregated landscape. It would also lead to sweeping changes in how people in the United States fought for, or against, racial equality. In *Brown*, the Supreme Court declared that racially segregated schools violated the Constitution. Under our constitutional regime, separate could never be equal. With the Supreme Court's rejection of *Plessy* and the legal basis for America's racial caste system, many were optimistic that other pillars of racial inequality would soon fall beside it. For civil rights lawyers and activists, *Brown* provided the legal and moral framework to galvanize support for efforts to desegregate housing and other public accommodations.

While millions celebrated the *Brown* decision, to millions of others it was akin to a declaration of war—an attack on their way of life, their power, and their privilege. The decision threatened racial segregation writ large and the ability of the government to label Black people with badges of inferiority. *Brown* outraged much of white America and led many to make a fierce recommitment to segregation. Segregationist public officials vowed to protect racial segregation with every tool available to them.

Elected officials in the South were vociferous in their denunciations of *Brown*. James Eastland, a powerful senator from Mississippi, declared that "the South [would] not abide by nor obey" the *Brown* decision. Senator Harry Byrd of Virginia called *Brown* "the most serious blow that has yet been struck against the rights of the states in a matter vitally affecting their authority and welfare." As he said: "If we can organize the Southern States for massive resistance to this order, I think that, in time, the rest of the country will realize that racial integration is not going to be accepted in the South."

White people throughout the South responded to their elected leaders' calls for massive resistance to *Brown*. White citizens harassed, threatened, and beat Black families who tried to exercise their rights. Plaintiffs who brought lawsuits to enforce *Brown* received death threats and suffered physical and economic reprisals. People lost their jobs, their sense of safety, and sometimes their lives. White parents sickened by the image of their children sitting in a classroom next to Black children organized private, whites-only academies, often using public funds to do so until that practice was challenged in court.

Government officials resorted to drastic measures to fend off integration, demonstrating the extreme lengths they would go to and the profound sacrifices they would demand in order to resist change. Prince Edward County, Virginia, closed its entire public school system rather than integrate. The schools remained closed for the next five years. Similarly, just as court orders requiring integration in Norfolk, Charlottesville, and Warren County, Virginia, were set to be enforced, state officials closed the schools. After the Virginia Supreme Court overturned the school-closure law, the Virginia General Assembly made school attendance optional.

Orval Faubus, governor of Arkansas, infamously promised that "blood will run in the streets if Negro pupils should attempt to enter Central High School." He backed up that promise with action, deploying the Arkansas National Guard to block nine Black children from entering Central High School on the first day of school on September 2, 1957. Eventually, President Eisenhower called in the National Guard and sent 1,000 paratroopers to escort these children to school and enforce integration. The troops remained in Little Rock for the rest of the school year. Following their withdrawal, Governor Faubus closed all of Little Rock's high schools.

The November 1954 midterm elections brought Strom Thurmond, the 103rd governor of South Carolina, to the United States Senate. Thurmond would become one of the staunchest opponents of civil rights legislation. He won notoriety for conducting the longest filibuster ever by a lone senator—twenty-four hours and eighteen minutes—in opposition to the Civil Rights Act of 1957, which expanded federal supervision of integration in southern states. In one campaign speech during his third-party 1948 presidential campaign, Thurmond had declared: "I wanna tell you, ladies and gentlemen, that there's not enough troops in the army to force the Southern people to break down segregation and admit the Negro race into our theaters, into our swimming pools, into our homes, and into our churches." He felt no differently about integrating public schools.

In February and March 1956, more than one hundred United States senators and representatives from southern states drafted the Declaration of Constitutional Principles, known informally as the Southern Manifesto. Thurmond wrote the first draft. Although other senators worked behind the scenes to tone down his rhetoric, the final version asserted that the *Brown* decision was "a clear abuse of judicial power" and promised to use "all lawful means to bring about a reversal of this decision." The Southern Manifesto also defended the legality of segregation and opposed any integration in public places. It was introduced in Congress on March 12,

1956, by Representative Howard Smith of Virginia. Following his speech, several members of the House applauded, but not a single one rose to speak against it.

The Southern Manifesto was presented in both the Senate and the House, inserted into the Congressional Record, and was the focus of a national publicity campaign. The signatories—all from former Confederate states—included the entire congressional delegations of Alabama, Arkansas, Georgia, Louisiana, Mississippi, South Carolina, and Virginia, as well as most of the Florida and North Carolina delegations. The Southern Manifesto helped to further convince the region that *Brown* was a violation of their rights and an existential threat to their way of life.

It was the very effectiveness of the modern civil rights movement—of which *Brown* was a critical milestone—that inspired such committed resistance by southern whites. Indeed, the Southern Manifesto was written during the Montgomery Bus Boycott, which was triggered by Rosa Parks's arrest for refusing to yield her seat to a white passenger. That protest would introduce the world to the Rev. Dr. Martin Luther King Jr. It remains perhaps the paradigmatic example of the reality that transportation was and is at the heart of Black Americans' demands for justice and the right to live their lives with dignity. By the time congressional hearings on the Federal-Aid Highway Act of 1956 began, the modern civil rights movement, as well as the massive prosegregation resistance that it inspired in reaction to it, were both in full swing.

THE NEW LAW LAUNCHED WHAT WAS THEN THE LARGEST PUBLIC WORKS program in the history of the world. It allocated approximately $25 billion to construct a 41,000-mile network of interstate highways that would span the country and link metropolitan areas. The new system of highways would alleviate congestion and make coast-to-coast travel easier and safer. Although the federal government picked up 90 percent of the tab, leaving states to kick in only the final 10 percent, the states would maintain control over construction of the highways.

The newly built highways facilitated the flight of white Americans to the growing suburbs and the development of largely whites-only communities. They would also restructure the urban communities those new suburbanites left behind. The interstate highway system was not built on a blank slate; its spurs were routed through existing neighborhoods. In 2017, the United States Department of Transportation estimated that more than 475,000 households and more than a million people were displaced nationwide as a direct result of the original construction of the highways. Millions more were left living in hollowed-out communities after the bulldozers finished their work. The neighborhoods that were destroyed, the families that were forced to move, and the communities that were physically quarantined, were overwhelmingly Black and poor. So, just as the interstate highway system facilitated the development of white suburbs, it also drove the physical and economic destruction of Black communities.

The nation's interstate highway system's routes were adjusted, finalized, and ultimately built against the backdrop of *Brown*'s promise of racial equality. But they were also built against the backdrop of the massive resistance to integration that *Brown* inspired. The highway system could have been constructed in a way that furthered the promise of *Brown*. Instead, it became an essential element of the resegregationist agenda. Just as the laws and norms that provided the legal and intellectual basis for segregation were falling to the civil rights movement, the Interstate Highway Act presented many governors, mayors, and city planners with a means of fighting back.

In the event, a disproportionate number of highways displaced Black people, were built through Black communities, or were constructed in ways that isolated those communities from other neighborhoods, entrenching racial inequality and protecting "white spaces" and privilege. The physical boundaries they created would withstand the adoption and evolution of civil rights laws that followed the decision in *Brown*. Segregationists may have had to comply with new civil rights laws, but the highways became a new body of "laws" unto themselves.

IN THE YEARS LEADING UP TO THE PASSAGE OF THE INTERSTATE HIGHWAY Act, from Congress to state houses and local communities, talk about race, segregation, and inequality was never far from the surface of public discourse. Although the congressional debate on the Act steered clear of explicit discussions about race, behind the scenes, government officials and power brokers talked about how to use highways as a means of removal and as a wall to shield white communities from Black migration.

A notable precursor to such discussions—and a window into how the federal government thought about race across this era—was the Federal Housing Administration's *Underwriting Manual: The Underwriting and Valuation Procedure Under Title II of the National Housing Act*, published in 1936. It includes the policies and regulations that Federal Housing Administration (FHA) staff were to use in determining the eligibility of nonfarm mortgages for insurance under Title II of the National Housing Act. Ultimately, the Manual provided guidance on how to assess mortgage risk. One of the primary factors in assessing mortgage risk was race—the race of the borrower, the racial makeup of the community in which the house was located, and the racial makeup of the nearby communities. The Manual encouraged valuators to investigate not only the community in which the property was located, but the surrounding area as well "to determine whether or not incompatible racial and social groups are present." It further advised the valuator to make "an intelligent prediction" regarding "the possibility or probability of the location being invaded by such groups." It went on to opine that "If a neighborhood is to retain stability it is necessary that properties shall continue to be occupied by the same social and racial classes. A change in social or racial occupancy generally contributes to instability and a decline in values."

To help valuators guard against the risk of insuring a home in a community that might later be "invaded" by Black people, the Manual advised that aggressively enforced deed restrictions that limited occupancy to "the race for which they were intended," coupled with racial zoning laws that limited the neighborhoods in which people of color could live, could effectively protect the value of homes.

The Manual also recognized the power of physical barriers in maintaining racial segregation and the value of white-owned property. In a section titled "Protection from Adverse Influences," it counseled that "natural or artificially established barriers will prove effective in protecting a neighborhood and locations within it from adverse influences. Usually, the protection from adverse influences afforded by these means includes prevention of the infiltration of businesses and industrial uses, lower class occupancy, and inharmonious racial groups." The Manual highlighted how the presence of highways and roadways could be particularly useful in this assessment, suggesting that "a high speed traffic artery or a wide street parkway may prevent the expansion of inharmonious uses to a location on the opposite side of the street."

The FHA was not alone in recognizing the potential of highways to block Black migration to historically white communities. In 1945, Joseph Barnett, the chief of the Urban Road Division of the Bureau of Public Roads, presented an article at the annual meeting of the Highway Division of the American Society of Civil Engineers, titled *Express Highway Planning in Metropolitan Areas*. Harkening back to the FHA's underwriting manual, he recommended that highways passing through the central business district be located to function as "the divider between neighborhoods or between a neighborhood and an area of a different type."

A decade later, in the early post-*Brown* era, many local, state, and federal highway builders now hid their intent behind nominally race-neutral criteria. Chief among them was the language of urban renewal—the promise to clear "blighted" areas and "slums." The terms "blight" and "slums" had no fixed meaning yet were incredibly effective instruments of power, best understood not for what they meant, but for what they could do.

The idea of urban renewal, and the economic investment it would bring, was deployed first to build support for the highways and then to justify the widespread destruction of Black-owned homes and Black communities. In theory, urban renewal is the process by which the government works to improve neighborhoods by seizing and demolishing decaying private and public property and building new and improved buildings in their stead, including affordable housing. In his 1949 State of the Union address, President Harry S. Truman called on Congress to enact legislation that would create "low-rent public housing" and speed up the process of "slum clearance." Congress would pass the Housing Act of 1949, which funded urban renewal through a grant and loan program administered by the Department of Housing and Urban Development (HUD) and promised to dramatically increase the availability of affordable housing by replacing slums with new housing. The Act effectively spread urban renewal across the country. As with the Highway Act some years later, the federal government would foot the bill while state and local governments retained almost complete control over how and where the funds were deployed.

In practice, the Act funded the destruction of more affordable housing units than were ever built. During the 1950s and 1960s, nearly "ninety percent of low-income housing destroyed by urban renewal was not replaced." Indeed, urban renewal funds were frequently used to attract commercial development: cities would demolish aging homes and replace them with high-end housing, hotels, and retail. The federal government essentially empowered local governments and private companies to develop downtown neighborhoods and disproportionately displace the mostly poor residents of color who lived there. From 1949 to 1973, 2,532 urban renewal projects were carried out in 992 cities around the country. These projects displaced a total of one million people, two-thirds of them Black. At a time when Black people were only 12 percent of the population in the United States, they were five times more likely than others to be displaced by urban renewal.

Although race-neutral on the surface, urban renewal was infused with racial thinking. It was no secret that "blighted neighborhoods" and "slums" were euphemisms for Black neighborhoods—especially not to residents of such neighborhoods. A popular phrase used by people and organizations protesting the displacement was "urban renewal means Negro removal." In the summer of 1963, James Baldwin gave an interview in which he spoke to the emotional experience of confronting policies of mass dislocation and demolition, and the consequences for feelings of belonging, citizenship, and agency. He said: "A boy last week, he was sixteen, in San Francisco, told me on television . . . he said 'I've got no country, I've got no flag' . . . and I couldn't say 'You do,' I don't have any evidence to prove he does. . . . They were tearing down his house, because San Francisco is engaging—as most as all Northern cities now are engaged—in something called urban renewal, which means moving the Negroes out. It means

Negro removal, that is what it means! And the federal government is an accomplice to this fact! Now this … we are talking about human beings, there is not such a thing as a monolithic wall or some abstraction called 'Negro Problem,' these are Negro boys and girls who at sixteen and seventeen don't believe the country means anything it says and don't believe they have a place here, on the basis of the performance of the entire country."

"Blight" was also used to describe the impact that predominantly Black communities could have on white neighborhoods, if those Black neighborhoods were not somehow kept in check. Blight was likened to a cancer that would spread from poor minority districts and infect the surrounding communities if not removed. With federal money in hand, municipalities turned to eminent domain—the right of the government or its agents to expropriate private property for public use. Eminent domain was used to seize the homes of poor people of color with little payment and no relocation assistance, all in the name of urban renewal. And all of this was done with the approval of the United States Supreme Court. In 1954, shortly after their decision in *Brown*, the Supreme Court decided *Berman v. Parker*, another landmark case, though lesser known today. It sanctioned urban renewal and eminent domain in Southwest Washington, DC, and ultimately, around the country. Southwest Washington, DC, was part of Pierre L'Enfant's original plans for the city and was home to some of its oldest buildings. While people outside of the community might have seen nothing but deteriorating buildings, the area was a vibrant community. In fact, prior to the start of urban renewal, Southwest DC was home to a thriving commercial district with department stores, boutiques, grocery stores, and a movie theater. Wealthy Black people called it home and lived in large, ornate houses that were the envy of many others, of any race, across the city.

Southwest DC was also where many of the city's poorest Black residents lived, crushed by the weight of segregation and racial oppression. Their homes were not the kind that most white residents of Washington, DC, found attractive. More than half had outside toilets, and almost 30 percent had no electricity. The businesses located in the community were not often visited by white patrons. But the homes and businesses mattered to the thousands who called Southwest DC home. In the name of urban renewal, virtually all of the mostly Black, low-income homeowners, tenants, and businesses were evicted. Parks were destroyed, businesses were shuttered, and streets were torn up so that the federal government could rebuild.

The feared destruction of the Black community of Southwest Washington, DC, in the name of urban renewal was at the heart of the Supreme Court's decision in *Berman*. That decision upheld the use of eminent domain to displace individuals and whole communities for urban renewal projects in order to maintain "desired housing standards." The plaintiff in the case was Max Morris, the owner of a successful department store in Southwest DC. Although his store was not labeled as blighted, it was still slated to be taken via eminent domain under the authority of the District of Columbia Redevelopment Act. Morris objected to his private business being taken by the government and given to private redevelopers for private use. In his complaint, Morris asserted that the government could not constitutionally "tak[e] from one businessman for the benefit of another businessman." He insisted that the government's intervening to increase the wealth of one man by taking the wealth of another was unconstitutional. The Supreme Court disagreed.

In his majority opinion, Justice William O. Douglas acknowledged that the population of the urban renewal district at issue was 97.5 percent Black. But he and his fellow justices saw no significance in that fact. The court unanimously held that the Takings Clause of the United States Constitution allowed private property to be seized for public purposes. It did not matter that Southwest DC was home to many people, because those in power viewed the homes as a cancer, liable to infect the communities that surrounded it. The language the court used is astonishing to read today:

> Miserable and disreputable housing conditions may do more than spread disease and crime and immorality. They may also suffocate the spirit by reducing the people who live there to the status of cattle. They may indeed make living an almost insufferable burden. They may also be an ugly sore, a blight on the community which robs it of charm which makes it a place from which men turn. The misery of housing may despoil a community as an open sewer may ruin a river.

The court ruled that the legislature had immense power "to determine that the community should be beautiful as well as healthy, spacious as well as clean, well balanced as well as carefully patrolled." In pursuit of this purpose, not only could the government condemn the buildings—homes, community institutions, parks, and private businesses—but it had authority to take complete title to the land with "just compensation."

Before urban renewal came to Southwest Washington, DC, 70 percent of its residents were Black. After the predominantly Black sections of the community were carved out and removed, 70 percent were white. Highway development followed a similar pattern. Transportation infrastructure worked in tandem with urban renewal to restructure the country's physical landscape. Even well before the passage of the Interstate Highway Act, business and political leaders around the country had touted highways as a powerful weapon for clearing slums and aging neighborhoods. Over the next decades, highway builders often appropriated the language of urban renewal to gain support for targeting and removing low-income communities of color that officials considered "undesirable," whether or not those communities were actually in designated urban renewal areas. Highway engineers came to speak of "killing two birds with one stone": they could improve traffic conditions while simultaneously removing Black communities. The 1956 Act was in some senses the culmination of this ethos, not the beginning of it.

In 1938, nearly two decades before the adoption of the Interstate Highway Act, the federal government began exploring the creation and funding of an interstate highway system. Secretary of Agriculture Henry Wallace, who would soon be vice president—and who is remembered as a staunch left-winger—argued that highways should be routed through central cities to further "the elimination of unsightly and unsanitary districts."

Those early discussions resulted in a bill, the Federal-Aid Highway Act of 1938, that directed the Bureau of Public Roads, the predecessor of the Federal Highway Administration, to study the feasibility of creating an interstate highway system and to submit its findings to Congress. In 1939, the Bureau published a report called *Toll Roads and Free Roads*, urging public officials to avoid any further delays in the expansion of the highway system, specifically because the automobile had made the migration of white residents to the suburbs possible. Those white residents' former homes were now "occupied by the humblest citizens, they fringe the business district, and form the city's slums—a blight near its very core!"

In 1941, President Roosevelt appointed the National Interregional Highway Committee to evaluate the possibility of building a national highway system headed by the federal commissioner of public roads, Thomas H. MacDonald. Roosevelt warned those exploring the various possibilities to keep the planned routes "fluid" to keep the price of rights of way low. Roosevelt believed that "it hardly seems fair that the hazard of an engineering survey should greatly enrich one man." "After all," he said, "why should the hazard of engineering give one private citizen an enormous profit? If there is to be an unearned profit, why should it not accrue to the Government—State or Federal, or both?"

In 1944, the Committee issued its report to Congress, entitled *Interregional Highways*, touting the potential of highway construction through blighted areas. Highways would allow the government to clear those areas and "employ its powers of eminent domain in the public interest." In a section titled "Locating the Interregional Routes in Urban Areas," *Interregional Highways* predicted that blighted areas surrounding slums would themselves become slums if they were not replaced by highways. The report said these areas were of "a very low order of development—neighborhoods of cheap, run-down houses and shacks, abject poverty, squalor, and filth." The report concluded that locating city-entering routes through these communities would not only improve the flow of traffic, but also help the "eradication of a long-standing eyesore and blight upon the city's attractiveness and health."

Officials at the state and local levels frequently embraced the segregative potential of highways as they planned for the new construction. For example, the Cleveland City Planning Commission began mapping out the city's freeway routes in anticipation of the availability of public funds to build highways. In 1950, the Commission included the proposed freeway routes in its city plan, which it called *Cleveland Today . . . Tomorrow: The General Plan of Cleveland*. The plan touted the potential of highways to "check blight and prevent the spread of slums." Echoing some of the racist tropes often used to describe Black communities, the report described the targeted communities as unhealthy slums that "breed crime and delinquency—and all of us pay the resulting police, court, and prison costs."

But it was Thomas H. MacDonald and another bureaucrat, Robert Moses, who most effectively popularized the idea of linking the building of inner-city expressways to the destruction of urban housing, and they embarked on a campaign to spread their vision across the country. Mac-Donald was the public roads commissioner who led the committee that issued the *Interregional Highways* report. In a 1947 article, he conceded that while a lot of property would need to be destroyed to clear space for the highways, "In most instances, routes selected for expressways, as they approach the center of the city, pass through 'blighted' sections where property values are low, and most of the buildings are of the type that should be torn down in any case, to rid the city of its slums."

Moses was an influential New York public official who shaped urban development and public works projects both in that state and around the country. Moses was also a bigot. He believed that infrastructure projects like highways could not only be used to clear blight and slums, but that those same highways could also provide semi-permanent physical barriers to keep people of color separate from white communities, ensuring that the blight that they produced would never harm white communities again. Moses built New York's parks, roads, and highways in ways that put his racism on full display. He built Lincoln Center for the Performing Arts in a densely populated urban area known as San Juan Hill, displacing almost 7,000 mostly Black and Latino residents and 800 businesses. He built the Cross Bronx Expressway through a vibrant, low-income community in the Bronx, destroying one of the country's most integrated neighborhoods—Black, Puerto Rican, Jewish, Irish, and Italian—without remorse. According-ing to one, perhaps apocryphal, story, Moses instructed highway engineers to build the bridges across the new Southern State Parkway with one foot less clearance than bridges on the Hutchinson, Saw Mill, and Bronx River Parkways. The bridges were thus too low for buses coming from New York

City to pass under. Moses believed that Black and Puerto Rican New Yorkers would most likely use buses to access the beach. As a result, the low clearance on the Southern State would force buses to use local roads to access the beach, making the trips "discouragingly long and arduous." Moses could not legally prevent people of color from using the beach, but he could make it extremely difficult for them to do so.

Today, many historians question the authenticity of this story. Whether true or not, it is told and retold because it represents the more documented history of Moses's intentions. It remains a revealing anecdote about how transportation infrastructure has been used to force segregation when other tools were failing, both by Moses and his acolytes. Moses became a leading advocate for displacing Black communities to build the highway system, and his ideas were widely adopted around the country.

In a 1954 statement to the President's Advisory Committee on a National Highway Program, Moses argued that new urban expressways "must go right through cities and not around them if they were to accomplish their purpose" of removing unwanted communities. And, in 1956, just as the country was launching the construction of the interstate highway system, Moses published an essay in *Harper's Magazine* where he predicted that "this new highway program will affect our entire economic and social structure. The appearance of the new arteries and their adjacent areas will leave a permanent imprint on our communities and people. They will constitute the framework within which we must live." He was right: Black communities around the country still bear that imprint.

BY THE 1960S, BLACK ADVOCATES AND ORGANIZERS SAW THE URBAN renewal MacDonald and Moses promised for what it was: building "white men's roads through Black men's homes." This became the rallying cry for some communities fighting against their own displacement. In states across the country, highway builders went out of their way to avoid white homes and community institutions and run the highways right through the heart of Black communities. Government officials defended their siting decisions by saying they were focused on the areas in need of revitalization and that entailed the lowest costs for acquiring the right of way to build.

In practice, this meant targeting Black communities that were long segregated and starved of resources, essential infrastructure, and economic
investment—communities where federal policies such as redlining deliberately kept property values low and eminent domain more affordable. It
also meant that highway builders were targeting neighborhoods with less
political power to fight eminent domain and challenge the destruction of
their homes, businesses, and communities.

By the time the interstate highway system was completed in the early
1970s, it had linked much of the country—and fundamentally restructured
urban America. In almost every region of the continental United States,
the new interstate highway system uprooted, displaced, and isolated hundreds of thousands of people. The toll was devastating. As mentioned
above, the United States Department of Transportation estimates that
more than a million people were displaced nationwide as a direct result
of interstate highway construction. But even that high number severely
understates the legacy of the Interstate Highway Act. Beyond the people
who were directly displaced, the highways changed the lives of the people
who remained.

Michelle Alexander's modern classic, *The New Jim Crow*, argues that
the prison system took over when the legal reign of Jim Crow was coming to an end. The education system would undergo a similar evolution to
ensure the future of racially segregated education both before and after
Brown v. Board. After Congress adopted the Fifteenth Amendment to provide Black men access to the ballot, grandfather clauses, poll taxes, and
literacy tests did the early work of blocking access to our democracy, followed by new and evolving measures to deny and dilute the right to vote.
The highway system, though less studied than these other systems, played
a similar role. Certainly, it did so for its architects, who no longer could
segregate their cities and towns legally. Highways became segregation by
another means. And the effects would be enduring. The next chapter tells
some of their stories.

Chapter 2

Substance over Form

A segregated bus station in Durham, North Carolina.

Generations of advocates and communities have fought to force this country to live up to its promises of equality and dignity for everyone. Yet racial inequality persists. Racism's power derives, in part, from its ability to adapt. Black people have faced ever more creative and effective government-authorized or government-enabled tools to segregate, exclude, and devalue. From chattel slavery to Jim Crow, and from state-sanctioned brutality to more subtle forms of oppression, the history of racial oppression in America is a story not of stasis but of transformation, with the oppressors' tools evolving as the law changed.

In combatting racial inequality, judges and policymakers have too often focused on form over substance. They may try to dismantle a particular tool of discrimination but lose sight of the larger system of white supremacy. Frequently, the result is a short-term victory when a particular law or rule is invalidated, followed by the adoption of new and even more pernicious tools that effectively achieve the same inequitable outcome. On the flip side, those set on perpetuating racial inequality often focus on substance over form. The forces that support white supremacy do not worry too much about the specific route they take to get there. White supremacy may be a constant in American history, but it is also a shapeshifter. That is one of its great advantages.

Birmingham, Alabama; Atlanta, Georgia; and Indianapolis, Indiana, provide powerful examples of how the highway became a tool of a post–Jim Crow segregationist agenda. In Birmingham, racial zoning laws created an invisible line dividing Black and white neighborhoods. Once a federal appeals court struck down Birmingham's racial zoning law in 1950 in *Monk v. City of Birmingham*, and the Supreme Court declined to hear an appeal, white residents and city officials sought to replace the invisible dividing lines with visible ones. Similarly, Atlanta substituted highways for racial zoning laws and legal segregation.

In Indianapolis, the city government and private actors systematically underinvested in Black communities and then used the challenges those communities faced as a reason to justify their further devastation. In the words of Langston Hughes, such policies transformed Black communities into the "land of rats and roaches, where a nickel costs a dime."

BIRMINGHAM, ACCORDING TO DR. MARTIN LUTHER KING JR., WAS "THE most segregated city in America." The title was well-earned. Following the end of Reconstruction, the city turned racial segregation and oppression into a science. In 1910, Birmingham adopted laws requiring racial segregation on public transportation and banning Black people from using city-owned parks, while providing no parks designated for Black people. Step by step, Birmingham expanded segregation in both public spaces and private interactions. By the 1930s, the city required racial segregation in everything from public transportation to restaurants and public restrooms. It even banned Black and white people from playing in the same pool halls or playing checkers, dice, or dominoes together. And to ensure that they left no stone unturned, Birmingham officials passed a law requiring segregation in "any room, hall, theatre, picture house, auditorium, yard, court, ball park, public park, or other indoor or outdoor place."

But the city was still not done. Next, it turned to ensuring that the residential segregation that had been enforced through brutality, intimidation, and custom was codified into law. It did so through racial zoning laws. In the early 1900s, cities across the country—from Baltimore, Maryland, to Atlanta, Georgia, and from Richmond, Virginia, to Louisville, Kentucky—adopted residential segregation ordinances. These were a bastardization of general zoning laws that were intended to help homeowners protect their neighborhoods from encroaching industrial and commercial districts. Segregationists quickly saw the power in the laws and co-opted them to prevent integration and block Black migration from rural areas into majority-white cities and towns.

The birth of the racial zoning movement occurred not in the Deep South, but in Baltimore in 1910, when the city passed "an ordinance for preserving peace, preventing conflict and ill feeling between the white and colored races in Baltimore city, and promoting the general welfare of the city by providing, so far as practicable, for the use of separate blocks by white and colored people for residences, churches and schools." The law was a response to a Black couple moving into a white neighborhood. Following Baltimore's lead, cities across the South adopted racial zoning laws under the guise of protecting the peace and property values by keeping the races separate.

Although city officials explored the possibility, Birmingham was not an early adopter of racial zoning laws. In 1913, City Commissioner James Weatherly proposed a racial zoning law, citing its ability to protect white property values. He noted that city officials "had several complaints that a man building a nice home has had its usefulness and value partially destroyed by negro dwellings near there." Although the city studied and debated the idea, it did not act before the National Association for the Advancement of Colored People (NAACP) intervened to stop the growing proliferation of racial zoning laws across the country.

Shortly after the NAACP was founded in 1909, it focused its advocacy on challenging racial segregation broadly and racial zoning laws in particular. In 1917, it won the case of *Buchanan v. Warley*, in which the US Supreme Court barred municipal ordinances that required segregation. *Buchanan* began when William Warley, president of the Louisville, Kentucky, NAACP branch, made an offer to buy a plot of land from Charles Buchanan, a white realtor. The lot at issue was on a street zoned for white occupancy. Buchanan accepted Warley's offer, but filed suit when Warley was prevented from occupying the land because of Louisville's racial zoning law.

Following the Supreme Court's decision, W. E. B. Du Bois, who was one of the founders of the NAACP, said *Buchanan* signaled "the breaking of the backbone of segregation." But the court's decision was not about racial justice or equality, nor did it lay the groundwork for integration. The decision was about protecting white people's property interests. The unanimous opinion focused on the fact that Buchanan, the white realtor, was unable to sell his property because of the ordinance. As the court said, "the case presented does not deal with an attempt to prohibit the amalgamation of the races. The right which the ordinance annulled was the civil right of a white man to dispose of his property if he saw fit to do so to a person of color." The ruling left the larger ecosystem of white supremacy untouched.

The *Buchanan* decision may have complicated Birmingham city officials' plans to adopt a racial zoning law, but they were not deterred. White residents who lived in neighborhoods adjacent to historically Black neighborhoods continued to demand protection from the perceived dangers of Black encroachment. City officials continued to believe that legal separation was the most effective way to protect white people and white property values, and to block demands for school integration.

Ultimately, the city implemented a two-part strategy to overcome the legal hurdle posed by *Buchanan*. First, city officials invoked the twisted logic of *Plessy v. Ferguson* and the separate but equal doctrine, which had allowed them to impose comprehensive segregation across the city. Birmingham's city attorney, W. J. Wynn, believed that a racial zoning ordinance had a chance of withstanding legal challenges despite *Buchanan* because under *Plessy* "the federal constitution prohibits discrimination, not segregation." Here, Birmingham sought cover from the state of Alabama. In 1922, with the help of Wynn and the Birmingham Real Estate Exchange, the Birmingham City Commission drafted a state zoning-enabling statute that purported to protect "the public peace, order, safety, and general welfare" of municipalities by allowing those municipalities to regulate "the different class of inhabitants" that could live together, provided that any regulation did not "discriminate in favor of or against any class of inhabitants." Essentially, municipalities would be allowed to provide "separate but equal" housing to Black and white people.

In September 1923, the Alabama legislature passed a zoning enabling act permitting residential racial segregation, using the language that had been proposed by Wynn and the Birmingham City Commission. This opened the door for Birmingham to act directly. Wynn and other city officials knew that the statute was on legally shaky ground but believed the potential benefits outweighed the risks of a legal challenge. In an interview

about the state law, Wynn said that there was psychological value in passing the bill. Moreover, he believed that even if the law was ultimately held
to be unconstitutional, it would take a long time for any litigation to be
resolved by the US Supreme Court. In the meantime, segregation would
become further entrenched, physically and psychologically. The work of
white supremacy would move forward even if the statute were eventually
overturned.

The second step in navigating around *Buchanan* was for the city to
adopt its own racial zoning law that could comfortably sit under the cloak
of *Plessy* but also fit into any openings left by the *Buchanan* opinion. The
city leaned into the aspect of the Supreme Court's ruling in *Buchanan* that
focused on the unconstitutionality of restrictions on owning and selling
property because of race. The City Commission crafted an ordinance that
allowed Black people to own property in districts zoned for white people
but strictly prohibited where Black and white people could live, whether
they owned the property or not. And with that, on July 13, 1926, the Birmingham City Commission enacted what would become the South's
longest-standing racial zoning law.

Decades of brutally enforced racial segregation had left Birmingham's
Black residents with insufficient public services and substandard housing. They were concerned that racial zoning would cement their current
condition as their permanent lot in life. They opposed the zoning law,
not because they wanted to live next door to white people, but because
they knew intimately the devastating realities of racial segregation for
Black people and Black communities. Oscar W. Adams, publisher of the
Birmingham Reporter, a local Black newspaper, organized a committee
of prominent Black Birmingham residents to block the ordinance. The
committee published an open letter in the *Birmingham Reporter* explaining the community's opposition. They noted that although Black people
would prefer to live in Black communities, they knew that Black communities would continue to be neglected by city officials. Even without the
stamp of approval provided by the racial zoning law, racial segregation had
left Black neighborhoods "without the necessary sanitary arrangements,
street improvements, lights, police protection and the necessary comforts

given other peoples in the municipality." The committee feared that the adoption of a racial zoning law would only worsen the existing conditions.

In another editorial published in the *Birmingham Reporter*, advocates made clear that "some might get the impression that the Negro would oppose the bill because they desire to live with or near white people. Nothing is further from the truth. They oppose the measure because Negroes are unprotected when they are not near white people. They don't have police supervision, lights are not given, streets are not kept up and a general lack of interest is exercised in any absolute Negro community."

They were right, of course. The areas in Birmingham that were zoned for Black people were places where no one else wanted to live. The newly adopted racial zoning map locked in historic racial segregation and relegated Black people to flood-prone areas and blighted neighborhoods. Black people were largely restricted to living near commercial or industrial areas with no place to build homes and raise their families. Just a single neighborhood—Enon Ridge—was designated for Black single-family homes. During the 1920s, Birmingham's total population was roughly 40 percent Black. Yet the racial zoning ordinance designated less than 20 percent of the city's residential land for its Black citizens.

Emory Jackson, executive secretary of the Birmingham branch of the NAACP, would later write that city officials and white residents were unbothered by "the fact that Negro citizens are bottled in the slums and restricted to the blighted area." He went on to explain that the Black citizens of Birmingham "are zoned near the railroad tracks, near the overflowing creeks, near the shops. This is their lot in Birmingham as citizens of a democracy on an earth God made for all, and all alike." For decades, Black people in Birmingham lived their lives and raised their families according to those invisible—yet painfully real—boundaries.

Some of the most significant racial boundary lines were in and around the Smithfield neighborhood. Center Street ran down the middle of Smithfield. Black families lived on the east side of Smithfield and could not move within one hundred feet of Center Street. White families lived on the west side of Smithfield and similarly could not move within one hundred feet of Center Street. The Center Street area also helped to separate the white-zoned Graymont–College Hills neighborhood from the Black-zoned sections of Smithfield. Finally, there was North Smithfield, a white-zoned neighborhood surrounded by Black-zoned neighborhoods to the north, south, and east. Center Street would come to be known as both the line of demarcation between the Black and white communities and "the spine" of the Black community that led the movement to desegregate Birmingham.

In the 1940s, Black people began to challenge Birmingham's racial zoning law with new force. They sued in federal court. But they did not wait on the legal system. Some Black people simply ignored the racial zoning ordinance and moved into white-zoned neighborhoods, purchasing homes from sympathetic white people. The response, as it often is when Black Americans resist their oppression, was a combination of racist violence and political maneuvering. Black people who dared to cross or even approach the demarcations between neighborhoods were met by ruthless city officials and white terrorists aided by notorious segregationist Eugene "Bull" Connor. As Birmingham's public safety commissioner, Connor controlled the city's police and fire departments and had an outsized influence over Birmingham city government. He used his power to deny Black people their civil rights and strictly enforce racial segregation. He would later gain international infamy for using fire hoses and attack dogs against civil rights protesters in front of television cameras. But decades earlier, going back to 1939, Bull Connor was already laser-focused on enforcing segregation in Birmingham by any means necessary.

As Birmingham's Black people pushed back against racial segregation and defied racial boundary lines, they were met with vigilante violence at the hands of their white neighbors, harassed by Connor's police force, and impeded by city officials. There would be fifty bombings of Black homes and churches between 1947 and 1966, including one in 1963 that infamously took the lives of four Black girls in the Sixteenth Street Baptist Church. The racial terror campaign earned Birmingham the nickname "Bombingham." The bombings began in response to efforts of the Black community to challenge the racial zoning law. Most of these attacks, especially in the '40s and '50s, took place in North Smithfield as Black people moved into the white neighborhood and bordering areas, and white supremacists responded with violence. The neighborhood would come to be known as "Dynamite Hill."

The Birmingham NAACP turned to Arthur D. Shores, the only practicing Black attorney in Alabama, to lead the legal battle against racial zoning. Shores's first legal challenge was on behalf of Alice Allen, an administrator at a local college. Allen purchased a home in North Smithfield, in a commercial area with no racial occupancy restrictions. White residents of North Smithfield complained. In response, the City Commission voted to rezone the area surrounding her property as a white-only district and told her she could not move in. Two weeks after Shores filed his legal challenge, the Commission reversed the measure to avoid a direct attack on the ordinance.

The next case was filed on behalf of Samuel Matthews. In December 1945, Matthews and his wife Essie Mae bought two lots in the North Smithfield buffer area that were zoned for single-family white occupancy. The lot was on the west side of Center Street, about half a block from a Black neighborhood and three blocks from the nearest white residences. The city gave the Matthews family a building permit but, once the house was built, denied them a certificate of occupancy because of the racial zoning law. Shores filed suit challenging the law. On July 31, 1946, the judge in the case ruled in favor of Matthews and acknowledged that the racial zoning law impinged on the rights of Black people in violation of *Buchanan v. Warley*. But he limited the ruling to the Matthews residence; he did not attempt to strike down the state's zoning law.

On August 18, 1947, just two weeks after the judge's ruling and before the Matthews family could settle into their new home, the house was bombed. The walls were blown out, the roof collapsed, and most of the house was crushed. The police never charged or arrested anyone for the crime.

The more members of the Black community ignored the racial boundaries, the harder the white community fought to preserve segregation. In response to the Allen and Matthews legal victories, the Birmingham chapter of the Ku Klux Klan formally incorporated, with defending residential segregation at the top of their list of priorities. In 1947, the Ku Klux Klan began aggressively lobbying city officials to defend the sanctity of the racial zones. They threatened the NAACP, including by sending a menacing letter demanding the organization stop its legal challenges, and burned crosses in various neighborhoods. At every turn, they were protected by Connor and his police.

In 1948, four Black families moved into homes formerly occupied by white people in the area near Center Street. In March 1949, a fifth Black family joined them. In response, the Graymont–College Hills Civic Association demanded that the city commission stop issuing permits allowing Black people to build homes or move into houses formerly occupied by white people west of Center Street. The city ordered the five Black families to move. Later that month, three of the houses were bombed. Again, no arrests were ever made. The Graymont–College Hills Civic Association continued to press the city to enforce the racial zoning laws.

On the night of August 12, 1949, the Center Street homes of two Black ministers—Rev. Milton Curry Jr. and Rev. E. B. DeYampert—were destroyed by bombs. The houses were just one block away from the three homes that had been bombed earlier that year. Again, no one was charged.

Rather than protect the lives and property of Black families who were being terrorized by the string of bombings, Bull Connor blamed the racial violence on the people selling houses to Black people. His solution was to make it a criminal offense for members of one race to move into neighborhoods "generally and historically" belonging to another race. The attorney who drafted the ordinance for Connor said, "If you let the situation disintegrate and negroes continue to infiltrate white areas and whites infiltrate negro areas so that your lines of demarcation become broken down, you are in for disorder and bloodshed and our ancient and excellent plan of life here in Alabama is gone."

The final challenge to the law came in a 1949 lawsuit filed by the NAACP on behalf of Mary Monk and fifteen others. Mary and her husband Monroe Monk purchased a lot in North Smithfield on the west side of Center Street, in the area zoned for white people. On December 14, 1949, a judge finally ruled that Birmingham's racial zoning ordinance was unconstitutional and enjoined the city from enforcing it. While the city appealed the ruling, two additional North Smithfield homes owned by Black people were bombed. Then, in December 1950, one day after a federal appellate court ruled in her favor, Mary and Monroe Monk's home was bombed as well.

The city appealed, and the Supreme Court ultimately struck down the Birmingham ordinance. But the white leadership of Birmingham remained undeterred. They replaced the invisible boundary lines with more durable, physical ones: Interstate 59 and Interstate 65.

AFTER BIRMINGHAM'S RACIAL ZONING LAW WAS STRUCK DOWN, WHITE RES-idents feared the end of their segregated way of life. The Interstate Highway Act would open the door for highways to finish the job that racial zoning and racial terror had started. Although the new highway construction was not singularly driven by racial animus, city and state highway planners used Interstate 59 and Interstate 65 to advance their segregationist agenda where possible. White Birmingham was able to abandon house-by-house combat and remove entire Black communities instead. I-59 travels north to south, while I-65 runs east to west. They meet in the heart of Birmingham at an intersection often referred to as Malfunction Junction.

The state and local highway department built I-59 to serve as a boundary between College Hills, a previously white-zoned neighborhood just west of the Smithfield neighborhood, and nearby Black neighborhoods. Under Birmingham's racial zoning ordinance, Eleventh Avenue had served as a boundary line. After the racial zoning law was struck down, white College Hills residents feared that Black people would move into their neighborhood, and petitioned Birmingham's city commissioners to adopt new demarcations. Mayor James Morgan and members of the City Commission, while acknowledging the limitations put in place by the Supreme Court's rulings, pledged to "explore all possible routes to aid white property owners in the preservation of the character of their neighborhood," which white residents believed was being threatened by "the influx of Negroes." Interstate 59 was ultimately built along Eleventh Avenue. Its route followed the old racial zoning boundary, creating a massive, elevated physical buffer between the white and Black communities.

Southwest of Smithfield, I-59 runs along the southern border of Ensley, creating a racial boundary line separating the predominantly Black Tuxedo community and white Ensley Highlands. An invisible boundary between the two communities had been codified in the city's racial zoning law. Now, planning for the highway proceeded alongside planning for an Ensley Highlands urban renewal project. Birmingham commissioned a feasibility study that touted I-59's planned route as a barrier between the blight and "detrimental influences" of the Black community and white Ensley Highlands. In addition to serving as a barrier, the highway and its accompanying surface street connections would be critical to removing the "blighted" Black neighborhoods that would otherwise "remain between the expressway and the sound neighborhoods to the south." The report's authors noted that this additional benefit of neighborhood removal "represents an example of the value of close coordination between urban renewal and urban highway projects."

In the center of the city, I-65 was built to track historic racial boundaries. One portion of the highway followed Sixth Street, mimicking the racial boundary created by the 1926 zoning map and separating the Black neighborhood of Enon Ridge from the white community of Fountain Heights. Interstate 65 also became a buffer between Birmingham's west side neighborhoods and the central business district, and between the University of Alabama and the Black Titusville neighborhood.

The highways stood as monuments to past segregation and evidence of its perpetuation. In a 1958 story in the *Birmingham News*, residents compared the impact of the freeways slicing through Black Birmingham to the devastation left by a bomb blast. The immediate impact of highway construction was the displacement of thousands of mostly Black residents and the decimation of an entire community in Malfunction Junction. That area alone lost almost 5,000 residents who were forced to relocate.

LIKE BIRMINGHAM, ATLANTA USED RACIAL ZONING LAWS TO ENFORCE THE legal separation of Black and white neighborhoods and to "protect" white property owners from Black migration. Less than a decade after a violent white mob attacked Black residents and murdered more than two dozen in what came to be called the Atlanta Race Riots, Atlanta adopted its first racial zoning law in 1913. It was quickly struck down by the Georgia Supreme Court in *Carey v. City of Atlanta*. But city officials did not give up. They adopted a new, revised racial zoning law in 1916, and in a reversal, the Georgia Supreme Court upheld the new law in a ruling that relied on the logic of *Plessy* and glorified segregation:

> Courts are not blind to the fact that by nature there are several races of people, and that the conditions of civilization compel certain regulations relating to the contact of the races. . . . The white and black races have been forbidden intermarriage, and have been separated in public conveyances, inns, hotels, theatres, and public schools. If it be justifiable to separate the races in the public schools in recognition of the peril to race integrity, induced by mere race association, then we cannot see why the same public policy cannot be invoked to prohibit the black and white races from living side by side.

Following the US Supreme Court's 1917 ruling in *Buchanan*, Atlanta kept revising its racial zoning law in an effort to preserve housing segregation—for example, by adjusting the law to allow servants' quarters to be open to anyone regardless of the race of the zone—but the Georgia Supreme Court finally struck the law down in 1926. Following the ruling, Atlanta officials began exploring the possibility of using roads and highways to contain Black migration and create buffers between Black and white residents. It was not an entirely new idea. In 1917, city officials had proposed building a 180-foot-wide parkway that would separate Black and white neighborhoods. The parkway, which was to be called the Grand Boulevard, would allow city officials to designate the area east of the parkway for Black people, and the west side, adjacent to the business district and access to economic opportunities, for white people. According to the plan, this would make the Grand Boulevard "a great parked thoroughfare, which would distinctly divide the negro population of the fourth ward from the white." The Grand Boulevard was never built, but the proposal planted a seed in the minds of city planners. That seed would continue to germinate as

Black people migrated through the city, unconstrained by the vacated racial zoning law.

As Atlanta embarked on extensive highway construction in the 1950s and 1960s, planners generally focused on facilitating commercial activity and neighborhood development, but also took advantage of opportunities to promote segregation whenever they could. White Atlanta residents called on the mayor and city officials to use the highway system as a series of racial barriers, and the city leadership openly committed to doing just that. One clear example is Interstate 20. In addition to tearing through the heart of several Black neighborhoods and forcing several thousand Black residents to move, I-20 was used to limit Black access to the white Adamsville community, serving as a wall between Black neighborhoods to the north and the white neighborhoods to the south. In 1952, the *Atlanta Daily World* published an article titled "Southwest Citizens Group Discloses 'Barrier' Plans Endorsed by City Officials." It reported that the chairman of the Southwest Citizens Association Contact Committee told a crowd of more than 1,500 "cheering white citizens" that the mayor and city council had agreed to five proposals that "would serve as 'barriers' between white and Negro residential areas." One of them was a six-lane highway that would guard against "Negro encroachment."

The city did not hide its segregationist agenda. In a 1960 report, the Atlanta Bureau of Planning acknowledged that "approximately two to three years ago, there was an 'understanding' that the proposed route of [I-20] would be the boundary between the White and Negro communities." By the time that report was issued and the city's intentions were laid bare, I-20 had already been built, and the damage was done. Black developers who sought the planning bureau's permission to build low-to-moderate-income housing south of the planned I-20 were denied. The planning bureau justified its refusal by explaining that the city "had obligations to the [white] Adamsville citizens to adhere to the expressway route boundary" and could not allow housing for Black people to be built in the protected community. Such a move would undermine the goal of building the highway there in the first place. A similar pattern was repeated around the city.

IN MARCH 1926, INDIANAPOLIS'S KU KLUX KLAN–AFFILIATED CITY COUNCIL passed a residential segregation ordinance. The ordinance was a response to the Great Migration and the resulting explosion in the city's Black population, as Black people moved north to escape southern racism. From 1910 to 1930, the Black population of Indianapolis increased from 21,816 to 43,967—the latter number representing 12 percent of the city's population at the time. Fleeing Jim Crow, in Indianapolis Black people faced a new kind of racist oppression and a powerful Klan.

The first Indiana Ku Klux Klan chapter was organized in 1920 and quickly gained power through an 1870s-era state law that permitted citizen vigilantes to become certified constables for the purpose of arresting "horse thieves and other felons." Under the cover of that law, the Klan engaged in a reign of racial terror, stopping and searching cars, conducting raids on businesses, and riding through Black Indiana communities with their guns drawn. By 1923, the Klan boasted 28,000 members in Indianapolis alone.

In municipal and statewide elections held in 1924 and 1925, the Klan's popular support translated into sweeping victories. In the 1924 Republican primaries in Marion County, which includes Indianapolis, Klan-endorsed candidates won nominations for sheriff, Congress, and governor, among a host of other state offices. They ultimately secured both the governorship and a majority of seats in the state legislature. In 1925, the Klan added to its political power when the vociferously anti-Klan Indianapolis mayor Lewis Shank was replaced with the Klan-endorsed John Duvall. Making matters even worse, Mayor Duvall secured the Klan's endorsement in an explicit quid pro quo with Indiana Grand Dragon D. C. Stephenson. In exchange for the Ku Klux Klan's support, Duvall promised to let Stephenson handpick the chief of police, police captain, and the entire Board of Public Works. These victories helped clear the way for enactment of the segregation ordinance.

The Klan was far from the only white supremacist force in Indiana, nor was it the only one focused on maintaining residential and educational segregation. The White People's Protective League emerged in 1926 to champion racial segregation and prevent the migration of Black people into "white territory." In a February 1926 letter to the editor for the *Indianapolis News*, Omer Whiteman, an attorney for the League, bragged that "several leagues and civic associations" were drafting a racial zoning law. He added that the White People's Protective League itself was drafting such a measure. More than a mere citizens' interest group, the League was actively engaged in racial terrorism, much of it focused on "protecting" white communities from Black migration. In 1927, League members reportedly bombed a home in their campaign to ensure that no Black residents lived on or above Twenty-Ninth Street.

The Klan and the White People's Protective League were joined by another organization, the White Supremacy League, in championing the segregation ordinance. The White Supremacy League was founded by Daisydean Deeds to fight for school segregation but quickly joined the push for residential segregation. In a January 1923 article in the Klan's newspaper, *The Fiery Cross*, Deeds said that the only resolution to "the race problem" is to "confine both races separately into their own distinctive realms of literacy, morality, sociology, and politics. It can be accomplished no other way." After the ordinance's passage in March 1926, a columnist for the *Indianapolis Recorder*, a local Black-owned newspaper, wrote that it was "the immediate work of the distorted ill-conceived child of ignorance and bigotry (the so called White Supremacy League)." The White Supremacy League was also responsible for distributing handbills in white communities that asked "Do you want a nigger for a neighbor?"

As Black Hoosiers continued to challenge the boundary lines between Black and white neighborhoods, white residents and civic associations pushed back. When Dr. Lucien B. Meriwether, a Black Indianapolis dentist, purchased a home in the Capitol Avenue and Twenty-Third Street neighborhood, a white civic association called the Capitol Avenue Protective Association offered him well over what he paid for the home to prevent him from moving in. Dr. Meriwether refused the association's offer. In response, the Capitol Avenue Protective Association erected a ten-foot-tall "spite fence" around his property.

At least five of the nine members of the Indianapolis City Council that passed the Indianapolis Segregationist Ordinance—its official name—were Klan-affiliated. A May 1925 article in the *Indianapolis Times* identified the five Republican members of the council as being endorsed by the Klan, and indicated that they were all featured speakers at a members-only Klan event. All but one of them voted in favor of the segregation ordinance. (The vote was five-to-one; three of the members were absent, including one of the Klan-affiliated Republicans.) When Mayor Duvall signed the measure into law, he claimed that it was a race-neutral ordinance that contained no intent to discriminate against members of either race, despite the clear message of its title.

Of course, there was nothing race-neutral about the law. It declared that "in the interest of public peace, good order and the general welfare, it is advisable to foster the separation of white and negro residential communities." The law embraced *Plessy v. Ferguson*'s ethos that governments could not force people of different races to interact socially if they chose to live separately:

> That it shall be unlawful for any white person to hereafter establish a home-residence on any property located in a negro community, or portion of the municipality inhabited principally by negroes, or for any negro to establish a home-residence on any property located in a white community or portion of the municipality inhabited principally by white people, except on the written consent of a majority of the persons of the opposite race inhabiting such community or portion of the city to be affected.

By including a provision allowing Black people to live in white communities with permission, the city council and its white supremacist allies believed they were evading *Buchanan*'s prohibition on racial zoning laws. The NAACP immediately brought a legal challenge modeled on its challenge in *Buchanan*. It was successful: in November 1926 an Indianapolis state judge ruled the racial zoning law unconstitutional. Soon afterwards, the United States Supreme Court reviewed a parallel New Orleans ordinance, striking it down in March 1927. After the issuance of the decision in that case, Indianapolis segregationists decided not to appeal the local judge's ruling. In the end, the Indianapolis Segregationist Ordinance was in effect for only eight months.

But in Indianapolis, as in other cities around the country, redlining, urban renewal, and public works programs picked up where racial zoning left off. These three strategies combined with private discrimination to lock in segregation, devalue Black Indianapolis communities, and then destroy and depopulate those communities. As one Indianapolis resident presciently said following the law being struck down, "the Ordinance is the outcome of a movement which has been on for a decade or more, and the worse [sic] is yet to come."

Redlining had a particularly devastating impact on Black communities in Indianapolis. Redlining was a practice that guided which communities had access to federally funded mortgages and related economic investment. The Home Owners' Loan Corporation (HOLC) was a federal agency within the Federal Housing Administration formed in 1933 to regularize the mortgage market. The HOLC created "Residential Security" maps of major American cities that documented how loan officers, appraisers, and real estate professionals should evaluate mortgage lending risk during the era immediately before the surge of suburbanization in the 1950s.

Rather than assess every individual house or parcel of land for a mortgage, the HOLC sought to systematize the property appraisal process by classifying neighborhoods based on their likelihood for foreclosure risk. Neighborhoods were rated from green to red. Green neighborhoods were deemed to be "Best" and blue neighborhoods were "Still Desirable." Black people were labeled an "undesirable element" and anywhere Black people lived was coded red to indicate to the FHA appraiser that the neighborhood was too risky for a federally funded mortgage. As a result, neighborhoods considered high-risk were "redlined" by lending institutions, denying residents of those neighborhoods access to mortgages and capital investment. Some of the maps even said "Negro dominated" or "Negro Colony" in the red areas. Yellow neighborhoods were considered declining, in large part because of their proximity to redlined neighborhoods.

The FHA used HOLC's classification system to discourage lending in Black neighborhoods. Furthermore, in 1936 the FHA published its *Underwriting Manual* and explicitly warned of the dangers of "lower class occupancy and inharmonious racial groups." The race of the hopeful borrower, the racial composition of the community, and the probability that a neighborhood might be "invaded" by people of color, were among the primary factors in assessing mortgage risk. The result was predictable. People of color were denied access to mortgage financing and federal underwriting opportunities that were readily available to people seeking to live in predominantly white communities. Between 1934 and 1962, a mere 2 percent of $120 billion in Federal Housing Administration loans went to nonwhite families.

Redlining triggered a cascade of harm and inequity in Black communities. The harm was not limited to the denial of federally backed mortgages, which alone had a substantial impact on the ability of Black people to build wealth by purchasing property. Redlining also helped spread the notion that residents of color were financially risky and a threat to local property values. This limited the availability not only of mortgages, but of home insurance. More broadly, the systemic undervaluing of Black communities, and the federally imposed principle that Black communities were inherently risky, discouraged investment in Black communities by businesses and made it harder for those businesses that were in Black communities to access the capital they needed to grow and thrive. Redlining provided an infrastructure for the devaluation of Black communities.

Redlining also locked in the racially segregated landscape. It helped to limit the ability of Black people to move homes, including from one Black community to another, unless they could do so without help in financing the purchase. It also created additional barriers to moving into white communities that feared new Black neighbors would decrease or eliminate their own ability to get financing. The HOLC helped to codify into federal policy what realtors, neighborhood associations, and racial terrorists had been seeking for decades.

Indianapolis was indelibly shaped by redlining. Black residents faced land devaluation, severely limited outside economic investment, and intense racial segregation. They struggled to get loans to purchase homes or to repair their property. Starved of capital, Black neighborhoods deteriorated, while large numbers of white residents moved out of the city and into second-ring suburbs with the help of the federal government.

Indiana Avenue provides a telling example. Beginning in about 1900, as racial segregation took hold of Indianapolis, Black businesses and leisure started to concentrate along Indiana Avenue, a main thoroughfare downtown. The avenue was surrounded by pockets of Black residents. Because Black people were physically segregated from whites, and because white businesses refused to cater to Black customers, Black people spent their lives on Indiana Avenue and in the communities that surrounded it. Black businesses arose to meet their needs, and Indiana Avenue flourished as a center of Black commerce and community. As one historian of Indianapolis put it, "every sort of Black expressive culture was available on Indiana Avenue." Black entrepreneur Madam C. J. Walker, who went from being the first child in her family born into freedom to the country's first self-made female millionaire of any race, arrived in Indianapolis in 1910 to establish the headquarters of the Madam C. J. Walker Manufacturing Company and the Walker Drugstore. She was drawn to Indianapolis by Indiana Avenue.

But the Black neighborhoods surrounding Indiana Avenue were redlined, devaluing the land and making it easier for public works officials to justify cutting through the community to build a highway. Interstate 65 and Interstate 70 are two major highways that merge in the heart of Indianapolis. When you are downtown, the highway comes at you from all sides. It is confining and overwhelming. The construction of the intersection, known as the Inner Loop, alone displaced 8,000 businesses and homes and 17,000 people. Most of the residents who were forced out were Black, and the displaced businesses were predominantly Black- and immigrant-owned. City planners constructed the Inner Loop on the guiding theory that people could work in downtown Indianapolis and then easily travel home to the suburbs along the highways. City planners apparently forgot about the lives and well-being of the people who *lived* downtown and would continue living there after the highways were constructed.

The Interstate 65 and Interstate 70 Inner Loop bisected some communities, cut others off from surrounding areas, and created both physical and psychological barriers between Black communities and the cultural and economic life of the city. I-65 and I-70 left behind a foreign landscape. The Inner Loop did not physically tear through Indiana Avenue itself, but its construction removed many of the people and institutions that helped make it what it was. The Indiana Avenue area was forever changed. Many of the once-vibrant thoroughfares serving the Indiana Avenue community now serve as exit and entrance ramps to the massive highway interchange. Other nearby streets are now dead-ended or effectively dead-ended. And much of the wealth of the largely self-sufficient and self-sustaining community that supported Indiana Avenue businesses was destroyed, often through the seizure and demolition of Black-owned homes.

Thomas Ridley was born in 1922, just three blocks from Indiana Avenue. The avenue played a central role in his life; he considered himself to be an "Indiana Avenue person," strolling "The Avenue" just about every day. But when I-70 came through in 1956, "Indiana Avenue died." At the time, Ridley was working for the post office, his wife was a schoolteacher, and they had made a home for their family on Ralston Avenue in a working-class Black community. I-70 ran east to west, completely cutting his and other neighborhoods off from Indiana Avenue. The trip to The Avenue became long and arduous, requiring them to navigate spiderwebs of streets to complete what was once an easy trip. The highways made it easier for some people to travel through and out of Indianapolis. But, for many others, the highways made life a daily challenge.

The word *displacement* can carry multiple meanings. The people who were forced to leave their homes and communities were not the only ones displaced. While thousands of people were uprooted by I-65 and I-70, many more were left to live in their shadow. They, too, were displaced, living in a community that was no longer their own. It was now dominated by a highway. Although they were not forced to move, they were left feeling isolated, unmoored, and discarded.

I-70 runs for a long distance without any underpasses or pedestrian bridges, leaving the community north of the highway separated from neighbors, shops, and restaurants. In May 1972, Ann May and Flora

Spurlock wrote to the chair of the State Highway Commission to complain about the lack of through streets between S. West and S. Meridian Streets. They pleaded for the state to build a pedestrian bridge to reconnect the separated sections of the neighborhood. But their request was rejected and their isolation ignored; they were told that there was neither enough traffic nor pedestrians to warrant the new construction.

Other residents circulated a petition requesting that a "walk" be built because community members were "fenced in." And in June, residents organized a protest, carrying signs that read "Don't Fence Us In" and "The Old Folks Want to Walk Through the Neighborhood"; a sign held by a child said "I Want to Go to Grandma's." Indeed, as the *Indianapolis News* reported as I-70 was being constructed, "now that the interstate is being constructed, a physical wall is being built . . . there is no overpass on I-70, and between 400 and 500 persons who live north of the interstate are isolated." Some trips that had been a three-minute walk would now take thirty minutes on foot. Eventually, a through street was built, but meaningful access was never restored.

Some members of the community were displaced multiple times. William Craig grew up on the South Side, selling newspapers every Sunday before church and playing in the wading pool at Miekel Street Park, later renamed Babe Denny Park. He was "raised at South Calvary Baptist Church," and his family had deep roots in the neighborhood. They owned a funeral home at 1002 South Senate that opened in 1936. The property was taken by eminent domain for the construction of I-70 in the 1960s. The Craig family then bought a grocery store at 826 South Capital, an area that they thought was safe from the highway's reach because it did not appear in any of the plans that were shared with the community. They expected to reopen their funeral home there. Yet soon that property was taken for the highway as well.

At a public meeting before the highways were built, but after the routes were announced, a Black chiropractor named Robert O. Pettiford asked the questions that were on many residents' minds: "Where will the people move, if the State Highway Commission runs a freeway through our neighborhood? How can older residents, many of whom own their homes, buy new [ones] with the money they would get on a 20-year-depreciation basis?" He put his finger on the exact problem the highways would result in: "The neighborhood is an old one and many of the residents have their homes paid for. If the government takes off on the values of homes over 20 years old, how can these residents, many on pensions or with other types of limited income, buy homes equal to theirs with the money they would get? Take a fellow neighbor I know. He owns a nice house that's worth maybe $3000 on the market. He can't get another house for $3000. And he wouldn't have enough to make house payments."

Although the state did not technically take Mary Brame's home to build I-65, in many ways it took her life, at least the life on 439 West Fifteenth Street she had known since 1945. Brame's husband Clarence died in 1952, and after his passing she continued to live in her home along with her sister and elderly mother. When I-65 was built through her neighborhood, the homes of her neighbors were all demolished. In 1966, there were a mere five other homes in what was left of her community. Just one year later, Brame's home stood alone; her only neighbors were the highway and a church. The highway cut off West Fifteenth Street, leaving her on a now dead-end street. Construction closed down all of the streets leading to Brame's home, except one extremely short road. The state took much of her backyard and erected a fence up against her home. The highway was destroying her life—the noise disrupted her sleep, deeply impacting her health—while the vibrations from traffic were literally destroying her home.

In June 1973, Brame's attorney wrote to Indiana governor Otis Bowen, pleading with him to purchase Brame's home. On July 23, 1973, the State Highway Division's executive director R. H. Harrell wrote back and argued that "proximity to a highway is not a compensable damage consideration," and concluded that "In good conscience [the state] cannot spend taxpayer money for land or improvements that are not needed for a public facility." They left Brame to wonder where their "good conscience" was when they made the decision to leave her isolated in the shadow of a highway.

Paula Brooks, an Indianapolis community organizer and advocate, grew up in a neighborhood near Indiana Avenue that was likewise decimated by the highway. Decades later, she can still recall everything in vivid detail. She describes how the construction turned the homes of her neighbors and the streets where she once played into a jumble of highways and access roads, separating her from family and friends. One by one, the buildings of her childhood were torn down, rending the fabric of her community. Even as a child, Brooks linked the construction of the highway with the push for segregation and attacks on school busing that were happening at the same time in Indianapolis. She knew that the highway was just another way to "get the Black people out by any means necessary." She and the community continue to feel those injuries today: "four generations of wealth wiped off the map and we haven't yet recovered."

On the North Side, Robert Edwards and three generations of his family lived on Shriver Street. They were part of a middle-class Black community then known as Unwa, short for United Northwest Area. They owned several duplexes and single-family homes; some they lived in and others they rented out to supplement their income. They wanted to solidify their place in the city. For the extended Edwards clan, it was all about creating their redoubt—a safe haven for their family—and realizing their version of the American dream: work hard, build a home, invest in your community, and leave something of value to your children. They thought they had found that on Shriver Street.

When I-65 came through the North Side, the Edwards family initially thought they had dodged a bullet because they did not lose their homes, as thousands of others would. But still, the highway upended all they had built, demolishing everything on the opposite side of Shriver Street and removing an entire side of the neighborhood. The highway literally sat across the street from their home—a six-lane highway and a concrete wall that separated them from friends and basic services. Their deep family and community connections were replaced by a concrete wall and highway connector streets, courtesy of I-65. Their family fortress was no match for the highway builders.

In addition to being isolated, the Edwards family's property values plummeted, despite the investments they made in maintaining their homes. No one wanted to buy a home across the street from a concrete wall and six-lane highway. No one wanted to invest in property where they would be forced to breathe in exhaust fumes and hear the constant drone of cars just feet away from their porch. People who had means moved to what were called Indianapolis's Golden Ghettos—racially segregated suburban communities. Those who could not afford to move stayed. In a vicious irony, because the Edwards family lost significant wealth due to I-65, they could not afford to create a similar family enclave in one of the Golden Ghettos.

The Edwards family saw cruelty in the process. The highway builders had options that could have lessened the impact of I-65. They could have narrowed Shriver Street slightly and installed trees in front of the highway wall to give the remaining homeowners a small measure of protection and a less jarring view. But that would have been incongruent with the planners' modus operandi. The builders destroyed the homes of some Indianapolis residents and made no effort to mitigate the damage to those homes that were "spared." Their properties stayed in the Edwards family. While other family members moved away, Robert Edwards's older sister Virginia Mae Edwards lived there until she passed in 2019 at the age of 101—living her life in the shadow of the highway. This was not the legacy Robert Edwards had imagined for his family.

PLANNERS WERE ABLE TO BUILD HIGHWAYS THROUGH THE HEART OF BLACK communities while providing home and business owners next to nothing for their family's primary asset. The low value of these assets was itself the result of federally mandated redlining that contributed to the devaluing of the community and everything in it—both economically and socially. Defenders of the highway system often argue that these communities were targeted because of low land costs, not because of the race of the people who lived there. But this argument falsely treats those reduced land costs as a coincidence, or as the fault of those living on that land, rather than the predictable consequence of public policy. Land costs were low in predominantly Black communities in large part because they were the targets of discriminatory redlining, neglect, and disinvestment.

In 2020, architectural historian and archivist Jordan Ryan created a series of overlay maps, taking the 1937 HOLC Redlining Map of Indianapolis and combining it with the maps of I-70 and I-65. The result shows that highways almost exclusively tore through formerly redlined communities, taking twists and turns to avoid the white communities that surrounded the Black neighborhoods. Although the Black communities were devalued because of redlining, it would be a cruel caricature—and deeply misleading—to call them slums. In Indianapolis, as in much of the rest of the country, residential segregation meant that Black communities were home to people of varying economic means living and working alongside each other. These were vibrant communities—and while racism impacted them negatively, they and the people who lived there deserved better.

When I visited Indianapolis, Indiana, to see firsthand the impact that the construction of I-65 and I-70 had on historically Black communities, many of the people I spoke with told me that their family homes were "underneath the highway." Initially, I took this as a metaphor or exaggeration; I imagined homes so close to the highway that the residents could almost reach out and touch the road. But the homes were no longer there. I soon learned that they meant it literally—the foundations of their homes had become part of the foundation of the highway. The trauma and impact of the highway is always with them. Of course it is. The highway not only sits on top of their family home like a gravestone, but on top of their history, wealth, connections, and potential.

Today in Indianapolis, there is little physical evidence to remind us of the bustling Black communities that once stood where the highways now stand. The sounds of life in those lost communities have been replaced by the sound of cars racing to, from, and along the highway. Before I-70, on the South Side of Indianapolis, Sephardic Jews and Black people lived alongside one another from the 1920s to the 1960s, when the Jewish residents began to migrate north for better education and better homes with the assistance of the GI bill, and the remaining Black residents lost their homes to I-70. Although many were displaced and scattered by the highway, every year, on the first Saturday in August, former residents of the community gather in Babe Denny Park—a veritable urban island, surrounded by I-70 and its on-ramps and off-ramps—to remember and celebrate the lost neighborhood. Many still feel deeply connected to their former neighbors. For more than thirty-five years, between two hundred and three hundred former residents have come from near and far to share memories of their beloved community. When asked why they continue to come back to the community, to stand in the shadow of the highway, they say that the neighborhood was a special place, and talk about their desire to keep their "family" connections. Even as I-70 looms over them, they refuse to let the highway take even the intangible things from them.

Across the country, highway development and the broken promises of urban renewal dealt a devastating double blow. Black families were promised that the homes that were demolished for highway development and "slums" would be replaced with public housing. But their homes were often bulldozed before the construction of new public housing even began. Many Black residents tried desperately to find new homes nearby, but racial zoning, redlining, and segregation left very few options available to them. True, the interstate highway system did not cause every problem that urban communities face. But its construction compounded discrimination, exclusion, and exploitation, and the boundaries the highways created—physical, psychological, and economic—were and remain durable monuments of white supremacy.

Just as many segregationist government officials hoped, these physical boundaries have so far withstood the adoption and evolution of civil rights laws. Rather than be forced to comply with the law, the highways became the law.

Chapter 3

It's Just a Highway

A sign from a segregated bus in Nashville, Tennessee.

n November 2021, Transportation Secretary Pete Buttigieg launched a media blitz to promote the Infrastructure Investment and Jobs Act, more commonly called the Bipartisan Infrastructure Law. To the surprise and appreciation of many whose lives had been affected by the highways, Secretary Buttigieg crisscrossed the country speaking about the racism that shaped the interstate system. He did not mince words, saying that the bill would "deconstruct the racism that was built into the roadways." Buttigieg was mocked by conservative lawmakers and commentators whose critiques of his statements amounted to: "It's just a highway." Indeed, an all-too-common retort to people who talk about the impact of highways on minority communities is to ask, simply, "How can a highway be racist?"

It is easy to dismiss the impact of the highways on communities—unless, of course, it was your community that was destroyed. "It's just a highway"—unless it was your home, your community institutions, and your business that were destroyed. It is easy to ask, "How can a highway be racist?"—unless your community was targeted.

For the people of Birmingham, Atlanta, and Indianapolis, it will never be just a highway. And sadly, the people of Birmingham, Atlanta, and Indianapolis are not alone. Communities across the country have stories to tell about lives and neighborhoods destroyed.

Neighborhoods play a central role in Black America. Sugar Hill in Harlem, Tremé in New Orleans, Baldwin Hills in Los Angeles, The Hill in Pittsburgh, and other similar communities are where the stories of Black identity, Black life, and Black independence played out. Facing racial violence and oppression, these neighborhoods became storied places where many Black people felt safe and respected, where they could express themselves without judgment or fear. In many cases, highway construction robbed them of that feeling. It wasn't just that the highways reinforced segregation. It is that the highways destroyed Black communities.

In the mid-1960s, Interstate 95 was built through the center of Overtown, then considered to be the heart of economic and cultural life for Black Miami. By 1930, much of Miami's Black population had been segregated by local racial zoning policies into Overtown, originally called Colored Town, and a handful of other racially segregated neighborhoods. The destruction of Overtown that followed was the realization of a decades-long campaign by white business leaders to remove Black residents and claim Overtown for themselves, to expand Miami's central business district.

The first attempt was made when Miami's white elites conceived of using undeveloped land five miles outside of the central business district to build a New Deal–funded public housing project for Black residents called Liberty Square. The city's white elites hoped that this new housing development would replace Overtown as the center of the Black community. Although many middle-income and upwardly mobile Black residents did move to Liberty Square, its creation did not lead to wholesale Black migration from Overtown. And many of the people who did make the move to Liberty Square returned to Overtown for their shopping, banking, and socializing.

Miami's power brokers did not give up. In 1936, the Dade County Planning Board proposed a "negro resettlement plan." It called for the removal of Overtown's residents and their involuntary resettlement on the agricultural fringes of the city. In a 1937 speech to the Miami Realty Board, George Merrick, a prominent local developer, suggested "a complete slum clearance effectively removing every negro family from the present city limits." His plan never materialized. But the passage of the Federal Highway Act would finally provide the opportunity Miami's leaders needed to seize Overtown and push out its Black residents.

The Miami Planning and Zoning Board was out of step with the conventional thinking of highway builders around the country. It valued neighborhood preservation, and that extended to the Overtown neighborhood. But the Board was ultimately cut out of the final decision-making. Downtown Miami business leaders, realtors, and politicians joined forces in 1955 and formed the Miami First Committee to help push an alternative plan, one that would not respect the Overtown community. When the federal Highway Act was passed the next year, Florida state highway planners quickly developed their own plan for Miami, rejecting essential portions of the 1955 Miami Planning and Zoning Board plan and adopting much of the alternative.

Powerful city interests got to work promoting the new plan, and Miami's major newspapers and media outlets endorsed it. Members of Miami's Black community did not have the political power to stop it, and the new plan was adopted.

In 1957, the Miami Slum Clearance Department estimated that 5,700 people would be displaced from their homes to build the highway. That same year, the *Miami Herald* published an article titled "What About the Negroes Uprooted by the Expressway?" that noted that no agency was planning for the relocation of Black people in Overtown.

By 1959, the Dade County Manager's office had increased the estimate to 10,000 people displaced. Yet the city ignored questions about where removed Black people would live. Black housing density was rising long before the highway was built through Overtown, and there was already pressure to build more housing for Black people. With the impending highway, that pressure understandably increased. The Greater Miami Urban League urged the government to plan for housing dislocation and the resulting social consequences of expanding I-95 through Miami. Despite many promises, no such relocation program ever materialized. Very few housing units were built to replace demolished homes, whose residents received little or no relocation assistance. Most of them ended up settling in other Black neighborhoods in Miami, especially in Liberty City.

Elizabeth Virrick, a housing reformer and activist in Miami, wrote about the displacement in her monthly newsletter:

> With shocking ruthlessness, the expressways slash through our city without regard to the grim results . . . building an impenetrable wall that will cut the city in half, will separate many stores from the people who deal there, will uglify pleasant areas and make bad areas worse. We are told to take it or leave it.

By the late 1960s, Overtown was dominated by the highway. A single interchange took up forty square blocks, devoured the Black business district, and took the homes of about 10,000 people—for a total of eighty-seven acres of housing and commercial property. Large parcels of land in Overtown were also seized for parking lots and garages. Overtown was once called the Harlem of the South, but there is painfully scarce evidence of that history today. The *Miami Times* observed that no corner of Overtown "seemed to have escaped the angered wrath of the bulldozers and wrecking cranes that have been busy at work demolishing homes, churches, apartment houses and business places." It reported that "a drive through the downtown Negro section gives one the idea that something like a king-size tornado had hit the place."

The residents who could not or did not want to move remained in the hollowed-out community adjacent to the highway, trying to rebuild. To this day, they bear the marks of decades of accumulated disadvantage. Although Overtown is now experiencing a period of reinvestment, the community is finding that the consequences of the highway, though built more than sixty years ago, remain hard to overcome.

THE DEMOLITION OF BLACK NEIGHBORHOODS ALSO INTENSIFIED RACIAL segregation and the concentration of poverty by forcing dislocated Black people deeper into inner cities. Housing displacement was particularly hard on inner-city Black residents because the housing supply was already inadequate before the arrival of the highway, and the boundaries of Black neighborhoods were vigilantly policed. Black property owners were rarely paid the true value of the property that was taken from them, and the federal government seldom provided relocation assistance. In addition, significant time would often elapse between condemnation orders and actual demolition, leading to deteriorating neighborhood conditions and making it even more difficult for property owners to sell their homes or businesses and move to a new community. Some remained in place, feeling stuck. Others just abandoned their property, fleeing without selling.

Many displaced residents wanted to remain close to the network of support and daily assistance that made survival possible. Some of them were lucky and found housing close to their old, fractured neighborhoods. But the destruction of Black homes to build highways depleted the overall housing stock in these communities, leading to overcrowding and homelessness.

To this day, people living in the communities cordoned off by highways face the stigma of state-sponsored racial segregation. Stigmatization assaults one's self-respect and dignity. Living in a segregated community can impose a sense of "otherness" on the segregated group, harming physical and mental health. Erecting highways separating Black and white communities sent a clear message of racial hierarchy. It demonstrated the establishment's power over the lives of Black people, ensuring that they understood "their place." Segregating communities using highways created a "badge of inferiority" for the people who lived there, a badge that remains.

For most displaced people, the only housing options were in other racially segregated and economically struggling communities. These included so-called second ghettos, a term often used to describe the expansion of low-income, Black neighborhoods after World War II through conscious, racist efforts by federal and local governments as well as private entities that had the government's support. Others moved to "transitioning" neighborhoods—working-class white communities that were beginning to experience white flight, a trend that hastened as Black people moved in. As white residents fled to suburbs made newly accessible by the highways, racially restrictive covenants kept Black people from buying in those communities, and the federal government denied home loans to Black people looking to live in white suburban communities in any case. Even setting aside these barriers, Black people often lacked the financial resources to improve their housing conditions. Hiring discrimination and a second-class education too often kept Black people from well-paying jobs. And in many cases, the highway had claimed the most significant financial asset Black families owned—their home. In the end, this web of restrictions left Black people crowded into small, poor neighborhoods.

In Iowa, local newspaper articles in the late 1950s focused on how the planned freeway through Des Moines would affect white homeowners, businesses, and leisure activities. The articles explored the projected impact the highway would have on the Waveland Golf Course and the Des

Moines Golf and Country Club, but not on the Black people who stood to lose their homes. And, of course, those were the people who had the most to lose.

A three-part series in the *Des Moines Tribune* in 1956 reported that even without segregation laws, the division of races in Des Moines was "nearly 100% effective." After redlining was made illegal, many white people shifted to using then-legal methods like "steering": refusing to show Black people homes outside of the inner city and drastically increasing home prices if a Black family wanted to make an offer.

These practices would only make it harder for Black families to find new homes once the highway took theirs. One Black homeowner who would lose his house to the highway said, "When I told people I was looking for a house which would cost what the highway commission paid me, they laughed at me." Another Black man, whose home was located on Martin Luther King Jr. Boulevard, which the new I-235 intersected, shared that he and his family "were paid only $5500 for our three-bedroom house and now are forced to buy a two-bedroom house, not as good for $9500."

THE LEGACY OF THE HIGHWAY SYSTEM IS CLEAR. IN A 2016 DEAR COLLEAGUE Letter, the then-secretaries of the United States Departments of Housing and Urban Development, Education, and Transportation acknowledged that the intersection of transportation, housing, and education policy helped to create and sustain concentrated poverty and racial segregation. According to the letter, "children raised in concentrated poverty or in communities segregated by socioeconomic status or race or ethnicity have significantly lower social and economic mobility than those growing up in integrated communities." They also noted that "rising economic segregation means that an increasing number of low-income households are located in distressed neighborhoods where they face challenges such as failing schools, high rates of crime, and inadequate access to services and jobs, making it harder for individuals and families to escape poverty." Transportation policy, including the interstate highways, is a significant cause.

There are also significant health impacts. The increased traffic from the highways coursing through Black communities has led to disproportionate air pollution, particularly in the Northeast and Mid-Atlantic. Going to school or living near a major highway increases your risk of asthma, lung disease, heart disease, adverse reproductive outcomes, and death. And once the highways were built, many of the affected communities became so-called sacrifice zones, forced to accept transportation hubs, landfills, power plants, and oil and gas refineries, with further impacts on physical and socioeconomic well-being.

In Syracuse, New York, Interstate 81 cut through the center of the city, decimating a primarily Black and Jewish neighborhood, the Fifteenth Ward. The ward was a half-square-mile area where Black and Jewish people built a community after being shut out of other neighborhoods by bigotry. By 1950, eight out of every nine Black residents in Syracuse lived in the Fifteenth Ward.

In 1964, the city began to bulldoze the neighborhood to make way for the highway. When the displaced Black residents from the Fifteenth Ward moved to other city neighborhoods, white residents fled to the suburbs. And today, Syracuse has among the highest rate of Black concentrations of poverty in the nation and bears the hallmarks of multigenerational poverty—few businesses, lack of economic opportunity, poor-quality schools, and violence. Housing for poor families remains crowded around I-81's elevated overpass, and nearly two-thirds of poor Black people in Syracuse live in high-poverty neighborhoods. Only about 30 percent of Black people in the Syracuse metro area own their own homes, while 71 percent of white people do.

Syracuse is also intensely racially segregated, with I-81 serving as a "line of demarcation." The highway separates the city's "best" neighborhoods from less resourced communities via up to six lanes of traffic, feeder ramps, and access roads. Notably, I-81 erects a barrier between University Hill—which includes several hospitals, Syracuse University, and some schools within the State University of New York system—and a low-income neighborhood. Some have compared I-81 to the Berlin Wall, dividing "the haves and the have nots."

NEIGHBORHOODS ARE MORE THAN THE BUILDINGS THAT COMPRISE THEM. They can encompass a sense of connection and common purpose among the people who live and work there. Too often, a highway took that, too. My research and advocacy have allowed me to spend time with so many wonderful people who were willing to share their stories in the hope that their trauma, and the trauma of their ancestors, might be a catalyst for change. When people speak about the many ways their neighborhoods were harmed by a highway, they often linger on the experience of watching their community fall apart over the days, weeks, and months after the construction of the highway was announced. They speak of seeing their beloved neighborhood dismantled building by building; of watching their friends, family, and favorite businesses and institutions leave each day. The arrival of a highway often created a clear "before" and "after." But it is also true that a major highway construction project is an ongoing process that many Black residents have experienced. Unlike with a bomb, the demolition did not come quickly or out of nowhere—it was something to dread over the course of months and years as the tragedy unfolded before you.

Many residents talked about a personal sense of loss. I spoke with one woman whose family still refuses to drive on I-81 in Syracuse, decades after the highway was built, because of all the things that the highway took from them. Another woman recalled her parents' shame and despair at seeing their beloved home and neighborhood overrun by rats because the highway construction had displaced the rats, too. I met people who recounted their parents' pain over losing their homes, the one real asset they had and their one opportunity to pass any wealth on to their children.

FOR MANY OF THE PEOPLE WHO LIVED IN COMMUNITIES TARGETED BY highway builders, their world was grounded in their familiar surroundings. In St. Paul, Minnesota, a Black neighborhood called Rondo was destroyed to make room for Interstate 94. In the 1930s, Rondo was the heart of St. Paul's Black community, not only home to the majority of Black residents in the city, but also to Black-owned grocery stores, credit unions, and social clubs. The neighborhood's center was Rondo Avenue, a prosperous corridor of Black-owned businesses. The Hallie Q. Brown Community Center was important to the social life of Black St. Paul, and the Sterling Club became a networking hub for Black professionals who could not join white groups. In 1928, the Credjafawn Social Club began playing a similar role for younger members of the Black community, and would later launch a credit union and food cooperative.

By the 1960s, the neighborhood's business core was gone, replaced by the newly constructed interstate. One in every eight Black residents of St. Paul lost their home to I-94. Homes that used to be a short walk to the nearby stores and restaurants were now blocked in and overlooked a six-lane highway shuttling commuters between the Twin Cities. Homes and businesses were seized using eminent domain. The neighborhood was split in two and the spirit of Rondo was gone. A resident of the neighborhood described the lingering consequences:

> As a community we had a geographical bond. Rondo was the thoroughfare, the main drag, the main contributory, the focal point, the center, the epic center [sic], the nexus. . . . When you walked down that street you walked past people you knew, places you ate, places you partied at, and everybody knew you. A common thread ran through everyone and when they tore that street up, it was like ripping your arm off. People were floundering. We were castaways. Where was our Rondo?

Nathaniel Khaliq was raised by his grandparents in a home they owned in Rondo. It would become the last house standing when the highway came through. In Rondo, he felt safe and loved, protected from the racism that surrounded him. Khaliq's grandfather, Rev. George Davis, held Sunday services for his congregation, Union Gospel Mission, in the house, which doubled as the mission's sanctuary. It all changed when Khaliq was thirteen years old. Police officers came into his home and removed his grandfather, who was eighty years old, and his grandmother Bertha. Reverend Davis and his wife had refused to leave their home to make way for I-94. Khaliq remembers the police holding axes and sledgehammers, knocking holes in the walls, breaking the windows, and tearing up the plumbing to ensure that Reverend Davis and his family could not move back into their home. His grandparents had to move into a rental home on the other side of town. When Khaliq arrived there, he found them sitting in the dark, crushed by the weight of all that had been taken from them. Remembering that day, he said, "It broke my grandfather's heart because the only thing I think a black man had back then was his dignity, his pride, self-worth, and independence. He didn't ask anyone for anything. He was a Pastor, and people in need would come by and he would help them out with prayer, food, or a word of encouragement."

Some residents managed to stay behind. Margaret Anne Ponder Lovejoy has lived her entire life in Rondo on the same plot of land. She watched as her parents' home and the homes of many others were taken down for the construction of I-94.

> I especially remember when they tore down my sister girlfriend's house on the corner because I sat out front and watched. They would bring in these big balls, huge destruction balls, and they hit the house. They hit it several times before it gave way. It was so horrendous to watch, to see properties destroyed like that. I remember the quietness when everybody was gone. . . . It was hard to move and it was hard to be left behind.

Samuel Fulwood III felt the pain of being left behind when a highway was built through his Charlotte, North Carolina, neighborhood. He said that he grew up believing that he "lived in a near-perfect world,"

> but that was in the early 1960s, before the bulldozers uprooted the dogwoods and oaks; gobbled up wide paved streets; and turned my playmates' homes into rubble. I vividly remember the change, in terms that a little boy can understand: Jimmy Don Arnold, who had the largest and best comic book collection, tearfully told me he couldn't hang with the fellas anymore because the mysterious "They" were tearing down his house. William "Beegee" White's huge front yard, where we played pickup football games, became a mound of dirt for an embankment to support an off-ramp to I-77. . . . Biddleville Elementary School, where I attended first and second grade—and heard about President

John F. Kennedy's assassination—was no more, gone to make way for the Brookshire Freeway, which connects I-77 and I-85.

The federal highway law was not the only source of destruction. The nation's highway system is made up of a complex web of federal interstate highways and state highways, and the latter were no kinder to Black neighborhoods than the federal ones.

James Wilson was finishing up junior high school when a state highway was built through his Toledo, Ohio, neighborhood in the early 1960s. It swallowed every house on both sides of Oakwood Avenue, including his family's home at number 639. His was a Black working-class community, with a mix of beautiful houses and some in need of repair. But everyone was working hard to maintain or renovate their homes, including those that, according to James, were not in good condition when they were purchased. As James pointed out, "by the time a Black family got a house, it was already run down. That's why they were able to get it." And "when you start at the back, it is hard to get to the front." This made the dismantling of the community even harder to watch. He knew what it took for people to make it to where they were—to own a home and get their piece of the American dream. Like so many others in this era, James watched the dismantling of his community, house by house, piece by piece, over the course of years.

It had been a tight-knit community, full of longtime residents. James and his closest friends had grown up together since kindergarten. Shortly before the freeway took his family home, he and his friends were preparing to move up from Robinson Junior High School to Jessup Scott High School. They all dreamed about playing on the Jessup Scott football team together. It was a dream they would never realize. Although James's older sister Pamela was able to attend Jessup Scott until her junior year, the construction of the state highway forced the family to move before Pamela had the chance to graduate with her friends. She was devastated. Pamela was an active member of the school's yearbook committee. Jessup Scott included her picture in the yearbook during her junior year since she would not have the opportunity to be a senior there.

Their parents had only bought their house a few years before it was taken for the freeway. They were proud of what they had accomplished—it was a big deal for Black people to buy a house in that era—and they loved their house.

Being forced out of it was particularly hard on James's father. He felt the weight of responsibility to take care of his family and find a new home. But he struggled to determine a clear path forward. On Sundays, the family would go house shopping. James, his mother, and his sister would all wait in the car while his father would knock on the door of a house they liked to express interest and ask if Black people were able to see it. He remembers the hurt on his father's face when he would return to the car and say to his family, "This one is not for us. We don't want this house." He and his sister knew what that really meant.

Chapter 4

Berlin Walls

Main Street in Buffalo, New York, is the color line. Locals speak of the "Main Street Divide." Most Black residents live to the east of Main Street and most white residents live to the west, with significant inequality of all kinds across the divide.

Eight Mile Road in Detroit, Michigan, separates Detroit, one of the most segregated cities in the United States, from the predominantly white suburbs to the north in Macomb, Oakland, and Livingston Counties. These counties are among the top ten in per capita income in Michigan. Predominantly Black Wayne County, home to Detroit, ranks thirty-fourth. Black people from south of Eight Mile Road often report increased police harassment when they cross the dividing line.

Troost Avenue in racially segregated Kansas City, Missouri, divides white residents to the west and Black residents to the east. The average life expectancy on the east side of Troost Avenue is fifteen years less than it is on the west side. A person walking along Troost Avenue could move from a census tract where the unemployment rate is below 20 percent to one where it is more than 45 percent simply by crossing the street.

Or consider Delmar Boulevard in St. Louis, Missouri. One resident says that across Delmar, "you have a division between the haves and the have-nots. . . . People on one side are prospering and the people on the other side are not." Much of the area north of Delmar Boulevard is majority-Black with a median home value of $78,000. In the majority-white neighborhoods to the south, the median home value is $310,000. North of Delmar, only 5 percent of residents twenty-five years or older have a bachelor's degree. To the south of Delmar, 67 percent of residents twenty-five years or older have at least a bachelor's degree.

The interstate highway system made driving across the country easier and faster. With highways, a trip that used to take weeks could now be accomplished in a matter of days. But before the highways, one could always traverse the hodgepodge of state roads, city streets, and sometimes barely paved roads to get around.

Like much of the nation's interstate highway system, many roads were built to serve as physical boundaries to shield white communities from Black people who wanted to break free of their Jim Crow confines. In cities around the country, governmental powers were deployed under the guise of urban planning and street safety to build roads and street grids that appeased the segregationist desires of white citizens.

BEYOND ACTING AS LINES OF DEMARCATION THAT DETERMINED WHERE and how people lived, roads and street grids were manipulated to complicate the process of traveling from Black neighborhoods to and through white ones, locking people in or shutting them out, or both. Like a board game that becomes ever more difficult to play with each roll of the dice, roads and the layout of street grids did not enhance Black mobility in many cases, but made it harder. It was not just about restricting the areas Black people lived in; it was about controlling and curtailing Black movement. For many urban planners, it was not enough to keep Black residential communities separate from white residential communities. They had to create obstacles to keep Black people from even getting close to where white people lived, much less visiting those communities, or even just driving through them on their way to someplace else. It was as though Black people were a highly contagious airborne virus. Limited or transitory exposure at any proximity would be enough to sicken white neighborhoods.

The subtle and not-so-subtle uses of street-planning techniques included dead-ending streets; converting roads to one-way streets that repeatedly led drivers away from white communities; turning through streets into cul-de-sacs; changing the names of streets as they passed from white to Black communities; and refraining from paving streets as they approached racial boundaries. Sometimes, municipalities used subtle tactics to limit

Black access. At other times, localities made no attempts to disguise the segregationist intent behind nominally race-neutral practices.

Cities and towns across the nation used many of these strategies in concert to amplify their exclusionary effects. But Atlanta was in a league of its own. Georgia had a long history of removing people of color from land that white people wanted for themselves. As in so many other places in the United States, the tradition began with Indigenous people and blossomed into multipronged efforts to remove, isolate, and segregate Black people. Georgia was established on land that was already the home of the Muscogee (Creek) and Cherokee Nations. In 1838 and 1839, the state took part in the act of ethnic cleansing known as the Trail of Tears, with the federal government forcibly removing tens of thousands of Indigenous people to what is now Oklahoma.

After the Civil War, Black people began migrating from rural areas to urban centers such as Atlanta in large numbers, and Black neighborhoods started to coalesce throughout the city. Atlanta took action to restrict not only who could live in certain neighborhoods but where and how Black people could move around the city. Officials passed a segregation ordinance and racial zoning laws to control where Black people could live. As the Black community fought back and outsmarted many of these traditional methods, Atlanta's segregationists expanded their efforts. As in many other early segregationist communities, the strategies employed to regulate Black mobility continued to evolve based on Supreme Court precedent and the population growth of the city.

On June 16, 1913, the city enacted a segregation ordinance, frequently called the Ashley Ordinance, after Claude Ashley, the city councilman who spearheaded the legislation. Modeled after similar ordinances in Maryland and Virginia, the Ashley Ordinance forbade Black people from occupying homes on white-occupied blocks and white people from occupying homes on Black-occupied blocks, unless the majority of owners agreed that a house was open for occupancy by either white or Black people. The Ashley Ordinance was among the racial zoning ordinances invalidated by the Supreme Court's *Buchanan* decision in 1917.

Of course, segregationists did not give up. Following *Buchanan*, Atlanta turned to citywide "comprehensive zoning" to accomplish similar ends. This second wave of racial zoning ordinances arrived in earnest in 1922, when the city adopted a scheme that regulated "land uses, building types, and tenant categories," with explicit racial designations. These plans not only maintained racially identifiable neighborhoods but provided for commercial or industrial buffer zones between Black and white neighborhoods. Samuel Whitten was a prominent city planner who worked as a consultant to the Atlanta City Planning Commission during this time. He believed that "reasonable segregation is normal, inevitable, and desirable" and was "essential in the interest of the public peace, order and security." In 1922, while reflecting on the comprehensive zoning plan, he wrote that "establishing colored residence districts has removed one of the most potent causes of race conflict."

Despite the Supreme Court, or maybe because of it, city policymakers were well aware of which sorts of regulations would impact Black people most significantly. The Supreme Court had been compelled to rule on zoning ordinances and racial segregation so many times that racist city planners had a more refined sense of what was allowed and what was not with every subsequent court opinion. Indeed, the Supreme Court's decision in *Buchanan* offered a road map on how to avoid a constitutional violation. Subsequent racial zoning schemes were passed in 1929 and 1931 in Atlanta which managed to evade immediate judicial review. The 1929 law attached residential segregation to anti-miscegenation laws by prohibiting someone from moving "into a building on a street in which the majority of the residences . . . are occupied by those with whom said person is forbidden to intermarry." The 1931 law made it illegal for "any person of either the white or colored races to move into a . . . building last occupied by persons of a different race . . . if such . . . building is situated within fifteen blocks from a public school" of the other race. Although these laws were ultimately struck down, while they stood they helped to solidify the racial character of neighborhoods and created the footprint for future urban renewal, infrastructure, and segregation efforts.

Despite calling Atlanta "the city too busy to hate," white residents and local officials were obsessed with maintaining separate white and Black communities and making it exceedingly difficult for anyone to travel between the two. They supplemented strict housing segregation with infrastructure policy. Taking a belt-and-suspenders approach to racial segregation, Atlanta layered multiple road and street grid plans on top of each other, factoring racial considerations into virtually all major transportation infrastructure decisions. Officials openly acknowledged their intent to use city planning to segregate white and Black communities physically, socially, and economically. As civil rights activists fought to integrate lunch counters, public transportation, and schools across the South, housing in Atlanta grew increasingly segregated.

Still, with Black people no longer facing explicit racial zoning laws, they tried to move out of the overcrowded industrial and commercial areas to which they were confined. In 1959, Black people comprised 35.7 percent of Atlanta's population but were limited to 16.4 percent of its land, although many acres of land in Atlanta remained undeveloped. At the same time, Atlanta was witnessing a surge in Black political power— the result of the end of the all-white primary elections in 1946 and a substantial increase in Black voter registration. Black residents used their emerging political clout to force the city and white developers to come to agreements on "racial boundaries." They demanded more and better land for Black homes in exchange for maintaining all-white neighborhoods. Black residents hoped to improve their living conditions while avoiding the violence and racial terror that followed Black residents' attempts to integrate white communities.

These demands, and the resulting negotiations, were occurring alongside extensive highway and road building in Atlanta in the 1950s and 1960s. Local officials used the construction of new local roads, in addition to Interstate 20, Interstate 75, and Interstate 80, to go beyond the negotiated agreements and solidify the separation of Black and white neighborhoods. Not surprisingly, the white power structure sought to formalize invisible dividing lines by building physical ones, and by making it difficult to cross those newly strengthened color lines.

One example of how this worked in practice was Atlanta's West Side Mutual Development Committee. In 1952, the city established this biracial group and charged it with determining racial land agreements. The committee negotiated agreements covering which race would be allowed to live in emerging neighborhoods, the location of new roads to service and access these emerging neighborhoods, and commitments to preserve the racial character of established neighborhoods. Black residents agreed to be involved in the committee to make sure they had some say over where Black people could live, while hopefully stemming the racial violence they were sure to face if they moved into—or even close to—white neighborhoods.

Through the West Side Mutual Development Committee, Black leaders worked jointly with the city to determine where to place roads to *protect* Black neighborhoods from racial violence or decimation. The resulting agreements often created buffer zones between white and Black neighborhoods that ensured residents of different neighborhoods were rarely proximate. They also made it difficult for Black people to access white neighborhoods even to visit—whether for shopping or even just to get to other parts of the city. In 1954, the National Development Company, a Black-owned real estate development firm, planned to build west of Collier Heights, a traditionally white neighborhood. But white homeowners in Collier Heights were vehemently opposed to the development. The National Development Company worked with the West Side Mutual Development Committee, the Metropolitan Planning Commission, and several white neighborhood associations to settle on a plan that included building an access road, to be named Collier Drive, that would provide a wide buffer between Collier Heights and the planned Black community to the west.

Under the agreement, the National Development Company agreed to sell all the land it had acquired east of the proposed access road. In exchange, the white community groups would help the National Development Company secure the lots west of Collier Heights for Black residential development. Additionally, the City Planning Commission, Zoning Board, and Board of Zoning Appeals committed to developing sewage and water lines to the new area and paving Collier Drive to the western limits of the boundary line. The creation of Collier Drive would have the added benefit of diverting Black people away from Baker Ridge Drive, which ran through Collier Heights. The deal was made. Collier Drive was built and exists to this day.

Similarly, white residents of Mozley Park sought to formalize the north side of Westview Drive as an unofficial southern boundary for Black housing development. In 1952, the Empire Real Estate Board, a Black real estate group founded in 1939 to improve housing conditions for Black people in Atlanta, agreed to that unofficial boundary. However, the agreement also prohibited Black developers from offering housing within one hundred yards of Westview Drive. As a result, there were no paved streets within that zone that would connect the new Black developments to the north with Westview Drive and Mozley Park to the south. That made travel between the two communities difficult, and the unpaved swath of land and Westview Drive together became the unofficial boundary line for Black migration.

A related segregation technique commonly employed in Atlanta at mid-century was simply to abruptly end a street to prevent Black people from easily accessing a white neighborhood. In 1967, Samuel Adams, the former director of research for the Southern Regional Council, a civil rights organization founded in 1944 to stop racial violence and promote racial equality, noted:

> Drive from downtown Atlanta six miles southwest through Atlanta's bulging westside Negro community on out into the unincorporated areas of Fulton County, and you will find exactly three streets that provide fairly direct access between the Negro area to the northwest and the white areas to the southwest. In a city the size of Atlanta which always is struggling to relieve traffic congestion problems, this is a situation difficult to fathom on any sound or logical basis.

There was, of course, an unsound and illogical basis: the desire to block the expansion of the Black community. Leon Eplan, the commissioner of Atlanta's Department of Budget and Planning from 1974 to 1978, acknowledged that "streets were terminated as they passed from black neighborhoods to white ones," and that Atlanta's street grid now reflects "few continuous streets [that] traverse the urban community."

Consider Willis Mill Road, which connects to Martin Luther King Jr. Drive (formerly Gordon Road) in the north, where there was a growing Black population. To the south, a white community called Cascade Heights was accessible via Willis Mill Road. In the late 1950s the city agreed to abruptly dead-end Willis Mill Road five blocks south of Martin Luther King Jr. Drive to make it impossible to drive directly from Willis Mill to Cascade Road, the entry point to Cascade Heights. So, to inhibit Black people from traveling into the white neighborhood—not to live there, but simply to drive through it—a large portion of the road was abandoned between the two dead-ended stretches of Willis Mill Road. Today, the two Willis Mill Roads remain unconnected. The land between them is now an undeveloped walking path.

The best-known example of spatial racism in Atlanta is probably the Peyton Road "wall" in Atlanta. The wooden barrier created a physical divide between the white and Black neighborhoods within Cascade Heights. Although the barricade stood for just seventy-two days before it was ordered to be taken down, it was reflective of Atlanta's deep commitment to using infrastructure to protect inequality.

Peyton Forest was a wealthy, white section of the Cascade Heights neighborhood. The areas surrounding Peyton Forest were undergoing a racial transition that made white residents uneasy. At the same time, the white developer of Peyton Forest believed that its residents were standing in the way of his developing his land at a faster pace. He threatened to sell his properties to Black people if the barriers to development were not removed. Facing financial difficulties and not seeing the movement that he wanted, in December of 1962 the developer sold a home and twenty-acre lot to Dr. Clinton Warner, a Black surgeon, veteran, graduate of Morehouse College, civil rights advocate, and founding chair of the Morehouse School of Medicine.

The sale set off a white backlash. White Peyton Forest residents resorted to tried-and-true methods, deploying a racial terror campaign while enlisting support from sympathetic white government officials. White protesters dumped their trash on Dr. Warner's lawn, they left harassing messages on his office phone, and they tried to burn down his new house. Atlanta's mayor at the time, Ivan Allen, said that the sale set off "a holocaust among the whites there." They demanded not only that Dr. Warner be removed from his home, but that the city erect "racial buffers" to prevent more Black people from purchasing homes in Peyton Forest.

In particular, white homeowners asked officials to erect a physical barrier on Peyton Road and Harlan Road to prevent further "intrusion" into their community. Both roads served as north-south through roads, connecting the white and Black sections of Cascade Heights. Erecting the proposed barriers would sever a main artery, diverting drivers to various side roads—adding up to five miles to their journeys and generally making passage inconvenient.

Nevertheless, on December 17, 1962, the Atlanta Board of Aldermen approved legislation to do just that, and Allen immediately signed it into law. He was only a few months into his first term as mayor of Atlanta, having been sworn into office during a time of significant economic growth, infrastructure development, and racial justice protests. He considered Atlanta to be "the epitome of Southern womanhood." This sentiment was no doubt shared by other white Atlantans who sought to protect their property just as they had worked to "protect" white womanhood—by any means necessary. Mayor Allen believed erecting the barrier would be a "happy compromise" between "entrenched whites on one side, encroaching blacks on the other," in the tradition of other compromises around race that had been made around the city. He hoped the Peyton Road barrier would calm white residents while focusing attention on the potential to rezone vacant land to provide for much needed housing for Black Atlantans.

The following day, a crew of primarily Black city maintenance workers put up wooden barriers about three feet tall across Peyton Road. The barriers bore signs that read "Road Closed." Local and national newspapers called it Atlanta's Berlin Wall—a Cold War–era analogy that was used often when it came to racial dividing lines, as we've seen. The reference to the Berlin Wall surprised Mayor Allen. In his inaugural address, ironically enough, he had said, "It was in Berlin that the tragic and dramatic lesson of what happens to a divided city came home to me." He was also shocked to see the protests from the Black community, whose support had helped him win the election.

Indeed, blowback from the Black community was swift and furious. The barricade was challenged in court. Civil rights organizations formed a coalition to coordinate protests and picketed outside of city hall. There were calls for boycotts of white businesses around Cascade Heights that supported the barricade. Martin Luther King Jr. and the president of the Atlanta chapter of the NAACP issued a statement calling the barricade "one of Atlanta's gravest mistakes and a slap at our national creed of democracy and justice." The barricade was even set on fire. But the city quickly rebuilt the wall and then Klansmen dressed in their robes guarded it, with signs proclaiming that "Whites Have Rights, Too."

The controversy ended on March 1, 1963, when a Fulton County Superior Court judge ordered that the barricade be removed. Knowing that the court's decision would come down that day, and suspecting what the outcome would be, Mayor Allen had a crew waiting by the wall to remove it as soon as the decision was announced. He later recalled taking many lessons away from the debacle, including one that his predecessor William B. Hartsfield once told him: "Never do anything wrong that they can take a picture of."

Following the Berlin Wall debacle, Cascade Heights become a case study in white flight. By July 1963, only fifteen white families remained in the neighborhood.

A COUPLE OF DECADES LATER, MEMPHIS ATTRACTED SIMILAR NOTORIETY for blocking a single road. In 1981, following a protracted legal battle that would ultimately reach the United States Supreme Court, the city closed off West Drive, a main thoroughfare between an historically all-white community and a predominantly Black community, at the request of white property owners who wanted protection from "undesirable" influences. The closing of the road was not a part of a citywide plan, but a single act to protect one neighborhood at the expense of another. The result was a physical and psychological barrier that made a clear message about the relative value placed on a Black community and a white community.

It all started years earlier, on July 9, 1973, when a street closure application was filed by a representative of the Hein Park Civic Association and numerous residents. They wanted the city to close the north end of West Drive, an important thoroughfare that ran through Hein Park, right before it crossed Jackson Street. Hein Park was not just a predominantly white residential neighborhood when the application was made, but an exclusively white neighborhood.

Importantly, West Drive was also the main connection between Hein Park and a predominantly Black neighborhood to its north. The move would prevent Black drivers who used that stretch of road from traveling from their community through Hein Park to reach the city center. Instead, Black residents would have to drive around the white neighborhood. In their closure application, the Hein Park residents and civic association spoke of their desire to reduce traffic flow, increase safety, reduce traffic pollution, and stop the "interruption of community living." Of course, the traffic that they believed would threaten safety and interrupt community living would be overwhelmingly Black.

On April 1, 1974, Black residents led by Nathan T. Greene, a Black Memphian who lived north of Jackson Street, and two civic associations, brought a class action lawsuit seeking to stop the road closure. They argued that the decision to close the road and the juncture between the white and Black community denied Black residents the same rights as white residents to purchase, sell, and hold property. The closure of West Drive also promised to affect property values in both communities. It would negatively impact the property values in the Black community while demoralizing its residents. At the same time, residents of Hein Park would enjoy increased property values that would make it a "utopia" in Memphis. The group of plaintiffs also brought a claim under the Thirteenth Amendment to the US Constitution, arguing that the closure of a public street in a way that benefited white residents and negatively impacted Black residents, inhibiting access to the white community, was a badge or incidence of slavery.

The United States Supreme Court disagreed. Focusing solely on the number of minutes that would be added to the average trip for the predominantly Black commuters, the court found the street closure to be merely a "slight inconvenience to Black motorists," and a consequence of the location of their homes rather than the color of their skin. There was no mention of the manifest reality that, in the United States, those two things—where you live and your race—are hard to separate.

While the majority's opinion was detached from the fact of racism in America, Justice Thurgood Marshall—the first Black person to sit on the United States Supreme Court—dissented in an opinion that was grounded in a rigorous understanding of how government transportation decisions like the closure of West Drive can reinforce racial hierarchy and stigma. Justice Marshall pointed out that an analysis that focuses on the minutes or miles added or subtracted from a commute "ignores the plain and powerful symbolic message" the road closure sends to members of both communities. He noted that the curb Memphis erected to block traffic on West Drive was built at the precise point where the all-white neighborhood ended and the predominantly Black neighborhood began, sending a "clear, though sophisticated, message." He wrote: "The problem is less the closing of [the street] in particular than the establishment of racially determined districts which the closing effects," especially when the street closing was "one more of the many humiliations which society has historically visited" on Black Americans.

Justice Marshall grasped that the various justifications for the street closure were "little more than code phrases for racial discrimination." To him, the facts surrounding the closure told the story of "a white community, disgruntled over sharing its street with Negroes, taking legal measures to keep out the 'undesirable traffic,' and of a city, heedless of the harm to its Negro citizens, acquiescing in the plan." The Black residents were being told that "they are to stay out of the all-white enclave of Hein Park and should instead take the long way around." But Justice Marshall was able to persuade only two other members of the court to join him in his dissent.

Although West Drive was closed in a way that allowed access for emergency vehicles that needed to reach Hein Park, the message was clear to everyone else—Do Not Enter, as big red signs continue to read today. Black people would have to go around the white neighborhood. They still do.

ELSEWHERE, WHITE RESIDENTS TOOK MATTERS INTO THEIR OWN HANDS, erecting barriers themselves to enforce racial segregation. In 1971, the

Pattersons, a white family in Dadeville, Alabama, built a barricade across Patterson Street, the east-west public road they lived on. It was named for Will Patterson, an ancestor of theirs. The barrier denied a group of Black residents who lived at the opposite end of the street access to their own homes.

The Patterson family built the barricade along what had been the dividing line between two property tracts in Dadeville. Prior to their intervention, Dadeville officials had been paving sections of Patterson Street as homes were built along the road on the tract to the west of the section line. With every new home that was built, the city paved another segment of Patterson Street, until the paved portion reached Horace Dennis's driveway. He was the owner of the last lot in the tract, immediately to the west of the section line.

The forty-foot section of the road to the east of the section line remained unpaved. All of the remaining lots to the east of the section line were sold to Black people, except for the lot directly to the east of the section line, closest to the western portion of the road and next to Dennis's home, which was sold to a white man named James Shaddix.

Nearly two years later, Patterson family members took it upon themselves to enforce a racial boundary between Black and white property owners by constructing a barricade across Patterson Street right at the section line, preventing the Black residents to the east of the line from using the western portion of the street. Shaddix, the sole white resident whose access was blocked by the fence, was given permission to drive through an opening in it. The Black residents were given no such permission. Instead, they had to take a two-mile detour.

The Pattersons believed that they were entitled to put up the fence because, they argued, the small, unpaved strip of the street between Dennis's driveway and the section line was private property. Not surprisingly, the city of Dadeville endorsed the Pattersons' and Dennis's self-help strategy, arguing that the city lacked the authority to remove the fence from private property—all but abandoning control of the road to its white residents. The Black residents who lived to the east of the section line were forced to go to court to ultimately regain the use of the paved road that their taxes helped to maintain.

Six years later, in Nacogdoches County, Texas, a Black property owner named Odie Evans was similarly forced to go to court when a white neighbor, Lester Tubbe, erected a locked metal gate across the road Evans used to get to her home. Evans purchased her land in 1978, and the only access to her property was a road that passed through land owned by Tubbe.

According to Evans's lawsuit, after Tubbe put up the barrier, he "gave a key to the gate to all of the white people who owned property along the road but refused to give a key to Evans." Evans also reported that Tubbe and his sons threatened and harassed her and other Black people who were considering buying property in the area. Evans filed suit. But after an hour of deliberation, a local jury decided the case in favor of Tubbe.

In Georgia, in 1990, the city of Port Wentworth allegedly refused to reopen a road that had been blocked by a private citizen. Six Black residents of North Port Wentworth and the North Port Wentworth Citizens Council, an organization that sought to promote the interests of Black residents, alleged that the city abandoned a public road by allowing Lynn Jeffers, a white resident, to close off Coldbrook Road, a road used primarily by Black residents. Coldbrook Road had all the indications of a public road: it appeared on Department of Transportation maps as a county road, and there was a county road sign posted on it. Moreover, Jeffers acknowledged that he did not own the road.

Yet the city facilitated Jeffers's efforts by putting up a sign that designated it as a private road. The city council voted to change its name to Jeffers Road, a move suggesting that it was Jeffers's private property. The city also failed to take any steps to remove the fence or stop other alleged efforts to block the road, including when tacks, roofing nails, and large mounds of dirt were used to that end over the course of the next five years.

The Black residents ultimately settled the case with the city, with the city agreeing to request that a special master determine who owned the road and who might use it. Despite Jeffers saying he did not own the road in the original litigation, in January of 2013 a state Superior Court judge affirmed the finding of a special master that he did. The court also ordered that all the residents whose property was bound by Jeffers Road be given an easement by Jeffers to use the road to access their property. As in so many other stories we have seen so far, it is hard to talk about a distinction between history and the present. With transportation infrastructure, history *is* the present.

NAMES HAVE MEANING. CITIES OFTEN USE ROAD NAMES TO REFLECT A community's vision of itself. Main Street evokes classic Americana, a place where neighbors come to shop, eat, and share the news of the day. Fifth Avenue, Rodeo Drive, and Bourbon Street all prompt specific images for many Americans. Streets named after trees—Oak Road and Elm Street— are trying to communicate something about the nature of a given community. Municipalities have a long tradition of renaming streets—for example, to celebrate local heroes or to memorialize recent events. It is not surprising, then, that street names have also been wielded as a tool of segregation. In some cases, well-intentioned renamings have nonetheless come with a significant cost. In other cases, communities have intentionally renamed streets to isolate their neighborhoods from association with Black people.

A number of New York City avenues change names as they cross over from the Upper East and West Sides of Manhattan into Harlem. Most of these renamings happened in the 1970s and 1980s to honor Black leaders, some with important ties to Harlem. Seventh Avenue became Adam Clayton Powell Jr. Blvd. as it crossed 110th Street in honor of the first Black person from New York to be elected to the US Congress. Powell would represent Harlem in Congress for more than thirty years. Sixth Avenue becomes Malcolm X Boulevard in honor of the slain civil rights leader who considered Harlem his home. In tribute to the formerly enslaved man who became a famous abolitionist and writer, Eighth Avenue north of Central Park becomes Frederick Douglass Avenue. And much of Harlem's main economic and cultural thoroughfare, 125th Street, is conamed in honor of slain civil rights leader Dr. Martin Luther King Jr. These avenue names, and those of similar streets across the country, represent victories by community activists and political leaders who fought to ensure Black leaders were honored for their lives' work.

Today, many people question whether these streets honor the legacies of these leaders or make a mockery of them. Because racial segregation and material inequities are deeply connected, you can often guess a person's race by their address. The naming or renaming of streets in honor of Black leaders can trigger a process of racialization that marginalizes communities, leading to stigmatization and a lack of investment.

No example is more obvious than the Martin Luther King Jr. boulevards, avenues, and streets around the country. Many are in neighborhoods that are the antithesis of what he stood for, with high levels of racial segregation and less economic opportunity than surrounding areas. These areas do not make up the Beloved Community that Dr. King so often spoke of. With the notable exception of such roads in the state of California, study after study confirms that streets named after Dr. King are racially segregated spaces. In a 2020 study, researchers found that most Black people living in neighborhoods around a street named in honor of Martin Luther King Jr., particularly in southern and midwestern states, face extreme racial segregation. This segregation goes hand in hand with the creation of negative stereotypes about Black people and Black communities, grounded in false narratives of Black criminality and apathy. The vilification of these predominantly Black communities leads to property devaluation, economic disinvestment, industrial pollution, and other material consequences of racial stigmatization, which in turn lead to further vilification. Perversely, street namings intended to celebrate heroes of the struggle for Black freedom can sometimes trigger reactionary responses that undermine that freedom.

The 2020 study also points to the resistance of white residents to renaming efforts for streets that cut through both Black and white neighborhoods. An attempt to name Ninth Street in Chattanooga, Tennessee, after Dr. King failed. And residents were successful in getting Dr. King's name removed from one of Kansas City's historic boulevards: In January 2019, the Kansas City, Missouri, city council voted to rename Paseo Boulevard to Dr. Martin Luther King Jr. Boulevard. Before the name change, Kansas City had the distinction of being one of the largest cities in the United States without a street named in honor of Dr. King. Yet following a fierce backlash from residents, later that same year a proposal to change the name of the street back to its original name passed with 70 percent of the vote.

Decades earlier, in response to a 1988 campaign to rename upper Fifth Avenue in New York City in honor of Marcus Garvey, opposition came from all corners of the community. Many of the middle-class Black residents of the Riverbend Co-op, located on Fifth Avenue and 139th Street, publicly voiced a preference for the status quo. Ruth Richardson, a member of the co-op's management committee, told the *New York Times* that "Many vendors would say, 'Marcus Garvey Boulevard? I don't want to go up there.'" The vice chairwoman of the co-op board, C. Elaine Parker, stated bluntly that a street named for a Black historical figure in a predominantly Black neighborhood would struggle with marketability: "Imagine, 'Saks Marcus Garvey.'" More diplomatically, Uptown Chamber of Commerce president Lloyd A. Williams told the *Times* that "it's an excellent idea to honor Garvey," but "if there's one avenue we would like to maintain its name, its [*sic*] Fifth, for everything it connotes to the country and for the continuity between Harlem and the rest of the city." Members of this community understand the dynamics of racism and know that just replacing a sign that says "Fifth Avenue" with one that says "Marcus Garvey" will impact how their neighborhoods, homes, and businesses are viewed in the eyes of the world.

Well before the era when streets were being renamed in honor of Black heroes and leaders, Atlanta, so often in the vanguard of segregation efforts, was renaming roads to reflect the color line that city officials and white citizens were working so hard to protect. To further entrench the separation of the races, white Atlantans regularly collaborated with city officials to alter the names of streets that ran through both white and Black neighborhoods so that white residents would not share similar addresses with Black residents, even when both actually lived on the same road. Where streets were long, continuous, and passed through multiple one-race communities, the street names would generally change.

There were relatively few such streets to begin with; as we have seen, segregationist city planners placed physical obstacles—highways, dead ends, one-way streets, and roadblocks—to keep neighborhoods and commutes as physically segregated as possible. But where such thoroughfares did exist, renaming them based on demographics layered stigmatic harm on top of the myriad efforts to segregate and subjugate Black people. Renaming alerted others to the racial character of the neighborhood and allowed white residents to retain the "dignity" of supposedly not living on the same street as Black people.

Beyond the expressive dimension of forcing Black families to live on "different" streets, distinct street names for white and Black neighborhoods made it easier to discriminate based on address. Businesses, prospective residents, or anyone else for whom the racial character of the communities mattered could more easily identify the race of an individual or business owner. This opened the door to further discrimination against Black residents through reduced property values, denied loan applications and investments, or other policies of economic apartheid.

Consistent with the long-standing public-private partnership that helped to make and keep Atlanta segregated, the city made it easy for white residents to avoid the perceived plague of Black proximity. White residents needed only to petition the Atlanta–Fulton County Planning Board to rename a portion of a given street. White petitioners had little trouble gaining approval—a Black family moving to a street was enough to prompt a successful name change. The practice dated to the 1930s if not earlier. Name changes are visible in the 1938 Home Owners Loan Corporation map of Atlanta, which reflected redlining practices throughout the city. As discussed in chapter 2, such maps rated communities as green ("best"), blue ("still desirable"), yellow (definitely declining), and red (hazardous). Under this standard, predominantly Black communities, other communities of color, or neighborhoods that were too close to Black communities were designated as red or yellow, while white communities were rated as green or blue.

Much of the racialized renaming happened around Ponce de Leon Avenue, a major east-to-west thoroughfare, and occurred in response to the northward expansion of Black communities toward the road. Many (if not most) of the name changes were enacted as streets that ran north to south crossed Ponce de Leon Avenue and approached predominantly white neighborhoods to the north. Ponce de Leon Avenue does not perfectly match any line on the 1938 HOLC map of redlining in Atlanta. The road is not an exact boundary—the street runs east to west, while the boundaries of the racially segregated white neighborhoods sometimes run at a diagonal. But it is close enough, and the city treated it as the line of demarcation.

Today, within Atlanta's city center, a single road is named Juniper Street, then Courtland Street, and then Washington Street. The transition from Juniper to Courtland occurs at North Avenue, one block south of Ponce de Leon. Farther north, Juniper Street runs for only thirteen blocks, all in a neighborhood once designated as "declining" by the HOLC. Juniper terminates at Fourteenth Street, shortly below the white, "still desirable" neighborhood of Ansley Park, and becomes Courtland. The switch from Courtland to Washington occurs at Decatur Street, as the road enters a formerly redlined neighborhood. This pattern repeats as Ponce de Leon courses through the city.

On the east side of Atlanta, as Charles Allen Drive intersects with Ponce de Leon Avenue, its name changes to Parkway Drive for the portion of the road that is to the south of Ponce de Leon, an area of town that was predominantly Black-owned when built. One block to the east of Charles Allen and Parkway Drives is Monroe Drive. Monroe Drive intersects with Ponce de Leon, and the street that comes out to the south is simply called Boulevard. This change was made as Black migration on the east side of Atlanta began to move west. Six blocks north of Ponce de Leon, both Monroe and Charles Allen Drives reach neighborhoods that were formerly designated "best" and "still desirable" by the Home Owners Loan Corporation.

A few blocks further east, Briarcliff Road runs through a white community. After it intersects with Ponce de Leon, it becomes Moreland Avenue to the south as it runs through a Black neighborhood. Long after the legal racial boundaries between neighborhoods have been erased, these changing street names remain a monument to that history.

On the west side, as Hunter Street moves from a Black neighborhood to a white one, it becomes Mozley Drive. Hunter Hills, to the east of the HOLC's red line, was a prominent Black community, while the Mozley Park neighborhood was a white neighborhood that bitterly resisted integration. Today, the entire stretch from Mozley Drive to Hunter Street has been renamed Martin Luther King Jr. Drive.

Atlanta may have been an innovator, but it was far from an outlier in its use of street renamings to reinforce racial boundaries between neighborhoods as integration spread. Louisville, Kentucky, has followed a similar practice, as multiple streets change names at or just before Thirty-First Street—the boundary between a Black residential community and an exclusively white neighborhood.

Louisville's racial zoning ordinance had been struck down by *Buchanan v. Warley* in 1917. The case originated in the city itself. Under Louisville's racial zoning ordinance, the blocks between Twenty-First Street and Thirty-First Street were reserved for white people. In the decades after the *Warley* decision erased that legal boundary, the area just east of Thirty-First Street was the first location to which some Black families moved as they migrated west within Louisville.

White residents were determined to maintain Thirty-First Street as a racial boundary line and used street names as one of their tools. As in Atlanta, local whites secured name changes through city ordinances to further this effort. They wanted no ambiguity as to the physical location of the color line. Altering street names would ensure that Black people knew exactly what boundaries not to cross. At Thirtieth Street, Walnut became Michigan, Chestnut became River Park, Madison became Vermont, and Jefferson became Lockwood.

IN A NATION WHERE POLITICAL POWER IS DEEPLY INTERTWINED WITH race and economic power, it is not surprising that Black communities continue to disproportionately bear the burden of road development.

In 2019, then nine-year-old Amira Johnson learned that her great-grandmother's home would be taken to build a four-lane, high-speed road. She decided to take a stand and, in August of that year, sent a handwritten letter to the South Carolina Department of Transportation (SCDOT) to help her "crying great grandmother" and save the home Amira had lived in as a baby. Amira reminded officials of the history of Black oppression in the state, asking, "Did you know that black people did not have freedom?" On the impact the proposed road would have on her great-grandmother and her community, Amira wrote, "My great grandma is 79 years old and has no bisnus moving. When I was only a baby I lived with her. If you were me, you will be mad because they are taking away your homes. Be fair for once in your life."

At the time Amira wrote the letter, her grandmother lived in the predominantly Black community of Sandridge, a neighborhood in the city of Conway, which in turn is located in Horry County, South Carolina. That year, Horry County announced four possible corridors for the new Conway Perimeter Road—and all went through Sandridge, disproportionately affecting Black residents while sparing neighboring white communities. Unlike the infrastructure projects of the 1950s and 1960s, building Conway Perimeter Road would not destroy a thousand homes or displace thousands of families. Instead, the new road would swallow only twenty-one homes and three businesses. Yet the impact on Black families and a historic Black community will still be devastating. By the time this book is published, unless Sandridge is successful in fighting the Perimeter Road, construction may have already begun.

After the Civil War, Sandridge was founded as a close-knit community for people who had been enslaved in Horry County. Despite the long shadow of slavery and the violent realities of segregation and racial oppression, Sandridge residents created a place and a future for themselves. They built homes, established churches and schools, and started businesses. Some Sandridge men were lucky to get jobs at the lumber mill in nearby Conway. But most of the formerly enslaved people in the town were forced to sharecrop. By the early 1900s, a few of them managed to overcome incredible obstacles, including white terrorism, to gain ownership of land they could farm for themselves.

Today's Sandridge residents are the descendants of the sharecroppers who built a community in the face of white supremacy. Their history of collective struggle forged a tight-knit neighborhood where everybody knows everybody. The people of Sandridge are either blood relatives or chosen family. As the Conway Perimeter Road is built right through that community, these people stand to lose everything.

Some residents will lose their homes, a process that will tear apart their connections to their neighbors, their families, and their ancestors.

Displaced residents stand to lose land that has been in their family for over a century—land that sits near the roads, cemetery, and church named after their ancestors. Those directly affected will also be separated from family members who are able to remain. Residents who face dislocation know that the county and state will undervalue their property and refuse to provide them with the compensation necessary to relocate within Sandridge. They have seen it before and are experiencing it now.

Life in Sandridge will be harder for those left behind, and not only because they will be separated from some family members. Living with a four-lane roadway in their backyard will bring significant health and economic consequences—worse air quality, hazardous walking conditions, increased noise, more flooding, and decreased property values. They will be subject to hazards from the substantial increase in traffic that will be funneled through the Sandridge community.

Many people in Conway, South Carolina, were excited to hear that the new road was coming through. It would help alleviate traffic congestion and make the trip down to Myrtle Beach faster for them and the tourists who are vital to the local economy. But when Rev. Cedric Blain-Spain learned that the road was going to come through his beloved Sandridge, he knew he had to act.

Reverend Blain-Spain is a community activist and advocate born and raised in Sandridge. He sees his job as simply to protect everyone in the community. It is his "divine assignment," a charge that has been laid on him because of his deep connection to his ancestors. He is now part of the eighth generation of his family to live on this land. Originally, it was owned by his great-great-grandmother eight times removed, Hanna Hemingway, who was born on June 25, 1829, and passed on September 13, 1904. She was a sharecropper and ran her own farm. Through back-breaking work, Hanna Hemingway was able to acquire the land that she left to provide for her family. Reverend Blain-Spain's grandparents built homes on that land, homes where he and other members of his family continue to live.

In the late 1920s and early 1930s, Reverend Blain-Spain's grandfather, Arthur Blain, worked at the local bus station as a red cap. As he helped white travelers find their way and tote their luggage, they called him "nigger" and "boy." He had to enter the bus station through the back door and use a separate restroom behind the station. Arthur Blain's sons were not allowed into the station, so they would sit by the side of the building waiting for him to get off work or step outside to say hello. As they waited, white travelers and passersby would often spit on them and call them "nigger."

In an attempt to rally help to save his beloved Sandridge, Reverend Blain-Spain wrote to me, asking, "When will our Black communities be safe from our own governments and government agencies? At some point the universe shall turn in our favor and join the fight to help us save our Black Communities. Enough is enough." Reverend Blain-Spain understood how segregation's defenders had used highways and roads to destroy Black communities. He knew what was coming for Sandridge, so he began organizing to "arise and defeat these demonic forces known in this state as highways, freeways, roads, interchanges, expressways, [and] streets."

In choosing a path for the new road, SCDOT and other public officials are following a long history of discrimination in infrastructure programs at the hands of federal, state, and local officials—a history that has, in fact, already touched Sandridge. The town is near US-701 to the south and US-378 to the north, highways that contribute to poor air quality in the area. The Sandridge community is also located near a sixteen-mile liquid natural gas pipeline, trash disposal piles, a quarry pit, high-voltage electrical transmission lines, and an electrical substation.

As with countless other public infrastructure projects, local officials have targeted Sandridge in part because its residents' voices have been marginalized. The community does not have support from local, state, or national politicians. This Black community is believed to be the path of least resistance for the road project. Many residents work as housekeepers, cleaning the homes of white people and caring for their children. They are afraid to come to community meetings and to make their voices heard because they fear that public resistance to the road will cost them their jobs. They do not believe their local elected officials care about them. They recall a community meeting in 2010 when they sought help from their state senator. They retell the story of the senator turning to a community leader and asking, "Where them boys at?," referring to three Black pastors.

The struggle against the new road has taken an emotional toll on Reverend Blain-Spain and his neighbors. Many community members rallied to fight it, successfully convincing the United States Department of Transportation to open an investigation into SCDOT's decision to destroy Black homes and community institutions in Sandridge while white homes and business are spared. Others did not want to fight anymore because they believed they could not win. They felt they never have.

Sisters Irma Hemingway-Laws and Bobbi-Ann Hemingway-Jordan are both in their eighties now. Their ancestors helped to establish Sandridge when they purchased land in the community. Today, Hemingway Chapel Road bears the name of the local church their family founded. Irma and Bobbi-Ann lived in separate houses on their ancestral land, on property where they were born and raised, property their grandfather owned and farmed, property that was left to them by their grandparents. It is all that they have. The grief they feel as they face losing this family heritage has been overwhelming.

Hemingway-Jordan has more than twenty grandchildren, and they regularly visit with her. Her grandchildren loved that her backyard connected directly to Sandridge Park. They spent many days running among the trees that separated her backyard from the park, often only coming inside for dinner. At first, Hemingway-Jordan was told that her entire property would be taken to build the Conway Perimeter Road. After much confusion, she was given a glimmer of hope when she was informed that a portion of it might be spared. But she later learned that the piece of land they would leave her was too small to fit a house and would be virtually unusable. She would have to move. Just two years before, she acquired a reverse mortgage on her property to fund her retirement. Hemingway-Jordan intended to live in her home for the rest of her life.

Hemingway-Jordan chose not to continue to fight. She did not want to spend her remaining days in a battle with forces she did not believe she could overcome. So she sold her land to SCDOT, leaving behind her three-bedroom home and moving to a one-bedroom apartment downtown. Before the new road, she had been planning to expand her outdoor space to better accommodate her many grandchildren and other family members who often visited. She said that she "just wanted to leave a piece of me behind so that when I am gone, they feel me there, like I feel my parents." Instead, she was driven away from her ancestral home, a home that served as the haven where generations of her family came together.

Her sister, Hemingway-Laws, was told that her home would not be affected by Conway Perimeter Road. But she later saw plans that showed the road would run directly by her backyard. She wondered how the county could "build a four-lane road in our backyards and then say there's no impact?" Already distraught over her sister's fate, and missing seeing her sister and her grandnieces and grandnephews, Hemingway-Laws told me that she was worried about what further damage the threatened roadway would do to her quality of life. Would she still be able to enjoy her beautiful garden that she lovingly tended? What will it be like to live in a hollowed-out community and in a house whose value will decline precipitously? The Conway Perimeter Road will pin Hemingway-Laws between three roads. Her mobility will be affected—there is no sidewalk in any direction that will take her to her neighbors, to the park, or to the church. Instead of a three-minute walk, her twice weekly trips to church will become a ten-minute drive. And she worries about the noise, dust, and debris from the construction that will take place just a few feet away from her property.

Christine Williams's family has lived in Sandridge for as long as she can remember. Following her retirement in 2018, she decided to build a new home on property she had inherited from her mother and grown up on. She initially sought to purchase a mobile home to place on the land—a home that could have moved with her to another property. But Conway city officials told her that her land was not zoned for a manufactured home. So instead, she hired a contractor, secured the necessary permits, and built a new house on her lot. She thought she was living her dream.

Just one year later, Horry County and SCDOT released the Conway Perimeter Road plans, which showed that the proposed new road would run directly through her new home. Williams was heartbroken. She faced the loss of her dream home and would be forced to leave the community where she was born and raised. As is far too common for Black homeowners who lose their homes to eminent domain or infrastructure projects, SCDOT did not offer her enough compensation to pay off her home loan and still afford a comparable new home for her family in Conway.

Carmela Hemingway-Spain co-owns her home in Sandridge with her brother and sister. Their father bought the house in 1972 from her aunt. The Spains' property was not on the list of properties that would be taken to build the road, but her backyard was needed for the new road, and SCDOT and the county planned to take a significant portion of it. Worse than that, the dissection would cut her house off from its septic tank and render her home unlivable.

Government officials offered to pay Hemingway-Spain and her siblings $104,000 for the portion of land they needed, or to take the whole property for an insulting "higher" price of $105,000. Apparently, the state valued her home at just $1,000.

Hemingway-Spain has now sold her family home. Before moving, she lamented the destruction of her community and the loss of her "homestead." She now faces serious financial challenges because of the cost of relocating, the low appraisal for her former home, and the new burden of making house payments on a new one.

Carla Jean Ford is one of the oldest residents of Sandridge. She lives on Dirty Branch Road in a small home with a long and neatly manicured front yard. That yard affords her some privacy from the cars traveling along Dirty Branch Road, yet she still feels connected to the rest of the Sandridge community. Ford was originally told that the new road would pass directly behind her home, sparing both her home and yard. But that did not prove to be the last word. She was subsequently informed that the county planned to move her house to the back of her property in order to build a new road connecting the Conway Perimeter Road to Dirty Branch Road. This change meant that Ford would lose half of her property and be separated from the Sandridge community by the new four-lane roadway. Ford would no longer be able to walk to visit friends and family. She may be keeping her house, but she is losing her home.

While the county plans to permanently alter Ford's property, it chose to leave untouched a then-empty plot of land located directly next to her parcel. Developers have since turned that lot into a large storage facility to serve the neighboring white community.

It is not unreasonable for communities to bear some burden for progress. And roads, of course, can be a critical part of that progress. Change comes to every community, and it is not unreasonable to expect that the people of Sandridge would experience changes and bear some of its burdens. But as Sandridge's experience demonstrates, public officials can make choices about whether those burdens are shared fairly. The pain that Sandridge is being asked to bear is immoral—not only because of the devastation that the road will cause to people, their pocketbooks, their history, and their relationships—but because no other community is being asked to sacrifice itself in this way. Sandridge is another example of the fact that racism in infrastructure development is not ancient history—it is living history.

IN NORFOLK, VIRGINIA, IN THE EARLY 1920S, REAL ESTATE DEVELOPERS, members of the city council, and Norfolk's city manager decreed that Corpew Avenue would be the dividing line between a white community known as Brambleton and a predominantly Black community that was already partitioned off by three other roads. City leaders referred to Corpew Avenue as the "line of demarcation" between the two racial communities—Du Bois's color line made manifest. One immediate effect was white flight away from this dividing line as hundreds of families left the area for more distant communities.

A familiar story followed. When two homes on Corpew Avenue were sold to Black buyers, a mob of over one hundred white men marched to those houses and demanded that the new owners move out within twenty-four hours. They also demanded that the realty company that sold the houses cancel any other outstanding agreements to sell property along Corpew Avenue to Black families. Once city officials solidified the racial boundary, they systematically disinvested in infrastructure in this and other Black communities around Norfolk. Streets transitioned from pavement to dirt as they approached Black neighborhoods. Black neighborhoods were not provided with sidewalks, streetlights, sewers, or playgrounds.

One of the by-products of sustaining racial segregation through the development of roads and street grids has been economic disinvestment in the Black communities that were cordoned off. These lines were not only boundaries that Black people understood they should not cross. They were lines that local governments would not cross to provide essential city services and needed infrastructure. Regardless of class, Black communities did not receive the infrastructure investments and maintenance, sanitation services, fire protection, or recreation spaces that white communities did.

This disinvestment contributes to a vicious cycle. The deprivation of Black communities drives assumptions about the values and value of the people who live there. White people can point to dilapidated housing, poor educational and health outcomes, and other problems in Black communities and use it to justify their anti-Black prejudice, even though it is that very prejudice that drives the disinvestment and discrimination that leads to those outcomes. This remains a problem: today's public policy debates about conditions in Black communities often devolve into debates about "Black culture" to the exclusion of conversations about the centuries of public policies that cause those conditions.

And most tragically, perhaps, this disinvestment also has a detrimental effect on how residents feel about their own communities. This, too, is the legacy of racist city planning and street design.

Chapter 5

Still at the Back of the Bus

I n 1919, during a sweltering July heatwave in Chicago, a seventeen-year-old Black man named Eugene Williams went for a swim with some friends at the informally segregated Twenty-Ninth Street Beach. As they were enjoying some relief from the oppressive heat, Eugene drifted across an invisible color line to the white side of the beach. An angry white beachgoer hurled rocks at the group of friends, striking Eugene, who then drowned. The police were called. But rather than calming down, tensions between Black beachgoers, angry and shocked over Eugene's murder, and white beachgoers, angry over the violation of their white privilege, escalated. Although witnesses identified the man responsible for Eugene's death, a white police officer prevented a Black officer from arresting him and chose to arrest a Black man instead.

Eugene's murder and the police response triggered a week-long riot that resulted in the deaths of twenty-three Black people and fifteen white people. More than five hundred people were injured, and one thousand Black families were left homeless. It came to be called the Chicago Race Riot of 1919, and it was one of the deadliest riots of the so-called Red Summer, an outbreak of white supremacist racial violence against Black people that spread across twenty-six cities that year.

In the North, racial hostility toward Black people newly arrived from the South, as well as frustration within Black communities over a lack of affordable housing, helped fuel the Red Summer. Chicago was no exception. The city's Black population increased from 44,000 in 1910 to more than 109,000 in 1920. In response to the riot, Illinois governor Frank O. Lowden created the Chicago Commission on Race Relations and appointed a biracial committee—with equal numbers of white and Black members—to study the persistent conflict and propose solutions.

The Committee's work resulted in a report called "The Negro in Chicago: A Study of Race Relations and a Race Riot." One section, "Racial Contact on Transportation," examined Chicago's elevated train lines, with a specific focus on the twelve lines running from State Street on the South Side—an overwhelmingly Black neighborhood—to the manufacturing district where many new Black migrants were employed. Although Black people made up only about 4 percent of Chicago's population at the time, the report found that during rush hour, Black people made up a majority of El commuters. The El was one of the only places where white and Black Chicagoans consistently came into close contact with one another. It was also perhaps the only place where white people regularly found themselves outnumbered and surrounded by Black people. The results were predictable. The trains were frequent sites of racially motivated violence. The proximity to Black people fueled white prejudice, paranoia, and vitriol about the growing Black population. Many white people interviewed by the Commission described their mistrust of Black passengers, with one commuter saying that having to be with Black people on public transportation made her "all for moving them all out of the city."

From steamships and railroads to buses and subways, public transportation in the United States has long been a racial battleground. In segregated America, transportation was often one of the few spaces where Black people and white people found themselves in proximity; it is not surprising that these places have seen conflict as well. The tools of racism have evolved as public transportation has evolved, and the methods of promoting inequality have adapted as our laws and social mores have adapted. Public transportation systems that once operated under blatant racial discrimination and legal segregation are now shaped by dog whistles and false narratives of Black criminality, all presented as concern over public safety.

Class, too, has been central to the calculations of policymakers. Race and class have always been connected in the United States. But they come together in particularly powerful ways in public transportation. They shape decisions ranging from the way public transit systems are policed, to the placement of stops on buses and subways. Such decisions are often made in the service of the oppression and isolation of Black communities, and disproportionately, people of color living in poverty.

Prior to World War II, public transportation was generally viewed as the province of all races, with white and Black people regularly riding the same buses and trains, even though the seating was segregated and treatment was unequal. But after World War II, with the rise of personal automobiles and the interstate highway system, and expanding political challenges to racial segregation, public transportation increasingly came to be perceived as transportation for poor Black and Brown people. Highways facilitated white flight to new white suburbs, which in turn often blocked the expansion of public transit, with the explicit goal of preventing Black people—who frequently could not afford a car—from accessing the homes, schools, and jobs that lay at the other end of the expressway.

"TRANSPORTATION DESERT" IS THE TERM FOR COMMUNITIES WHERE THE supply of mass public transportation does not meet the demand, even as parts of the country continue to invest in highways and suburban commuter rail systems. And many of these "deserts" are Black communities that have been systematically targeted by policymakers. When Black neighborhoods were destroyed to make way for highways, roads, and urban renewal projects, the people who lived there found themselves scattered into transportation deserts. This has made everyday life infinitely more challenging. Residents have a hard time getting to work and school, going shopping for groceries or clothes, getting to the movies or the park, seeing a doctor or a dentist, and visiting family and friends. They may find themselves making unsafe crossings across high-speed roads—they are often forced to literally risk their lives.

The secondary effects, including on health, are numerous. People who rely on inadequate public transit often forgo needed services. Because getting to the doctor's office is much harder than it should be, medical appointments are delayed or missed, and emergency rooms are used more often. According to a 2022 study, nearly six million Americans do not get

medical care each year because they lack access to transportation, including public transit. And because communities of color are more likely to
depend on public transportation, they are at greater risk.

Inadequate transportation also worsens so-called "food deserts," which
are areas where residents lack access to healthy and affordable food. In
2009, the Department of Agriculture found that over 23.5 million Americans live in low-income neighborhoods located more than a mile from a
grocery store. And a study by the Urban Institute determined that one of
the biggest challenges for people in food deserts was the absence of adequate transportation to a grocery store. Once again, because Black people
are more likely to need public transportation and less likely to have access
to it, they are more likely to live in food deserts.

White communities can become transportation deserts, too. Some residents actually wish for that outcome, seeking to limit public transportation
in order to keep Black and low-income people from coming to, or merely
traveling through, their neighborhoods. For an example, let's return to
Atlanta. The city has some of the worst traffic in the United States. A portion of its traffic woes are linked to the city's history of using roads and
street grid layout to facilitate racial segregation. The 1980 Atlanta Comprehensive Plan listed traffic congestion on the Westside as a major concern, and a consequence of the "limited street network" and the "lack of
adequate north-south arterial capacity," relics of an earlier generation of
Atlanta's public officials intent on maintaining segregation.

Two decades earlier, as the Atlanta suburbs ballooned from white flight
and more and more people drove into and around the city every day, officials sought to address the growing traffic issues. In 1965, the Georgia
General Assembly voted to create MARTA, the city's mass transit system.
But MARTA's success has itself been limited, as transit officials have faced
fierce opposition to extending the system beyond Atlanta's borders, where
public transportation is equated with Black people, poverty, and crime.

The acronym MARTA stands for Metropolitan Atlanta Rapid Transit
Authority. But it has acquired a more derogatory name, too: Moving Africans Rapidly Through Atlanta. And suburban communities have waged an
all-out war against its expansion. In 1965, residents of the nearly all-white

Cobb County voted to reject MARTA. In 1971, the overwhelmingly white counties of Gwinnett and Clayton did the same and rejected MARTA by a four-to-one margin. In 1987, the chairman of MARTA, a white man named David Chesnut, shared his belief that suburban opposition to MARTA had been "90 percent a racial issue." Again in 1990, Gwinnett voted down the extension of MARTA into its community. A former Republican legislator noted that opponents "will come up with twelve different ways of saying they are not racist in public . . . but you get them alone, behind a closed door, and you use this old blatant racism that we have had here for quite some time." As recently as 2019, Gwinnett County voted MARTA down for a third time, by an eight-point margin.

BUSES CARRY A PARTICULAR RACIAL AND CULTURAL STIGMA, ONE THAT took shape during the civil rights movement and the white flight of the 1960s and 1970s. On November 13, 1956, the United States Supreme Court ruled that racial segregation on public buses violates the Equal Protection Clause of the Fourteenth Amendment to the United States Constitution. The decision led to the end of the famous Montgomery Bus Boycott but also helped code buses as "Black." The day after the decision, an article ran in *The Columbus Ledger*, in Columbus, Georgia, predicting that the decision would lead either to the end of bus service in southern cities or to white citizens' abandoning the bus system entirely to Black people. "The end result, we suspect, will be that intracity transportation facilities will become a thing of the past in the Deep South—or services patronized only by Negroes." It went on to predict that "as in the case of the Supreme Court decision, the Montgomery case foretells this in the hints of things to come. City busses [*sic*] lines all over the nation are undergoing severe economic challenge, any how. This decision might just be, at least in the Deep South, the death blow."

Cobb County had an opinion not just about MARTA but about buses, too. Many decades later, in 1994, former Republican Georgia congressman and Speaker of the House Newt Gingrich shared his understanding that "people in Cobb County don't object to upper-middle-class neighbors who keep their lawn cut and move to the area to avoid crime. . . . What people worry about is the bus line gradually destroying one apartment complex after another, bringing people out from public housing who have no middle class values and whose kids as they become teenagers often are centers of robbery and where the schools collapse because the parents who live in the apartment complexes don't care that the kids don't do well in school and the whole school collapses."

The stigma attached to buses is not limited to the South. Consider the death of a seventeen-year-old Black woman named Cynthia Wiggins in Buffalo, New York, on December 14, 1995. Cynthia worked at a fast-food restaurant in the Walden Galleria Mall, an upscale suburban mall in Cheektowaga. To get to the mall from the nearest bus stop, Cynthia had to sprint across a seven-lane roadway because the mall barred city buses, used primarily by Black commuters, from driving into its parking lot. Other buses—suburban commuter and tourist buses with greater white ridership—were permitted to enter. One day, as Cynthia made the dangerous run from the bus stop to the mall, she was crushed by a dump truck.

Cynthia's story made national headlines. Yet the mall's policy of excluding city buses would never have become news if it did not lead to such a tragic outcome. Cynthia's story was an extreme version of an all-too-common tale: Black people need to access jobs and opportunities that are located in white communities, and those white communities manipulate transportation policies to exclude them.

Consider a recent episode from Dayton, Ohio. One evening in 2010, Mark Donaghy, the CEO of the Greater Dayton Regional Transit Authority (RTA), attended a community meeting at a local church to hear hundreds of residents there talk about what it was like to risk their lives to get to work. One of those people was a young pregnant woman who spoke about her arduous commute to her minimum wage job in Beavercreek, Ohio, a suburb located about a fifteen-minute drive east of Dayton. She spoke about taking the Route 1 bus from Dayton to its last stop at Wright State University, then having to walk 1.5 miles into Beavercreek. Approximately half of that walk is along the six-lane North Fairfield Road, a stretch that includes an I-675 overpass. There is no sidewalk for long stretches, including the portion on the overpass; pedestrians must walk along the shoulder of the road as it passes over I-675. The overpass was not built for pedestrians: it has no sidewalks, crosswalks, or signs to help people navigate the road or to caution drivers. Instead, this woman, like other commuters, braved the commuters driving home, or toward the Fairfield Commons Mall or the other strip malls deeper into Beavercreek. The walk was treacherous on any day, and it only got worse in the winter when it was cold, windy, and icy. Moreover, the woman did the walk after dark, taking her life into her hands to provide for her family. Many other community members also testified about taking that long, dangerous walk to get to Beavercreek.

Donaghy left the community meeting committed to help. He decided to move forward with plans to establish an RTA bus stop in Beavercreek. The request was straightforward, and the need was clear; Donaghy believed the process would take about three months. But the RTA hit a roadblock Donaghy did not anticipate: the Beavercreek City Council and the forces that supported it.

In 1988, noted sociologist Douglas Massey found that housing in Dayton and its suburbs was more racially segregated than in all but two of the fifty largest metropolitan areas in the United States. The segregation was, in large part, the legacy of redlining and racially restrictive covenants that kept Black residents to the west side of the city and helped to create whites-only suburbs surrounding Dayton.

Even before the completion of I-75 in the mid-1960s and I-675 in the mid-1980s, Dayton's white population was declining, and the suburbs were growing quickly. The highways proved to be a powerful accelerant. As in other metropolitan areas around the country, the expansion of the interstate highway system funneled people, businesses, and jobs out of the city and into the nearby suburbs. After I-675 came through Dayton, dividing communities and destroying the Black business district, investors and developers decided that the city was no longer worth investing in and focused their resources on the communities that were now connected to Dayton by I-675. Ronnie Moreland, a longtime resident of Dayton and former president of Leaders for Equality and Action in Dayton (LEAD), a coalition of community-based organizations and religious institutions in

Dayton, lamented that "those living in the city of Dayton did not see the same America they did at the other end of I-675."

As economic opportunity left Dayton and was redistributed along the I-675 corridor, many Dayton residents were forced to make the long commute to the outer suburbs for better jobs. Yet RTA buses did not venture to the suburbs. When commuters reached the end of the bus lines, they often had to walk. In 2010, LEAD decided to take action. They focused on Beavercreek, which LEAD members knew as a "closed community." They committed to open Beavercreek up to the residents of Dayton. "We lost it all," said Moreland. "People who live in Dayton still want to feel safe, they want the opportunity to elevate their lives and get a quality education. They're competing for jobs that they can barely get access to here now. It shouldn't be a crime that you can't afford an automobile, and until you can get an automobile you need some way of sustaining yourself and giving your family hope."

There was hope and opportunity in Beavercreek. It had two large shopping centers that needed workers, The Green and the Mall at Fairfield Commons. Yet Dayton residents were turning down jobs in Beavercreek that they desperately needed because they could not get there. For those who relied on public transportation, a job at one of the malls in Beavercreek or at the nearby medical center meant taking the Route 1 bus to Wright State University and finishing the commute on foot, just like the woman who inspired Donaghy to action. It is a route that LEAD members aptly described as "an accident waiting to happen."

For LEAD, an RTA bus stop in Beavercreek was not merely an issue of transportation infrastructure, it was a fundamental issue of civil rights and racial justice. In a study commissioned by LEAD, it was shown that two-thirds of those who rode RTA buses did so to commute to and from work. Black people in the RTA service area disproportionately rely on public transportation compared to white people. In 2009, an RTA study on the racial and ethnic makeup of ridership revealed that in Montgomery County—where Dayton is located—about 73 percent of riders were people of color. Black people made up 64 percent of total ridership. At the time, Beavercreek was 3 percent Black and 89 percent white. In contrast, the city of Dayton was 43 percent Black and 52 percent white.

LEAD organizers were the ones responsible for contacting Donaghy and inviting him to the community meeting in 2010. Following the meeting, in March of that year, the RTA applied to add six bus stops to Route 1 along Pentagon Boulevard in Beavercreek in order to provide six or so daily trips to the Fairfield Commons Mall, Soin Medical Center, and DeVry University. But Beavercreek was not going to make it easy. Through an ordinance enacted in September 2000, the city required a transit agency to meet certain criteria before installing new stops. The ordinance included basic design criteria: a boarding pad, a bench, a sign, and a trash receptacle. Because Pentagon Boulevard was a heavily traveled street, the city also required a shelter, a transit pad, and a schedule holder. At the same time, the ordinance granted the city council power to "modify or expand upon the recommendations of the Director of Public Works prior to approval of any such application." The RTA's application complied with every one of the Beaverton ordinance's requirements.

Following pushback from Beavercreek officials, the RTA agreed to revise down the number of requested bus stops from six to three. In December 2010, the Beavercreek Public Works director accepted the RTA's modified application, and the city manager referred the application to the city council for a public hearing. In advance of the hearing, the Public Service Division sent an agenda to city council members noting that the proposal met "the City of Beavercreek Design Criteria for Public Transit Stops."

On February 14, 2011, the city council held its first hearing to discuss the RTA's bus stop application. The law ordered the city council to approve the application if it met their requirements—as the Department of Public Works had determined it did—unless they had a legitimate, nondiscriminatory reason to deny it. The hearing began with public comments from three people who all supported the RTA's application. The first city council members to speak at the hearing were also supportive. One member argued that the application was the best plan available and recommended approval, and then another confirmed that the RTA met all of the city's rules and that the plan must therefore be approved.

After that, the hearing took a dramatic turn. Some council members questioned whether the new bus stops provided any benefits to Beavercreek and noted that their job was to focus on the needs and wants of the citizens of Beavercreek, not those in nearby areas. Council members also raised safety issues and reported negative popular opinion among Beavercreek residents. City council members began to repeat the mantra that the bus stop was not what their citizens wanted. One claimed that his constituents "do not want this type of transportation in our community." At the end of the hearing, the city council tabled its decision until a later date, with the city attorney cautioning council members that they would need to find nondiscriminatory reasons to deny the application for the bus stop.

Following the hearing, council members met with private attorneys. They also received several emails from Beavercreek community members sharing their opposition to the application. Some of the emails suggested that some residents were motivated by a fear that adding the bus stops would open the door to more Black people moving into Beavercreek. In one email a resident urged the council not to "allow West Dayton to strong arm its way into Beavercreek" (West Dayton is a predominantly Black section of Dayton). Other emails suggested that buses traveling from Dayton would bring crime to Beavercreek.

The city council reconvened on March 14, 2011, with a long list of concerns, and ended up creating new requirements for the RTA. First, council members started to pick apart the application, looking for reasons to deny or delay voting on it. They asked for survey data and additional analysis. They wanted employment and ridership data. Essentially, they asked for data to support every assertion or representation that the RTA made in its application.

Some council members said the buses were too big and would create too much pedestrian traffic. And they raised questions about safety and the need for increased security if there were a bus stop. They talked about "issues" at other malls that had bus access from downtown Dayton. They said they did not want their community turning into the Salem Mall or the Dayton Mall, places where Black and Brown people shopped. Council members reported that residents believed the new bus stops would leave them less safe, lead to less investment in their city, and hurt their overall quality of life. They did not want the community near the proposed bus stop turning into what one resident called "the corner of chaos."

The city council also raised nineteen new requirements for the bus stop, eleven of which not only went well beyond Beavercreek's ordinance but beyond anything else the RTA had ever done in any municipality. The new criteria included: posting of Rules of Behavior and Consequences cards (in effect, an invitation to the police to selectively enforce the rules against Black riders who made white people uncomfortable); installing a police phone call box at each bus stop; installing "state of the art" surveillance cameras that provide full coverage of each transit stop and transmit real-time surveillance pictures to the Beavercreek Police Department; providing heated and air-conditioned shelters at each stop; providing a thickened concrete bus pad of eighteen inches instead of the required ten inches; using smaller buses; placing a deposit of $150,000 in case the bus stops resulted in the need to install new traffic control signals; and agreeing to pay Beavercreek for any police services directly related to the transit stops.

The RTA saw these conditions for what they were: pretexts to block the buses, and the people who rode them, from accessing Beavercreek. The RTA did not provide police phone call boxes at any of its existing 3,300 bus stops. And as for the installation of surveillance equipment, the RTA had no real-time feeds and only had security cameras at its transit hubs because of the volume of riders there. For example, the RTA had installed security cameras at its Dayton transit hub, which saw 1,200 bus trips per day. In contrast, there would be about six bus trips per day along the proposed Pentagon Blvd. Route 1 extension in Beavercreek. Moreover, the only fully heated and air-conditioned bus shelter in the world at that time was in Dubai. And eighteen-inch concrete pads were closer to the requirements for an airplane runway than a bus stop. At the end of the hearing, the city council once again tabled the decision.

On March 28, 2011, there was a third and final public meeting. City council members noted negative opinion among Beavercreek residents, citing a survey and constituent emails they received. They repeated their concerns about public safety and implied that a bus route connecting Dayton residents to Beavercreek would lead to increased crime, and that the

Fairfield Commons would fall victim to "all the issues that have been at the Salem Mall and Dayton Mall and downtown Dayton." At the hearing, Beavercreek's mayor, Arthur "Scott" Hadley, said that the city council speaks for the people and the people don't want the bus stops. The council then voted 6 to 0 to deny the RTA's application. Council member Julie Vann was the only one who had planned to vote in favor of the bus stop, but she was not present. The rest of the council thought it was important for the vote to be unanimous and were angry with Vann over her decision, which is why she decided not to attend the hearing.

One community member said the vote was "nothing but thinly veiled discrimination. *Very* thinly veiled." LEAD was obviously disappointed. Wilma Righter, a white woman and a LEAD member, said "it is good enough to have these people come out here, serve our food, empty our trash, scrub our toilets, but they are not good enough to have a safe, affordable, dependable ride to work." Her comment hearkened back to "sundown towns," common in the Jim Crow era, when white communities made sure that Black people never mistook those communities where they worked for home. Black people could come to sundown towns to serve white people's food and clean their homes but were required to leave town before the sun went down. When Mayor Hadley was asked about the council's decision to block the bus stops, he said that residents were happy with the way things were. They had good housing and excellent schools, and they simply wanted it to stay that way.

Following the vote, LEAD launched a public pressure campaign with the slogan, "Let the people ride!" LEAD requested a permit to march from the last bus stop on Route 1 along the path to the mall and across the overpass—the dangerous route that people were forced to walk to get to work. Ironically, or not so ironically, the city denied the permit, on the grounds that the route was not safe to walk.

On August 4, 2011, LEAD filed an administrative complaint with the Federal Highway Administration's (FHWA) Office of Civil Rights against the city of Beavercreek, alleging racial discrimination in violation of Title VI of the Civil Rights Act of 1964 and United States Department of Transportation regulations, a law that prohibits racial discrimination in programs that receive federal funds. Title VI prohibits intentional acts of racial discrimination as well as policies that, though racially neutral in their language, nonetheless result in racial disparities. LEAD stopped short of alleging intentional discrimination, instead arguing that Beavercreek's denial of the bus stop application had a disparate impact on Black bus riders and denied them equal access to roads funded by grants from the FHWA.

The goal of the FHWA's office of Civil Rights is to "ensure non-discriminatory, equitable, accessible, and safe public transportation in support of FHWA's mission to enhance the social and economic quality of life for all Americans." The FHWA launched an investigation and assigned it to Lester Finkle, its Title VI program coordinator. When Finkle first read the complaint and reviewed the case file, he saw the racial discrimination issues "right off the bat."

Finkle and the investigation team visited Dayton and Beavercreek in April 2012. On April 9, they met with Dayton community members in an open forum and listened to their concerns. At the request of the community, the team walked the I-675 overpass at 6:00 p.m. one evening. The investigators' experience confirmed everything they had heard from those advocating for the RTA's plan. They walked the overpass along the shoulder, fighting a cold wind while noting particularly dangerous sections where the shoulder became a ramp with cars turning into the lane. Finkle observed commuters on foot, carrying bags or packages. The investigation team concluded that "the Route is, by any reasonable standard, precarious in clear daylight, and even more dangerous in the dark and/or foul weather."

On June 26, 2013, the FHWA issued a letter of noncompliance and found that the City of Beavercreek violated Title VI of the Civil Rights Act by denying the RTA application without a substantial legitimate justification. Remarkably, it was the first time in its history that the FHWA, founded forty-seven years earlier in October 1966, determined a community to be in violation of Title VI. The FHWA would now require Beavercreek to develop a new process for evaluating bus stop proposals that was not driven by racial animus and did not have a disparate impact on Black riders. The FHWA would also require Beavercreek to reconsider the RTA's bus stop application, and it asked the Ohio Department of Transportation to monitor Beavercreek during the restarted process. Beavercreek never admitted to any wrongdoing.

On January 12, 2014, almost four years after Mark Donaghy filed RTA's request to add bus stops in Beavercreek, bus service from Wright State University to the Fairfield Commons Mall started. Early that Sunday morning, a packed bus burst into applause as it crossed over the I-675 overpass. It had been a long, hard fight.

THE DEVELOPMENT OF THE INTERSTATE HIGHWAY SYSTEM REFLECTED A shift in government resources away from building a robust public transit system. The growth of suburbs was made possible by massive investments of public funds into highways and by suburban mortgage guarantees. But it all came at the expense of investments in urban neighborhoods, a trade-off that left those neighborhoods poorer. Precious little public funding was set aside for urban mass transit.

These choices continue to disadvantage Black people who are disproportionately unable to afford a car and live in communities that are distant from work, school, and opportunity. The ongoing lack of adequate funding for these public services further aggravates the transportation-related hardships residents in Black neighborhoods face. To this day, states generally prioritize highway spending over transit investment in dense, diverse cities and suburbs. Indeed, according to one expert, "the lion's share of transportation dollars is spent on roads, while urban transit systems are often left in disrepair." This is not only the fault of the individual states, however; even the federal government keeps making the same decision.

A prime example is the Fixing America's Surface Transportation Act (FAST Act). The FAST Act was signed into law by President Obama in 2015. It was the first long-term national transportation spending package in a decade. It authorized $305 billion over fiscal years 2016 to 2020 for transportation initiatives. The act allocated $207.4 billion to highways and just $61.1 billion for public transportation, less than one-third of the total. That latter amount was split among several programs. For example, the State of Good Repair Program, which provides funding primarily for repairing and upgrading rail transit systems, got $12.9 billion; the Bus and Bus Facilities Grant Program received a paltry $3.74 billion.

This problem did not begin with the FAST Act. Within the realm of limited public transportation funding, buses are consistently shortchanged. Annually, bus transit receives only 31 percent of capital funds spent nationwide on transit, though buses account for more than 60 percent of trips. Of course, Black people are more likely than white ones to take the bus. And the issue appears in funding for other kinds of public transportation, too.

In Baltimore, Maryland, we can see how even generous federal funding for trains—resources that most cities fight for and welcome—can meet local opposition when those trains will make it easier for Black residents to commute to places where they are not wanted. Over the course of four decades, advocates and policymakers have put forward numerous proposals for rail lines that would serve some of the city's most congested and poorly served areas and connect members of Baltimore's predominantly Black neighborhoods to suburban communities. These proposals have been repeatedly scuttled.

In 1975, Maryland proposed the construction of a rail line between the predominantly white suburbs of Anne Arundel County and downtown Baltimore. The white suburbanites opposed the plan and encouraged their elected officials to block it. Researchers from Johns Hopkins University found that suburbanites believed the rail line "would enable poor, inner-city blacks to travel to the suburbs, steal residents' T.V.s and then return to their ghettos." Maryland's transportation secretary at the time responded to the opposition by stating that his office "would not force a transit line on an area that clearly does not want it."

In 1992, Baltimore's Central Light Rail opened, but it did not include stops in the affluent white neighborhoods of Ruxton and Riderwood because of local opposition. Gwinn Owens, a former editor at the *Baltimore Sun*, wrote that "beneath some of this opposition is a tinge of racism. One young woman told me, 'It will bring the wrong element into our community.'"

In Anne Arundel County, the county executive formally asked the transit agency to shut down two light rail stations, and run only peak service for white-collar office workers at two other stations, because of complaints from residents and John Grasso, a former councilman from the county who claimed that "drug addicts, crooks, and thieves" used the stations to "go out there, rob people, and hop on the train back to Baltimore City." Continued efforts to establish a rail line, and continued opposition, helped spawn the term "Loot Rail," a play on "light rail."

As a result of this backlash and stigmatization, residents of predominantly Black neighborhoods in Baltimore have some of the longest commute times in the city. In these same neighborhoods, nearly 50 percent of households lack access to a car and are entirely dependent on buses for travel. Rather than seeking opportunities to engage in criminal mischief, people are merely seeking opportunities to work.

In 2002, Maryland governor Parris Glendening, a Democrat, supported a plan to build the Red Line light rail system, an east-west transit route that would serve some of Baltimore's poorer communities. As scholar Sheryll Cashin noted, calling this proposed route the Red Line was more than a little ironic, given how the practice of redlining had helped impoverish and segregate much of Black Baltimore. For fourteen years, Maryland transportation officials studied, scrutinized, and planned the Red Line project, ultimately receiving approval from all necessary government agencies and securing a $900 million pledge from the federal government.

In January 2015, there was a change in the state's administration. Republican governor Larry Hogan and Secretary of Transportation Pete Rahn were sworn into office. Less than one month later, they announced a pause in all planning for the Red Line. Then, on June 25, 2015, Governor Hogan, citing cost concerns, announced the cancellation of the project, saying the funds would be redirected to a transportation initiative in rural and suburban areas outside of Baltimore. The cancellation meant that the state would forfeit the $900 million in federal funds that had been committed to the project in addition to the approximately $288 million the state and federal government had already spent on it.

In ordering the cancellation, Governor Hogan called the Red Line Project a "wasteful boondoggle," even though it was the result of decades of planning and demonstrable need. Notably, he did not cancel plans for the

Purple Line, a light rail line set to run through affluent Prince George's and Montgomery Counties near Washington, DC.

Many Baltimore residents who lived along the proposed Red Line corridor maintained that racial bias motivated the decision. The Red Line was slated to travel through some of Baltimore's poorest neighborhoods. It would have run just ten blocks south of the Gilmor Homes, where twenty-five-year-old Freddie Gray was arrested in April 2015. Gray's brutal death from injuries suffered in police custody led to widespread protests and uprisings for racial justice. While the circumstances of the Red Line's cancellation were striking, its timing was even more significant: it came just two months after the civil unrest stemming from Gray's murder, when images of protests and property damage in Baltimore captured national headlines.

Possible motives aside, the outcome was plainly a dismal one for the Black residents of Baltimore. The Red Line had been designed to improve life in some of the city's most isolated transportation deserts—neighborhoods with long commute times, that heavily rely on unreliable bus service and are disconnected from the region's job centers. The NAACP Legal Defense Fund challenged the decision and its racially disproportionate impact, on behalf of the Baltimore Regional Initiative Developing Genuine Equality, Inc. ("BRIDGE"), through an administrative complaint under Title VI of the Civil Rights Act of 1964. The complaint argued that

> The Red Line would also have served as the necessary link connecting West Baltimore's predominantly African-American neighborhoods to job centers. The Red Line corridor is sixty percent African-American.... Unemployment rates in the neighborhoods along Edmondson Avenue are extremely high: 17.5 percent in Poppleton; 17.9 percent in Allendale; 22.7 percent in Edmondson Village and in Harlem Park/Sandtown-Winchester; and 24.1 percent in Greater Rosemont—compared to the city's overall unemployment rate of 14.2 percent. Travel poses a barrier for jobseekers in these neighborhoods; less than two percent of jobs within the city of Baltimore, let alone the metropolitan region, are located in these communities. The regional job centers are located downtown, in Woodlawn, and

in other outlying suburban areas, which are difficult to reach on the public bus routes which are currently the only available form of public transportation.

The experience of Black Baltimore is far from unique. Cities will cut off their own nose to spite their face when it comes to federal funds for public transportation. The net result of such discriminatory policies is to limit the mobility of Black people, who are more likely than whites to rely on public transportation. The harms—housing segregation, the highways, the absence of trains and buses—compound one another. While much of this book so far has focused on highways and surface roads, the experiences of communities like Atlanta, Dayton, and Baltimore show that these problems cannot be understood in isolation.

EMBEDDED IN WHITE RESISTANCE TO PUBLIC TRANSPORTATION IS THE myth of excessive Black criminality. Although many policymakers point to crime as a primary motivation behind their opposition to mass transit, the problem is not actual crime, but harmful racist stereotypes. The narrative linking race and crime dates back centuries. And given the history of white people using notions of Black savagery to justify slavery and, later on, Black criminality to justify segregation, it should be no surprise that this narrative is now invoked as the basis of more modern tools of racial exclusion. From criminal justice reform, to education, to housing, this racialized narrative fuels a general state of fear and brands Black people as dangerous, even inhuman. It is a vicious cycle: white fear feeds mass criminalization, which helps contribute to the fact that Black people are locked up at higher rates than the general population, which in turn further feeds the original false narrative This self-reinforcing spiral drives much of our public policy, including in transportation. Many predominantly white communities and their political representatives view public transportation as a vehicle for criminality, and not what it actually is: a pathway to access and opportunity.

It is not just that white suburbs block buses and trains and roads. It is that they support a political system that harasses Black riders of public transit. Black riders face disparate treatment and overpolicing. Even as largely Black communities are blocked from accessing whiter, wealthier spaces, they are also subjected to state-sanctioned harassment.

Selectively enforcing the law and criminalizing Black riders is a powerful tool for keeping Black people in their place. New York City offers a telling example. In 2019, the *New York Times* reported that from 2011 to 2015 an NYPD Brooklyn Precinct commander directed his transit officers "to think of white and Asian people as 'soft targets' and urged them to instead go after blacks and Latinos for minor offenses like jumping the turnstile." This precinct commander oversaw the notably diverse Transit District 32, encompassing Sunset Park, which contains a large Latino community as well as Brooklyn's Chinatown, Flatbush and its vibrant Caribbean community, Russian-Americans in Brighton Beach, and a large Orthodox Jewish community. The members of those communities experienced widely different law enforcement as they rode New York City subways.

The disparate treatment was not unique to this commander's corner of Brooklyn. Across the city, between October 2017 and June 2019, Black and Latino people received nearly 73 percent of the tickets for fare evasion when race was recorded, despite accounting for only slightly more than half the population of riders. They also made up 90 percent of people who were arrested rather than ticketed. Nor are these trends unique to New York City. A 2021 report from the Transit Center, a foundation that advocates for public transportation, found that disparate enforcement is pervasive. In Seattle, from 2015 to 2019, Black riders received 22 percent of fare enforcement citations, despite making up just 9 percent of riders. In Washington, DC, from 2016 to 2018, 91 percent of fare evasion summons went to Black riders even though Black people made up just 50 percent of the population of riders. In Boston, a study in the *Boston Globe* revealed that from October to November 2019, 42 percent of subway citations were given to Black riders, although nearly two-thirds of riders were white. And in San Francisco between 2012 and 2017, Black riders were involved in 63 percent of "use of force" incidents despite representing just over 10 percent of BART riders.

These statistics illuminate the vicious cycle mentioned above. Fears of Black crime on the subways drive disparate enforcement, leading more

Black riders to be ticketed or arrested, which in turn feeds the myth of Black criminality. The very people who most depend on public transportation are the ones most harmed by it.

Racial disparities in law enforcement on public transportation are even more striking when compared to what drivers face. In Detroit, Atlanta, and New Orleans, all cities with predominantly Black public transportation commuters, the penalties for fare evasion are significantly higher than the penalties for violations of driving or parking rules, and often include criminal penalties, although both kinds of violations could be characterized as unlawful uses of public resources. In Detroit, fare evasion is a criminal misdemeanor, and fare evaders can be fined up to $500 or sentenced to up to ninety days in jail. By contrast, parking meter violations such as overtime parking or not paying a meter are civil infractions that result in a $45 fine and are not punishable by imprisonment. In New Orleans, fare evasion is also a misdemeanor crime; parking rule violations are civil violations with no criminal penalties imposed and subject to a $30 fine. In Atlanta, fare evaders can be suspended from the transit system for sixty days or assessed up to a $200 fine, and violations of the suspension can result in prosecution for criminal trespass, while overtime parking violations are subject to a parking citation and a $35 fine. New York City recently standardized the cost of its most issued parking fine—violating alternate side of street parking rules—at $65, but the penalty for turnstile jumping is $100.

Meanwhile, in three cities with predominantly white public transportation commuters—Seattle, Washington; Portland, Oregon; and Madison, Wisconsin—fare evasion is not immediately classified as a misdemeanor or criminal offense, and penalties are in line with those for parking violations. In Seattle, fare evasion on public transit is subject to an administrative fine assessed in-house by the Kings County Metro, the regional public transportation agency, rather than through the court system. First- and second-time violators are issued warnings, and the third violation leads to a $50 administrative fine, which can escalate to $124 for the fifth infraction. And individuals have several options besides immediately paying the fine, such as loading the citation amount onto a fare card, signing up for a course on fare evasion, or signing a pledge to pay the violation amount in the future. If a rider does not take advantage of any of these options, the citation can ultimately result in a misdemeanor.

Similarly, in Portland, fare evasion is subject to an administrative violation citation that can be resolved directly with the public transit system rather than the court system, and is subject to a $75 administrative fine, although this violation can also be resolved in ways other than paying the fine (such as community service), which reduces the burden of the violation. In Madison, fare evaders are first given a warning. Only if the individual refuses to comply after the warning will a supervisor be called to the scene; the supervisor can ask the passenger to leave the bus, and only if they refuse will the individual be subject to arrest. In short, there are several steps that precede arrest, and the individual is given a number of opportunities to change their behavior. In contrast to the harsh punishments for fare evasion in cities with high Black transit ridership rates, municipalities where riders are mostly white treat this infraction very differently.

THE CYCLE OF CRIMINALIZATION IS NOT ONLY VICIOUS BUT CAN BE DEADLY. Inner-city public transportation systems, often starved of necessary resources, nonetheless have adequate money to selectively overpolice Black riders, leading to expensive fines and dangerous entanglements with law enforcement. As we have learned all too often in recent years, those encounters can turn fatal. Oscar Grant was killed by a police officer on an Oakland, California, train in 2009—one of the first police shootings captured on video by bystanders.

But police shootings are not the only way that racist transportation policies can kill Black people. Earlier in this chapter, I shared the story of seventeen-year-old Cynthia Wiggins, the young woman who was hit by a truck while walking to work in a suburban mall, a journey she was forced to make because city buses were not allowed in the mall parking lot. Transportation policy did more than make Cynthia's commute difficult; it took her life.

Transportation is a life-or-death issue. It can kill you over time, by depriving you of what you need to live a decent, healthy life. It can kill through the wear and tear of a long commute, by making it hard if not impossible to get to the doctor, by exposing you to deadly traffic exhaust, by causing depression and anxiety as you experience your community being ripped apart or your home and your wealth disappearing, or by making it hard to secure healthy and affordable food for your family. Of course, because transportation involves large hunks of metal traveling at high speeds, it can also kill you in an instant.

Sometimes the language of "access" and "inequality" fails to capture everything that is at stake in transportation policy.

Chapter 6

The White Man's Right of Way

D. W. Griffith's *The Birth of a Nation* is an infamously racist film that follows two South Carolina families across the antebellum period, the Civil War, and Reconstruction. Released in 1915, it depicts emancipated Black people greedy for power as they try to assert dominion over white people. It shows what is, for Griffith, a horror story—a world where Black and white people live in close proximity and where Black people view themselves as equal to white people. The Black people in the movie, played by white actors in Blackface, are the boogeymen. They are opposed by the Ku Klux Klan, Griffith's heroes in an epic battle for the soul of the nation—protagonists in a righteous struggle against the existential threat of Black political and social power.

Alongside shoeless and barbaric Black legislators, the specter of miscegenation, and the rape of white women, Black control of the sidewalks is portrayed as a threat to white privilege. In one scene, a group of Black men are walking down a sidewalk with Lieutenant Governor Silas Lynch, a Black man who has risen to his high office during Reconstruction. Three white people—a couple and a character named Colonel Ben Cameron—approach them from the other direction. When the two groups meet, neither gives way to the other. While the white couple looks on in fear, Lynch raises his fist in anger and says: "The sidewalk belongs to us as much as it belongs to you, Colonel Cameron." To Griffith, Lynch's challenge was clearly a serious danger to the racial order.

Sidewalks might seem like a secondary concern; we might never think of them at all. Yet throughout American history, they have been an effective tool for making and shoring up racial hierarchies. Segregated sidewalks were a point of discussion in the Supreme Court's 1896 *Plessy v. Ferguson* decision. Curiously, the justices in the majority appear to have assumed that sidewalks in the South were *not* segregated and racially contested. Before the court, counsel for the plaintiff raised the hypothetical of a law "requir[ing] all colored people to walk on one side of the street and the whites on the other" as one example of a "parade of horribles" that might result if the court upheld the provision of "separate but equal" railway cars at issue in the case. The court's majority brushed off this argument on the grounds that "every exercise of the police power must be reasonable, and extend only to such laws that are enacted in good faith for the promotion of the public good, and not for the annoyance or oppression of a particular class." This is a low bar indeed, but one that a sidewalk segregation law, by implication of the court's opinion, would fail to meet. Thus, the *Plessy* majority appears to have implicitly presumed that public streets and sidewalks were integrated spaces, and that both Black people and white people enjoyed equal rights of access.

History tells us otherwise. In fact, sidewalks have always been contested public spaces that were shared by necessity, creating daily opportunities to reinforce racial hierarchy and the subjugation of Black people. The lone dissenter in *Plessy*, Justice John Marshall Harlan, relied on the same example to argue *against* "separate but equal" train cars, by stating his view that racial integration did not require absolute social equality: "The suggestion that social equality cannot exist between the white and black races in this country . . . is scarcely worthy of consideration; for social equality no more exists between two races when traveling in a passenger coach . . . than . . . when they use in common the streets of a city or town . . ."

During slavery, Black city residents—both free and enslaved—had greater freedom of movement compared to their brothers and sisters who toiled on plantations. Urban Black residents regularly shared the streets and sidewalks with white people. This relative freedom and frequent proximity prompted many southern cities to adopt laws legislating racial deference, codifying many of the unspoken rules in more rural areas. In cities like Richmond, Raleigh, and Montgomery, local governments made it illegal to disrespect white people and prohibited Black people from using or displaying things considered to be markers of white respectability. For example, Black people could not walk in the city square, smoke a pipe in the street, or carry a cane. These laws required Black pedestrians to look down or avert their eyes as they walked past white people as a show of respect to members of the privileged race.

The laws also made it undeniably clear that sidewalks were white spaces by ensuring that in the real world, the Lieutenant Governor Lynches of the world would be forced to cede the right of way to the Colonel Camerons. The sidewalks did not, as it turns out, belong to Black people as much as they belonged to white people. Black people were forced to walk in the gutter or the roadway when there was a conflict, much as the future Black citizens of Montgomery would be forced to move to the back of the bus whenever a white person needed a seat. As historian Richard Wade notes, by the late 1850s, laws regulating Black urban residents' behavior in public spaces in southern cities were ubiquitous. Richmond, for example, passed an ordinance in 1857 stating that "Negroes shall not at any time stand on a side-walk to the inconvenience of [white] persons standing by," and mandating that "a negro meeting or overtaking, or being overtaken by a white person . . . shall pass on the outside; and if it be necessary to enable such white person to pass, shall immediately get off the sidewalk." The Richmond ordinance also prohibited more than five Black people from standing together on a sidewalk at or near the corner of a street. Any violation was punishable by whipping.

After the Civil War, the use of social norms and codes of etiquette to enforce racial hierarchies on the sidewalks and diminish the new citizenship of Black people was pervasive. It continued into the twentieth century. Black Americans continued to experience relatively more freedom walking in public streets than they did in many other arenas, but the color line remained in place, and in force.

Jim Crow etiquette required Black people to yield to white people when walking—white people were granted the inner side of the sidewalk, further from the busy street, a practice informally referred to as "giving whites the wall" or "the white man's right of way." Today, many Black parents have a conversation with their children about how to deescalate interactions with police to increase the odds of surviving the encounter, something that has come to be known as "The Talk." For Black parents in the Jim Crow South, The Talk necessarily included how to navigate interactions with any white people, not just law enforcement, on sidewalks. For children, sidewalks were a fraught landscape and one of the more immediate experiences of segregation and racism. In an oral history of Jim Crow, former Louisiana resident Charles Gratton centered his recollection of growing up in a segregated society on his experiences of sidewalks:

> I can remember very close in my mind when my mother would have the occasion to send me to this grocery store I told you about that was approximately a mile away, which was the only grocery store in Norwood, uh, she would give me instructions before I'd leave home and tell me, say, "Son, now you going up to the store and get this or that for me, now if you pass any white people on your way, you get off the sidewalk. Give them the sidewalk. You know, you move over. Don't challenge white people."

Violating this racial etiquette—failing to give white people the wall—was to risk one's very life.

At the same time, refusing to yield the right of way on a sidewalk was a small way for Black people to preserve their dignity and humanity in public spaces. During the time between Emancipation and the solidification of Jim Crow, as historian Jane Dailey has observed, "the appropriation of public space was an important way for African Americans in this period to assert their humanity, demonstrate their political rights, and stake their claim to equal citizenship."

In 1883, a Black man refused to yield to a white man on a sidewalk in the city of Danville, a Virginia town near the North Carolina border. This dispute over sidewalk etiquette soon expanded into what became known as the Danville Riot.

The riot took place against a backdrop of a broader struggle over Black political power in the postwar South. The Readjuster Party was a biracial third party that had governed in Virginia beginning in 1877 until it lost control to white Democrats in 1883. The mission of the Readjuster Party was "to break the power of wealth and established privilege." The party invested in public education—especially public schools for Black children. It increased funding for Virginia Tech, and notably established Virginia State University, a historically Black university. The Readjuster Party also abolished the poll tax and took other steps to increase Black political participation.

Black members of the Readjuster Party filled Danville public positions, serving as police officers, schoolteachers, and city councilors. Indeed, because of the Readjusters' successful efforts to expand voting, Danville elected a Black-majority town council. White Democrats were unnerved by what they saw as a brazen assault on their privilege and pushed back, demonizing the exercise of Black power in local government and on the streets of Danville. In October 1883, the city's Democratic leadership published a pamphlet titled "Coalition Rule in Danville," later referred to as the Danville Circular. The Danville Circular was republished in various newspapers. It purported to outline "the injustice and humiliation to which our white people have been subjected and are daily undergoing by the domination and misrule of the radical or negro party." The authors lamented the empowerment of Black people in Danville and took special issue with sidewalk etiquette. They complained about Black people "who impede the travel of [white] ladies and gentlemen, very frequently forcing them from the sidewalk into the street." The Circular pleaded with white voters to continue to choose the Democrats, in order to save white people "from this awful state of humiliation and wretchedness."

On November 3, 1883, shortly after the Danville Circular was published, a young white man named Charles Noel was walking up Main Street when he tripped over the foot of Henderson Lawson, a young Black man walking in the opposite direction with his companion, another young Black man named Davis Llewellyn. The group exchanged words. Llewellyn maintained that he and Lawson had done nothing wrong, and Noel responded by striking him. Llewellyn defended himself and twice knocked Noel off the sidewalk and into the gutter. Noel eventually left, realizing he had been beaten. But he was not done.

Later that night, Noel returned with two friends, approached Llewellyn and Lawson, and assaulted the latter, leading to another fight. Although police officers eventually broke it up, a crowd of white and Black people had gathered. The police were able to separate Black and white people, yet they were unable to get the crowd to disperse, and tensions continued to rise. Without provocation, a group of white men fired shots into the crowd of unarmed Black people. As the Black people ran for their lives, some members of the white mob pursued and continued to attack them. Four Black men and one white man were murdered. In the aftermath of the riot, armed white patrols would roam the streets, intimidating Black residents and keeping most Black voters from the polls during the election that took place just three days later, helping the Democrats win control in the General Assembly.

BLACK PEOPLE WERE ONCE FORCED TO WALK IN THE STREET DUE TO THE racial hierarchy of slavery, and later because of the racial etiquette imposed by Jim Crow. For Black people who escaped *de jure* segregation by fleeing the South for northern cities during the Great Migration, as well as for those who stayed behind to overthrow segregation during the early civil rights movement, inequities in the pedestrian realm persisted.

Indeed, to this day the legacy of Jim Crow can still be felt in many formerly segregated cities and neighborhoods across the country that lack adequate pedestrian infrastructure. After city planners destroyed Black communities with highways and major roadways, they largely ignored not only the public transportation needs of those affected, but their pedestrian needs as well. How could residents safely navigate the area around the highways, overpasses, and access roads without a comprehensive system of well-maintained sidewalks? Walking in the street, and sharing the road with cars, motorcycles, and bicycles, is inherently more dangerous than traveling on a sidewalk. As we saw in the previous chapter, low-income Black people are more likely to rely on walking to get around. We should now add that they simultaneously live in neighborhoods without decent sidewalks. Black people are still being forced to walk in the street.

In many low-income communities, and for people with mobility disabilities, sidewalks are more than a helpful convenience for going for a jog or walking the dog. Open to everyone, they are public spaces and gathering places, sources of physical, social, and economic health. Sidewalks connect neighbors to neighbors, children to schools, and people to economic opportunity. They are a critical link to accessing public transportation and everything that public transportation in turn leads to. Missing or neglected sidewalks keep people from accessing the mainstays of an economically, politically, and socially vibrant life.

In many southern cities, poor sidewalk quality, or the lack of sidewalks altogether, is a legacy of racial segregation. Like their counterparts across the region, white supremacists in Starkville, Mississippi, imposed harsh segregation measures on Black residents. In addition to facing voting, employment, and educational restrictions, many Black Starkville residents lived in houses without running water or indoor plumbing. Starkville's sidewalk network was largely built during the 1940s and 1950s, when the city was fighting to maintain segregation in the face of Black resistance. The result was a patchwork of disconnected and poorly organized sidewalks.

Sidewalks line only about 14 percent of Starkville's roads, but to the extent that the sidewalks are well maintained, white people have the best of it. A group of scholars found a drastic difference in sidewalk quality between majority-white and majority-Black residential areas. Using compliance with the Americans with Disabilities Act as a measure of quality, the scholars concluded that about 70 percent of ADA-compliant sidewalks were on predominantly white blocks, compared to approximately just 22 percent on predominantly Black blocks.

Trimble Bottom, a Black neighborhood in Nashville, did not get any sidewalks until the 1970s. Today, about one-half of Nashville's roads have sidewalks, and roads in predominantly Black communities are much less likely to have them. Studies of sidewalks in New Orleans showed similar results. Professor Kate Lowe's research found that communities of color in the city have significantly worse sidewalks than white communities. Using a comprehensive inventory of bus stops and intersections that are connected by sidewalks, Lowe analyzed the access to sidewalks for low-income pedestrians and people of color and found notable racial and socioeconomic disparities in access to sidewalks, with white residents of New Orleans more likely to have continuous sidewalks in their communities.

Even in cities that were not segregated by law, sidewalks in predominantly Black neighborhoods are less common and of poorer quality, often as the result of a legal regime that places greater reliance on private property owners. More than perhaps any other means of transportation, pedestrian infrastructure is highly localized in its construction, funding, and maintenance; the federal government does little to oversee or force accountability on sidewalk quality or even whether sidewalks are required on a particular road. Sidewalks are in some ways "public," but are also closely associated with adjacent properties or lots.

The result is that neighborhood socioeconomic disparities map directly onto pedestrian infrastructure quality, as poorer neighborhoods that are disproportionately Black and Brown are less able to invest private capital into maintaining their sidewalks. Dallas is one of many American cities that requires adjacent property owners to fund sidewalks if they want them. And like many other cities, Dallas requires neighboring homeowners to repair or replace damaged sidewalks at their own expense.

Predictably, the city now has scattered patches of sidewalks that don't meet the needs of Dallas's communities of color. A 2021 survey commissioned by the city found that it had more than 2,000 miles of roadway that lack sidewalks, making it difficult for people who live near those roads to access public transportation, for children to walk to school, and for people with disabilities to get around. Dallas also has an additional 1,081 miles of broken and inadequate sidewalks. Those may seem like modest numbers given the sprawl of Dallas, but poor sidewalks create serious difficulties for the people who rely on them and compound other inequities.

None of these findings surprised people who live and work in Dallas. Throughout the city, there are long stretches of road without any sidewalks at all, forcing people to walk in ditches. Sidewalks often end abruptly, only to resume miles away. In many sections of the city where there are sidewalks, they are barely walkable, with cracks, crevices, and dangerously uneven joints. In some spots, the sidewalk looks more like a cobblestone path.

Municipalities that require private property owners to maintain sidewalks can worsen disparities when they enforce those rules in inequitable or unreasonable ways. For example, when cities pay for the cost of repairs themselves, they often will bill the adjacent property owner. This debt can be enforced through a lien that may ultimately result in foreclosure on the property. It should not be a surprise that Black communities bear the brunt of this practice. The City of Memphis handed out citations for sidewalk disrepair at a rate of one per day between 2018 and 2022. The zip code with the highest rates of such liens is in the city's overwhelmingly Black South Memphis neighborhood, which has a poverty rate of 40 percent.

A related problem comes when cities rely on private complaints to determine where and when the city should repair damaged sidewalks. Several cities use voluntary complaint systems like "311" phone calls to assess which sidewalks need work. Low-income communities of color are far less likely to call to request help. Seattle, Washington, switched from a 311 system to a fixed repair schedule after officials realized that relying on 311 led the city to make a disproportionate number of repairs in high-income, white neighborhoods. Those residents were more comfortable filing complaints and likely had higher expectations that those complaints would be addressed.

When Boston embarked on a citywide campaign to address sidewalk inequities in 2017, it opted not to use a 311 system. Instead, city officials went block by block over Boston's 1,600 miles of sidewalk to set repair priorities. But not all cities have the interest or the resources to follow Seattle's and Boston's leads.

Our national failure on sidewalks goes beyond impeding the welfare, mobility, and prosperity of residents of Black neighborhoods. America's willingness to deny Black people access to sidewalks has had dangerous, and sometimes deadly, consequences.

Black pedestrians have drastically higher rates of injury and death. Again: those living in poverty, in particular, are less likely to own cars and are thus more dependent on commuting by public transit or walking. And across the United States, lower-income communities and neighborhoods of color have disproportionately higher rates of pedestrian injury and death from automobile accidents. In 2018, Black pedestrians' fatality rate was roughly *twice* that of white pedestrians.

During the twentieth century, American cities systematically deprior-itized pedestrian infrastructure in favor of facilitating car travel. Plan-ners abandoned walkable street grids in favor of car-centric planning features like suburban arterials and cul-de-sacs. Cities that were built or significantly expanded during this era tend to have lower rates of side-walk coverage overall, larger and faster arterial roads, and fewer pedes-trian crossings. Such cities are concentrated in the American Southwest and Southeast, both of which saw high rates of growth during the early to mid-twentieth century. Unlike northeastern metropolitan areas, which urbanized in an earlier, pre-automobile era and were thus built more densely and with pedestrians in mind, southern and western cities were built to maximize traffic flow and encourage the fast movement of cars. As a result, these cities are much less safe on average for pedestrians. And rates of pedestrian injuries and deaths are on the rise, though exactly why is a confounding question.

Although the pedestrian safety crisis is a nationwide issue, its harms do not equally affect all Americans. Black people bear the brunt of road-way injuries because predominantly Black neighborhoods are less likely to have crosswalks, warning signs, and other basic safety measures. Many Black communities not only lack sidewalks but also have high-speed road-ways that are akin to mini highways coursing through their centers. The impact of discriminatory infrastructure planning is compounded by the prejudice of American drivers: numerous studies have found that drivers are less likely to slow down or stop for Black pedestrians than they are for white ones.

ALTHOUGH BLACK PEDESTRIANS ARE MOST AT RISK IN THE NEW CITIES OF the Southeast and Southwest, pedestrians in the Northeast face significant danger as well. New Haven, Connecticut, is home to Yale University, one of America's oldest and most prestigious universities. It also has some of the most impoverished urban communities in the United States. In its extremes of privilege and poverty, New Haven has long served as a sharp example of the disparities that exist across America. The area around the Yale campus is characterized by students walking to and from classes and other campus

0

activities. But those whose lives do not revolve around the Yale campus do not have as easy a time getting around their own city by foot.

New Haven is not one of the United States' most dangerous cities for pedestrians. It does not even make the top twenty, a list dominated by southern and western cities like Miami, Albuquerque, and Memphis—all cities that saw large waves of expansion in the post-1960 era of high-speed, multilane arterial highways. New Haven, in contrast, dates back to even before the country was founded. Its central street grid, built according to one of the country's first comprehensive city plans, was laid out in a pre-automotive era.

Yet among northeastern cities, New Haven nonetheless stands out as unusually dangerous. Based on data from 2016 to 2020, Greater New Haven was the deadliest northeastern metropolitan area for pedestrians. And as with other communities across the country, the city's accidents are disproportionately concentrated on arterial roadways: high-capacity, urban roads that are smaller than highways but much larger than local streets and collector roads.

Though the city and its grid are old, New Haven bears the legacy of a well-documented history of "urban renewal," and this is why pedestrian deaths in the city are relatively high. From 1954 to 1969, New Haven's municipal leaders mounted a campaign to reshape its built environment that was both unprecedented and unparalleled in its scope; in fact, the city accepted more federal urban renewal dollars per capita than any other in the United States. New Haven's infamous "Oak Street Connector project," for example, razed one of its poorest and most densely populated neighborhoods, home to a mix of Black, Jewish, Italian, and Irish residents, to make way for an extension of state highway Route 34 that was ultimately never completed, remaining a truncated stump off Interstate 95. The Oak Street Connector project was infected by racism and classism from the start. It continues to divide New Haven, separating its downtown area from its southern neighborhoods and the wharf and preventing residents from traversing from one area to the other on foot.

New Haven's urban renewal–era leaders inherited a city built for horses and carriages that suffered from worsening congestion since the arrival of the automobile at the turn of the twentieth century. To address the issue, officials sought to build fast-moving main streets. This would have the added benefit of attracting commercial road traffic from the city's booming suburbs to the shops and businesses in its downtown core, revitalizing its faltering economy. The magic solution was to make the city more "motor-friendly."

In a 1957 address to the city's board of aldermen, Mayor Richard C. Lee—the political face of New Haven's urban renewal program—listed among his administration's accomplishments for the prior year the paving of twenty-six miles of streets at a cost of $600,000, "more than twice the sum spent . . . [and] four times the miles of streets covered in any single year in the past." Lee argued that "a good system of streets will encourage shoppers to come downtown, thus assuring the continued prosperity of our central business district." He placed car transit at the center of his vision for New Haven's urban renewal, and linked it to his mission to cure the city's "blight." His words are worth quoting at length, in that they demonstrate how transportation was not incidental to urban renewal, but at the center of it:

I cannot impress too much the importance of modern highways, adequate off-street parking, and up-to-date traffic relocation in the orderly and sound development of a city. Streets designed for horse and carriage days cannot cope with present and future traffic needs. Traffic jams, inability to park easily, high volumes of heavy traffic are as an [sic] important a cause of blight as mixed-up land use and deteriorated, over-crowded housing. A program to rid a city of slums and blight must begin with an arterial highway program designed to take heavy through-traffic off local streets and provide commuters and shoppers with direct easy access to the central business district, where they must find ample and convenient parking space at prices they are willing to pay. Only in this way may a city expect to meet the ever increasing pressure of economic competition from the suburbs where large scale development parcels with free parking are readily available.

As officials saw it, traffic speed and "throughput" took precedence over safety and walkability. The city's leaders were laser-focused on widening and speeding up its streets and paid less attention to the potential safety issues that might result from their choices, especially for those who lived in the city itself.

In subsequent decades, the city's traffic safety issues became painfully apparent—particularly in its predominantly Black neighborhoods. Black residents had come to New Haven en masse relatively late in the city's history, arriving in large numbers during the Great Migration in search of jobs in the city's once thriving industrial sector, just in time to watch that sector's collapse. Because much of the city was closed off to them due to redlining, they settled in areas like the historically Black Dixwell neighborhood, as well as in Oak Street, Dwight, Newhallville, Fair Haven, and the Hill. Many of these areas suffered significant displacement and disruption as a result of urban renewal plans during the 1950s and 1960s. Today, they are among New Haven's poorest per capita and suffer from significant infrastructure gaps.

Several of the city's biggest arterial roads—including Whalley Avenue, Dixwell Avenue, and Ella T. Grasso Boulevard—cut through these neighborhoods. While these roads already existed at the time of substantial Black migration to New Haven, they were widened in the urban renewal era to make room for more suburban commuting traffic, and their pedestrian safety features have not been adequately upgraded or maintained since then. They lack adequate crossing points, street lighting, and traffic-calming measures. Even in sections that do have walk signals, the roads' multiple lanes make them too wide to safely cross in the allotted time. The sidewalks are aged (many date from the 1920s and 1930s) and are frequently in poor condition. Some places lack them altogether, and instead have "desire paths" (or "goat paths"), where pedestrians have created makeshift foot routes on unpaved areas along the roadside.

Today, these roads see some of the highest rates of pedestrian death not just in the city, but in the entire state. Ella T. Grasso Boulevard alone is responsible for such a high percentage of New Haven's pedestrian fatalities—nearly 50 percent in 2020—that it has been called "Death

Boulevard" by local media. And while the city and state have been aware of these roads' safety problems for decades, pedestrian deaths continue to occur with alarming frequency.

Residents have repeatedly advocated for the city to invest in better pedestrian infrastructure, often following another tragedy. In a community-led report on the Newhallville and Dixwell neighborhoods, a fifteen-year-old neighborhood resident named Andre responded to the question of "what can be done to make [the neighborhood] a better place for youth?" He answered: "In my perspective, I chose speed bumps because they would help a lot of pedestrians like myself have a safer walk across the street." After eleven-year-old resident Gabrielle Lee was struck and killed by a motorist while crossing Whalley Avenue in 2008, neighborhood advocates banded together to create the "Complete Streets Working Group," later renamed the "Safe Streets Working Group," to advocate for better safety features on New Haven's roads and sidewalks.

The city has responded to these calls by taking several steps to improve pedestrian safety. After the deaths of Lee and other pedestrians, in 2010 city legislators passed a "Complete Streets" policy that created a new road design manual intended to lower average vehicle speeds and improve pedestrian safety and walkability. Since then, New Haven has implemented a variety of traffic calming measures on its streets, including curb extensions, painted street lines, and new signage to slow vehicle speeds and reduce crossing times. In reaction to neighborhood advocacy, the city has also worked to build new sidewalks.

Many of these efforts are explicit reversals of the policies enacted during the 1950s and 1960s urban renewal era. Most notably, the city's Downtown Crossing project secured a $16 million federal grant in 2010 to convert the former Oak Street Connector back into two lower-speed multiuse roads capped off by a pedestrian bridge.

Though New Haven is taking meaningful steps to improve its infrastructure and reduce pedestrian deaths, some of its efforts seem misguided, such as its focus on enforcing traffic laws against pedestrians. In 2019, the New Haven Police Department used a state traffic grant to launch a pilot safety program that centered on "education" of pedestrians via increased ticketing. This program was almost immediately canceled after public outcry, but the city's police nonetheless continued to issue warnings to pedestrians, despite acknowledging that "giv[ing] tickets for jaywalking . . . [was] not having the desired impact," and that "a pedestrian crossing in a crosswalk does not pose the greatest threat."

In contrast, the city's police department has failed to strongly penalize *drivers* for endangering pedestrians. In 2018, three-year-old Jameson Jones was struck while crossing Howard Avenue in New Haven's City Point neighborhood with his daycare class and spent several days hospitalized for internal bleeding. The police who arrived at the scene issued the driver a citation and $265 fine for failure to grant the right of way but did not invoke a state "vulnerable users" law that would have authorized a much higher penalty. In fact, at the time only one person in the entire state had been found guilty of violating this law in the four years since its passage.

The Infrastructure Investment and Jobs Act of 2021 (IJA) could potentially help New Haven improve its pedestrian, cycling, and transit facilities. The IJA, one of the largest federal infrastructure bills in history, has the potential to fundamentally reshape the United States' roads, highways, sidewalks, and footbridges and change how people in this country traverse the built environment. The Biden administration made the redress of racial inequities a central tenet of the IJA's mission. Nevertheless, it remains to be seen whether the program will be successful at redrawing the dividing lines in New Haven and elsewhere.

IN NEIGHBORHOODS BISECTED BY HIGHWAYS AND ROADS, WHERE BLACK RESidents don't have many ways to move around safely, residents also face the threat of political systems that target, harass, and oppress Black people merely trying to navigate their own communities. As with overpolicing of Black people on transit, local governments often respond to their own underinvestment in sidewalks with over-enforcement of pedestrian traffic rules.

That is to say: The racial inequality faced by Black pedestrians also encompasses the web of laws and regulations governing how pedestrians move on sidewalks and roads, leading to more interactions with the police.

Pedestrian laws are one of the key legal contexts for racialized policing. As communities across the country debate how to reimagine public safety and end the overpolicing of communities of color, putting a stop to unnecessary police interactions and constraining the broad authority that has been ceded to law enforcement agencies must be a part of the solution.

The supposed crime of "driving while Black" has long been understood as one of the special burdens faced by Black people. Black drivers are disproportionately targeted and stopped for minor traffic violations such as having a broken taillight or an expired registration. In 2016, Philando Castile was shot and killed by a police officer after being pulled over for a broken taillight. He had been pulled over by police a staggering forty-nine times before this deadly incident. In January 2023, Tyre Nichols was beaten to death by Memphis police officers following a traffic stop.

"Walking while Black," though a less common idiom, can be just as dangerous. Pedestrian laws are also disproportionately enforced against Black people. This is not a coincidence, and it is not solely a matter of prejudiced behavior by individual officers. Black residents in areas with missing sidewalks, crosswalks, and crossing signals are more likely to break pedestrian traffic laws because they have few other options. And in response, city officials often choose enforcement over investment, leading to sometimes deadly consequences.

On August 9, 2014, Michael Brown and a friend were walking in the road on Canfield Drive in Ferguson, Missouri, when a police officer, Darren Wilson, drove by and ordered them to walk on the sidewalk. The situation escalated when Wilson confronted Brown, shooting and killing him. The killing would become international news and help spark America's ongoing reckoning with the role of racism in policing.

In Ferguson, a majority-Black suburb of St. Louis, many roads either lack sidewalks outright, have sidewalks that disappear into grassy fields, or have sidewalks that are cracked and buckling and therefore difficult to traverse. The city has chronically failed to invest in the infrastructure to support a population that uses walking as a primary means of transportation. Of the city's $21 million 2016 budget, a paltry $3,000 was set aside for sidewalk maintenance—enough, if you are lucky, to repair a few hundred square feet if the damage is not too bad. In 2017, it was $7,000, and in 2018, it was $3,500. Still, then, for many people the only place to walk is in the streets.

One of the main thoroughfares in Ferguson is West Florissant, a dangerous road with high-speed traffic. Many drivers on West Florissant are traveling between two of the three interstate highways surrounding Ferguson. Like much of the transportation infrastructure in the area, West Florissant is designed to cater to the drivers passing through the city rather than the people who actually live there. West Florissant has little usable pedestrian infrastructure. The sidewalks are often broken and disconnected, and so narrow that they typically fall below the standards required by the Americans with Disabilities Act. There are notably few crosswalks along the long, busy street. And in many places along the road, there are just no sidewalks at all.

West Florissant is not an anomaly; unusable or nonexistent pedestrian infrastructure is a problem throughout Ferguson. Many of its busiest streets have no sidewalks or traffic calming measures. On Chambers Road, a major thoroughfare running from east to west through Ferguson and one of the few streets with a bus line, crosswalks are sometimes as far as half a mile apart, forcing pedestrians to cross five lanes of traffic without the help of signals. Along Hudson Road, another busy street, there are no sidewalks, just signs warning drivers to "Watch for Pedestrians." The streets surrounding Griffith Elementary School have no sidewalks. The street directly in front of the school is exceptionally narrow and is blocked by utility poles and junction boxes, leaving little space for walking.

And yet walking in the street in Ferguson is illegal. Local laws require people to walk on the sidewalk or at the side of the road whenever possible, a rule that seems quite reasonable on paper. But "Manner of Walking in Roadway" charges, which can carry a fine of $1,000 and three months in jail, were commonly issued by Ferguson police officers to Black residents even when there was nowhere else to safely walk. In fact, the investigation by the United States Department of Justice following Brown's killing found that the Ferguson police department enforced the overly vague sidewalk law almost exclusively as part of a practice of discriminatory policing, in order to fill holes in the city's budget by extracting fines and fees from Black residents. From 2011 to 2013, Black people accounted for 95 percent of the charges for the offense of walking in the roadway. And it was that violation that led to the deadly encounter between Wilson and Brown.

Shreveport, Louisiana, has a similar law making it illegal to walk in the streets if a sidewalk is provided. In 2010, fifty-six-year-old Ola Mae Kelly was beaten and arrested by a Shreveport police officer after she was stopped for violating that law. She was charged with resisting arrest and walking in the street when a sidewalk was available. As in Ferguson, many roads in Shreveport lack sidewalks, and the ones that exist are often in poor condition, even in wealthier neighborhoods. In her suit, Kelly acknowledged walking in the street and claimed she was making her way to the sidewalk when the officer jumped out of the car and began yelling at her. She claimed that the officer ordered her to put her hands on the police car, to spread her legs, and put his hands in her waistband. When she asked why he was arresting her, the officer threw her to the ground and struck her repeatedly.

Even if Kelly violated the letter of the law, the beating she received shows the inherent dangers of laws that give police broad discretion to initiate contact with pedestrians. Kelly filed suit, the case was settled out of court, and the officer was ultimately fired.

If it is nearly impossible to walk in communities lacking quality sidewalks, consider the difficulties faced by people who use a wheelchair or other mobility aids. In 2015, fifty-eight-year-old Cedrick Murphy, another Black resident of Shreveport, was also ticketed for walking in the street because he could not use a badly broken sidewalk that was full of buckles and cracks large enough to allow big patches of grass to grow. Murphy has limited use of his legs and relies on a motorized wheelchair to navigate the city, a wheelchair that Shreveport's buses are not always able to accommodate. The sidewalk was a *danger* to him—it could cause his wheelchair to tip over or be damaged, something he could ill afford.

Following a common national pattern, Shreveport police have deployed the sidewalk law as a tool to stop, question, and arrest people, and disproportionately use that tool against Black residents. A 2014 study by the *Shreveport Times* found that between January 2011 and August 2014, 93 percent of the people ticketed or arrested in the city for walking in the street were Black. This was almost exactly in line with an earlier study covering January 1, 2005, to September 12, 2010, which found the figure to be 92 percent.

Those unsympathetic to the challenges facing Black pedestrians might accuse Kelly or Murphy of "jaywalking," arguing that there is good reason that walking in the street is illegal: it is dangerous. But there is little evidence that such laws have the intended effect, especially when they are enforced in a discriminatory manner and in communities where poor sidewalk infrastructure leaves pedestrians with few alternatives.

But we do have other evidence about jaywalking. Enforcing laws against jaywalking has become a central component of "broken windows" policing policies. Developed by Professors James Q. Wilson and George Kelling, the theory posits that minor crimes, such as vandalism and public intoxication, can promote a sense of public disorder that leads to more serious crimes. Police departments that adhere to this theory therefore target minor infractions in an effort to curb overall crime rates. New York City has been a testing ground for a broken windows policy, which can include heightened enforcement and penalization of pedestrian infractions. For example, in 1998, then–New York City mayor Rudy Giuliani increased the penalty for jaywalking from $2 to $50. At the start of his administration in 2014, Mayor Bill de Blasio, who ran in part *against* the NYPD's stop-and-frisk policies targeting young Black and Latino pedestrians, began increased enforcement of jaywalking violations as part of his Vision Zero initiative to eliminate traffic deaths, with the NYPD issuing fines up to $250.

Like other pedestrian laws and policies, laws against jaywalking have had well-documented, harmful effects on Black people and Black communities. Studies across the United States have repeatedly shown that Black pedestrians are disproportionately penalized for jaywalking infractions compared to white residents. In New York City, 90 percent of jaywalking tickets issued in 2019 went to Black and Latino residents, who represented about 55 percent of the population collectively. In Jacksonville, Florida, an investigation found that Black people received 55 percent of jaywalking tickets despite making up only 29 percent of the population. In Champaign-Urbana, Illinois, 89 percent of jaywalking arrestees from 2007 to 2011 were Black, and 91 percent of those cited were Black. In Seattle, Black residents received 26 percent of jaywalking tickets in 2017 while only constituting 7 percent of the population.

In California, Black residents of San Diego, Los Angeles, and Long Beach were stopped at a rate of between 17 and 22 percent above their share of the general population and were up to 4.3 times more likely to be stopped than white residents. In Sacramento, over 25 percent of jaywalking tickets went to Black residents in 2019 and over 40 percent of citations in 2019, even though the city's population was only 13 percent Black.

Walking while Black is a catch-22. Black people are penalized for failing to obey safety laws despite a lack of adequate infrastructure to help them comply with these laws. When sidewalks are decrepit, undersized, or intermittent, pedestrians are forced to walk in the street. When crossings lack sufficiently visible safety measures like crosswalks and lights, pedestrians are more likely to violate traffic safety laws—whether due to innocent error or necessity. Historically and to this day, disinvestment and biased law enforcement intersect. Rather than tackle the root of the problem by investing in public safety features—or penalizing wealthier and more politically powerful suburban car commuters—city officials attempt to address real safety issues by "cracking down" on Black pedestrians.

SOMETIMES, THE LACK OF SIDEWALKS IS AN INDICATOR OF A COMMUNITY'S poverty. At other times, it reflects a wealthy community's exclusion of those who rely on sidewalks to get around. In Connecticut, a road called Park Avenue separates the town of Fairfield from the city of Bridgeport. Fairfield is a community of 60,000 people that boasts parks, golf courses, and five miles of shoreline along the Long Island Sound. It is consistently included in lists of "top towns to live in" in Connecticut. And like most of Connecticut's wealthy towns, Fairfield is over 90 percent white. In 2022, the median household income in Fairfield was $165,316, well above the national median household income of $74,580 and the Connecticut median of $88,429. Bridgeport is Connecticut's most populous city—as of 2020, it

THE WHITE MAN'S RIGHT OF WAY   149

was home to 148,654 residents—and while it may be next door to Fairfield, in many ways it is a world apart. Although parts of Bridgeport bordering Fairfield are the wealthiest in the city, the former is a racially diverse city that has struggled with economic disinvestment and a crime rate above the state average. As you walk along Park Avenue, the side of the street within Bridgeport has a sidewalk and access to a bus stop. On the Fairfield side of the street, there is no sidewalk and no crosswalk at or near the bus stop.

Although he did not have the divide between Bridgeport and Fairfield in mind when he wrote it, in a famous poem Shel Silverstein described the place where the sidewalk ends as the divide between a bucolic community "where the grass grows soft and white," and an urban one "where the smoke blows black." The poem was written at a time when people were fleeing the perceived crime, chaos, and pollution of urban areas to suburban and rural communities accessible primarily to those with cars.

It is not quite that simple, however. In some jurisdictions, as we've seen, officials made decisions that promoted the development of pedestrian infrastructure in predominantly white communities but underinvested in that infrastructure in communities of color. But in other communities, race-based choices led to the creation of predominantly white communities with little or no pedestrian infrastructure. In these places, planners built with drivers in mind, acutely aware that those without cars—and therefore reliant on walking and public transportation—would more likely be Black. Sidewalks that end abruptly tend to be suburban phenomena or appear in mixed spaces where the urban bleeds into suburban. Here is yet another tactic policymakers in predominantly white communities used to keep their cities and towns racially segregated through infrastructure choices when they could no longer do so by legal fiat.

American suburbs built during the mid-twentieth century were designed to accommodate low-density housing. Private yards were placed behind homes, and socializing on the street was effectively discouraged. Developers were not entirely driven by the goal of racial exclusion. Many simply avoided the expense of sidewalks altogether, assuming that all residents would prefer to get around by car and seek to maintain a "high-class" appearance.

Some suburbs continue to this day to resist building pedestrian infrastructure and are focused on preserving their "park-like" feel. In these communities, sidewalks have come to be seen as an unwelcome symbol of urbanization and all the negative racial and class stereotypes that word entails. Sidewalks would interfere with suburban residents' idyllic vision of a privatized landscape of rolling green lawns and winding roads. Wealthy suburbs in the Northeast such as Nassau County, New York, and Darien, Connecticut, have taken exclusion to an extreme by creating what historian James Loewen calls "defended neighborhoods," making their streets and sidewalks deliberately hard for outsiders to navigate.

Today, cities around the country are experiencing reverse Black migration. As city centers become more attractive to the wealthy, we see more people with means choosing urban life over suburban life. This trend has led to the displacement of communities of color from urban centers by rising housing costs and gentrification. Black people, as a result, are migrating into cities' surrounding areas. These suburban communities—often built to be white enclaves—have thus become more diverse, both racially and economically. And they are now facing the consequences of past generations' hostile and exclusionary design choices. Black pedestrians are being forced to walk in places that were never designed to be walkable— with the expected consequences. Some newly diverse communities are struggling to handle the needs of Black families who are more likely to rely on walking and public transportation. Others are actively resisting the needs of these new arrivals.

Chapter 7

The Limited Reach of Traditional Legal Tools

I n chapter 5, we saw Black families successfully challenge the Beaver-creek, Ohio, city council's refusal to allow the transit authority to expand bus service to the city, despite the dangers to Black Dayton residents who had no safe way to get to work there. That success stands as an exception. Our legal system has not been widely receptive to challenges alleging racial discrimination in transportation infrastructure decisions and the resulting harms experienced by people of color. The legal challenge in Beavercreek worked, but it required herculean efforts on the part of community members and advocates and evidence of blatant racism on the part of public officials. The outcome says more about the years of organizing and the money spent by the community than it does about the efficacy of the legal tools those advocates had at their disposal.

American laws prohibiting racial discrimination in public decision-making often employ broad and powerful language that, in theory, covers racially oppressive transportation policy. The language of existing legislation *should* offer pathways to challenge the racial discrimination that has guided infrastructure decisions, and to challenge the decades of accumulated structural racial inequality that made Black communities the path of least resistance for planners and their bulldozers. In practice, however, the prevailing interpretations and applications of these laws by the federal courts have severely constrained those laws' potential. Far too often, courts have interpreted or applied the laws to *limit* their power within an ecosystem that gives undue deference to public officials, while placing undue burdens on community members who are challenging municipal actions. The courts have found that they can explain away the stark racial disparities and evidence of the intent to harm Black people and Black communities. Or, perhaps more accurately, they can explain away the intent to protect white communities at all costs.

A prime example comes from Nashville, Tennessee.

In 1967, a biracial group of civic, business, and education leaders filed a lawsuit against Tennessee governor Buford Ellington and other state and local officials to challenge the decision to build a portion of Interstate 40 through a Black community in Nashville. The group's leaders—calling themselves the Nashville I-40 Steering Committee—included educators from local colleges and universities, members of the NAACP, and religious leaders. The plaintiffs were represented by lions of the civil rights movement, including NAACP Legal Defense Fund attorneys Jack Greenberg and James Nabrit III. But their fight was unsuccessful. A federal judge rejected evidence of intentional racial discrimination and found that the devastation I-40 would visit on the Black community was beyond the court's concern and authority.

The challenged portion of the highway was a 3.6-mile-long stretch which was to be routed through North Nashville. By then, North Nashville was the center of social, cultural, and economic life for the Black people of the city, with Jefferson Street serving as the principal Black business district and heart of the community. North Nashville was also an organizing hub for the civil rights movement. College students, including John Lewis, Diane Nash, and Marion Barry, helped organize the sit-in movement in the early 1960s from Clark Memorial Methodist Church near Jefferson Street. Nearby was Hadley Park, the city's first park for Black Nashvillians. The planned route for I-40 would effectively eliminate Jefferson Street and the surrounding area.

Well before the Interstate Highway Act was officially adopted into law in 1956, city leaders started the process of drawing up plans for a proposed highway through Nashville. They wanted to be ready to move as soon as the Act passed. Back in 1946, a Chicago-based consulting firm completed a study and recommended a route along Charlotte Avenue. The route would have relied on widening an existing road, and it would have run along train tracks operated by the Louisville and Nashville Railroad so as to minimize the destruction of the surrounding community. Then, in the early 1950s,

Nashville city leaders contracted with a New York–based engineering firm, Clarke and Rapuano, to draw up potential plans for the proposed highway. The Clarke and Rapuano study was completed in 1955. The final report noted that it was "the result of detailed study based on criteria established by the Bureau of Public Roads for the Interstate highway system" and went on to endorse the Charlotte Avenue route proposed in 1946.

But city officials, even though they had commissioned both studies, were not happy with the outcome. Although the Charlotte Avenue route would minimize harm to existing homes and businesses, it would have brought the highway too close to Belle Meade, Nashville's most exclusive white community, and to institutions such as Vanderbilt University and Centennial Park. City leaders met with the engineers and consultants to voice their concerns, which included that the route would bring I-40 *too close* to railroad lines—something that had previously been touted as a benefit of the project—and that it lacked sufficient access points.

Three weeks later, the consultants shared a new route for I-40 that literally went out of its way to tear through the Black community of North Nashville. The route would include a hump, a stretch of road that abruptly reached up into and through North Nashville before coming back down to continue its original path. No one completed a feasibility study of the new route. There was no analysis comparing the impact of the newly proposed route to the original Charlotte Avenue route. A staffer with Clarke and Rapuano said such studies were not necessary because "the routing through the black community was the only obvious feasible alternative."

The new route would also allow the state to couple the highway project with an urban renewal project. Tennessee would save money by using the generous federal funds available for the highway construction to also condemn land for urban renewal projects—killing two birds with one stone. A Nashville planner involved in the I-40 route decision captured the broader thinking when he called for "aim[ing]" the interstate system like a gun, right at the heart of the slums."

On July 14, 1955, Nashville officials formally presented the new highway plan to the state highway planning commission while they waited for Congress to pass the highly anticipated new law. When the Federal-Aid

Highway Act of 1956 was enacted, it included a requirement that a public hearing on planned routes be held to discuss the economic impact, certification that the hearing had in fact been held, and submission of a copy of the transcript of the hearing to the federal commissioner of roads.

The required hearing for I-40 was scheduled for May 15, 1957. But state highway planners put up notices of the hearing only in post offices in white neighborhoods. They did not put any notices in local newspapers, where Black North Nashvillians might have seen them. Moreover, the notices that they did post had the wrong date, stating the hearing would be on May 14. At the hearing (on May 15), the discussion centered on the economic impact of I-40 overall. The specific question of the effect on North Nashville did not come up. Unsurprisingly, according to reports, no Black Nashvillians attended the hearing. In September 1958, the Federal Highway Administration approved the planned route.

The state of Tennessee waited seven more years before purchasing rights of way to build the highway. Some people believed the delay was intended to let the value of the North Nashville properties deteriorate— due to public knowledge of the impending construction—or to mislead residents about the planned route in order to run out the clock on any potential challenge. Both were likely true. During the delay, state policymakers actively misled North Nashville leaders about the route for the highway, stating that it was still preliminary and subject to change. The state highway department refused to release any plans and said they were still studying their options. One planner told citizens that "we can't give out any information. In fact, we don't know any of the designs, plans, or what." And when North Nashvillians questioned a land surveyor about why he was putting down stakes along the route, the surveyor told residents they had "no cause for alarm."

It was not until 1967 that the state officially announced that I-40 would run through North Nashville. Immediately, the president of Fisk University organized a meeting with local Historically Black College and University representatives and Black business leaders. This group was joined by residents and church leaders and became the Nashville I-40 Steering Committee. It filed suit in federal court bringing a claim under the

Due Process Clause of the Fifth Amendment to the United States Constitution against the federal defendants and claims under the Due Process and Equal Protection Clauses of the Fourteenth Amendment against the state defendants. The plaintiffs alleged that the route violated due process because state officials did not hold public hearings or provide sufficient notice. It further alleged that the proposed route discriminated against Black segments of Nashville because the destruction caused by the highway would disproportionately affect Black residents, businesses, and community and educational institutions, and because the choice of that route could not be explained by anything other than racial animus.

The plaintiffs were given a hearing before Judge Frank Gray Jr. of the federal district court in Nashville on October 30, 1967. They presented evidence of the procedural history and irregularities in the highway project; expert testimony by noted planning expert Yale Rubin, who talked about the planned Charlotte Avenue route and the insufficient process around development of the final route; and testimony from community members who would be affected. The plaintiffs also contrasted the lack of focus on the impact the highway would have on the Black community with the care that went into studying the impact on the white community. Indeed, city officials had gone to great lengths to avoid hurting white neighborhoods, and had even studied what the route would mean for campus parking at Vanderbilt. The plaintiffs argued that the impact on the Black community was so stark in comparison that only race could have motivated it.

At the conclusion of the hearing, Judge Gray found that the plaintiffs' evidence went to "the wisdom and not the legality of the highway department's decision." As to the latter, he first found that a public hearing had been held and any concerns about the adequacy of the hearing were better posed to the Bureau of Public Roads and the state highway department than to a court. Moreover, although he agreed that there was "inadequate consideration" of the impact on North Nashville, he also believed that there was no evidence of a "deliberate purpose to discriminate against the residents of North Nashville on the basis of race." Finally, the judge chastised the plaintiffs for not filing their lawsuit sooner. He believed that a newspaper article that ran in *The Tennessean* in 1957 discussing the plans for the route, combined with the state's ongoing acquisition of the rights of way before the suit was filed, should have prompted the plaintiffs to sue earlier. In the end, Judge Gray concluded that even though he had "grave doubts" as to the wisdom of building the highway through North Nashville, he could not conclude that the plaintiffs had made a strong enough showing to invoke the court's injunctive power.

The Nashville I-40 Steering Committee appealed the ruling to the United States Court of Appeals for the Sixth Circuit, and the appeals court upheld Judge Gray's decision. The higher court essentially shifted the burden onto the citizens of North Nashville to know what was happening and to understand the significance of the city's actions, rather than putting the burden on government actors to keep the community fully informed of its plans. The appeals court said that "no literate citizen of the Nashville Community" could claim they did not have notice of the proposed route.

Just as Judge Gray did, the appeals court pointed to several newspaper articles describing the proposed route of the highway as proof that the plaintiffs should have been on notice long before they filed suit. As to the sufficiency of the 1957 hearing that effectively excluded Black North Nashvillians, the court acknowledged that the notice was unsatisfactory, especially considering the incorrect date, and criticized the quality and comprehensiveness of the transcript of the proceedings.

However, the appeals court found that Judge Gray had been within his discretion in ruling that the hearing met due process and statutory requirements. The court pointed out that "neither the statute nor the regulations of the Bureau of Public Roads prescribed how notice of hearings should be given." It noted that the hearing was well-attended (albeit the appeals court did not note whether Black Nashvillians were in the audience) and described the widespread publicity surrounding the proposed route since 1957, including within the Black community.

The appeals court also found that Nashville fulfilled its statutory requirement of addressing the economic impact of the route because the attorney for the state highway department made a bland, contentless certification:

I certify that I am an official of the Department of Highways and Public Works of the State of Tennessee and that the above transcript of the public hearing heretofore conducted regarding the location of the above mentioned project has been read by me. I further certify that said Department has considered the economic effects of the location of said project and that it is of the opinion that said project is properly located and should be constructed as located.

In resolving the claims of intentional racial discrimination, the appeals court wrote "that the record fails to show any intent or purpose of racial discrimination in the selection of the proposed route." And: "In the absence of proof of racial discrimination, we do not consider this matter to be a justiciable issue. The routing of highways is the prerogative of the executive department of government, not the judiciary."

The appeals court believed that all parties should trust the decision-making process and defer to the good faith of the policymakers involved. Although the judges acknowledged the harm that would be visited upon the North Nashville community, the appeals court went on to say that "it would be virtually impossible to select a route for an interstate highway through a congested metropolitan area without working hardships upon many citizens. Appellants suggest possible alternative routes which they contend would avoid the unfortunate economic consequences which the proposed route will impose upon the North Nashville area. Alternative routes undoubtedly would impose hardships upon others. The minimizing of hardships and adverse economic effects is a problem addressing itself to engineers, not judges."

Construction of I-40 through North Nashville was completed by the early 1970s. The Nashville I-40 Steering Committee and the appeals court were both right about the hardships North Nashville would suffer. The highway took a large chunk out of the only park in the city serving the Black community. It destroyed more than six hundred homes, twenty-seven apartment buildings, Black churches, and most of North Nashville's Black businesses. Those destroyed Black businesses had nowhere to go, and Black North Nashvillians struggled to find new homes. What was left of the neighborhood was divided by the highway. In addition, fifty local streets were dead-ended. Fisk University, Meharry Medical College, and Tennessee Agricultural & Industrial State Normal School for Negroes (later renamed Tennessee State University), three historically Black institutions of higher education, were walled off from each other and the communities they served. The highway also physically constrained the growth of the three institutions. Moreover, the construction of the six-lane highway meant that many of the almost 20,000 people served by a hospital associated with Meharry Medical College, who did not own cars, were forced to cross the highway on foot to get to the hospital or seek care elsewhere.

Properties adjacent to the highways saw their values decline, and vacant plots of land located next to the highways could not be sold or developed, so they often sat undeveloped. The elimination of Black-owned businesses in North Nashville had a deleterious effect on a community already starved for economic investment. One North Nashville resident aptly called the highway routing decision "wretched, inhumane, illogical and an act of persecution" that "will emasculate the Negro community while leaving the white community intact."

The trial and appellate courts' opinions in the suit over the highway— *Nashville I-40 Steering Committee v. Ellington*—show the legal paradigms and analytical frameworks that courts have applied to beat back legal challenges to public infrastructure decisions. There was ample evidence of an irregular and nefarious decision-making process, including a shift in the highway route from running adjacent to a white community to running *through* a Black community following complaints from white leaders. The Black community had not been kept informed about what was going to happen to it, and worse, evasive actions had hidden the city's plans. Further, the courts employed unrealistic evidentiary standards to support their judgments that state and city leaders had not intentionally discriminated against the Black community. They assumed that a city and state with a centuries-long history of racial oppression had the best of intentions. They viewed racial discrimination through a narrow lens, demanding a "smoking gun" while ignoring a mountain of historical, expert, and circumstantial evidence.

The courts' opinions also speak to the challenge of civil rights protections that are triggered only *after* public officials have made and publicized their decisions. As Robert Moses said, "Once you sink that first stake, they'll never make you pull it up." It is difficult to challenge a public works decision once it is made and momentum is behind it. In the case of I-40, although Tennessee had not yet started construction when the lawsuit was filed, because the state had already begun to obtain rights of way, the courts felt that the wheels of bureaucracy were already spinning too fast to slow down. One could update Moses, who if anything understated the point: "Once a city has begun to act, it cannot be stopped."

The courts accepted the city's valuation of Black communities and their institutions at lower levels than white ones. When faced with the reality that a community would be negatively impacted, the court was willing to join with policymakers and view the marginalized community—the community with less political and economic power—as the obvious target. In essence, if hardships must be visited upon some community, then according to the courts there is no reason it should not be the Black community. They present the path of least resistance.

THE DECISION IN *Nashville I-40 Steering Committee* IS NOT AN ABERRATION, and in many ways it foretold the legal regime that would solidify in the ensuing years—the era right *after* the 1964 Civil Rights Act and the 1965 Voting Rights Act, the signal achievements of the civil rights movement. The problem is not the laws in themselves: there are constitutional provisions and causes of action under existing civil rights laws that have the potential to improve aspects of the decision-making process, laws that should have the teeth to challenge infrastructure decisions that disproportionately harm Black communities or that were motivated by intentional racial bias. In the context of transportation infrastructure, these include the Equal Protection Clause of the Fourteenth Amendment and the Due Process Clause of the Fifth Amendment, Title VI of the Civil Rights Act of 1964, and the Fair Housing Act found in Title VIII of the Civil Rights Act of 1968.

All are potentially powerful legal weapons, but they have been interpreted by courts in ways that do not allow advocates to unleash their full potential: courts limit their application to discriminatory decisions after they have already been made, when the momentum behind the projects is difficult to reverse. They place the burden of proof on members of the affected community rather than on government agencies responsible. And the courts require overwhelmingly clear evidence of racial intent and ignore structural and systemic concerns. Most officials are smart enough to avoid saying, "I'm making this decision because that community is Black." But evidence short of such admissions is routinely dismissed. In addition, many of these statutes, at least as they have been interpreted by courts, place the burden of enforcement on individual victims of injustice, who often lack access to the lawyers, research budgets, and other resources needed to enforce their rights.

Section one of the Fourteenth Amendment declares: "No State shall make or enforce any law which shall abridge the privileges or immunities of citizens of the United States; nor shall any State deprive any person of life, liberty, or property, without due process of law; nor deny to any person within its jurisdiction the equal protection of the laws." The Amendment, ratified in 1868, was intended to ensure that Black people were able to enjoy all the civil rights that white people enjoyed, and sought to end the political, economic, and social subjugation of Black Americans on the basis of their race. The Due Process Clause of the Fifth Amendment contains language nearly identical to the Fourteenth Amendment's, and similarly protects the right to due process before any deprivation of life, liberty, or property. While the Fifth Amendment restricts the actions of the federal government, the Fourteenth Amendment restricts the actions of states. Despite their broad language and purpose, in 1976 the United States Supreme Court enshrined the limits set by cases like *Nashville I-40 Steering Committee v. Ellington* and robbed the amendments of much of their potential.

The case of *Washington v. Davis* was brought by a group of Black men who wanted to join the Washington, DC, Metropolitan Police Department but were thwarted by a written test, known as Test 21, that disproportionately blocked Black people from serving as police officers in Chocolate City. The plaintiffs filed a lawsuit using the Fifth Amendment to challenge the stark statistical disparity in test scores between Black and white applicants. From 1968 to 1971, 57 percent of Black test takers failed the test, compared to 13 percent of white applicants. Test 21 had been developed by the United States Civil Service Commission and was widely used throughout the federal government. It was designed to test verbal ability, vocabulary, and reading comprehension. But it was never linked to the essential job functions of being a police officer or validated as a reliable predictor of success on the force. Yet it was used to screen out the majority of Black applicants. Two questions from Test 21, evidencing the exam's disconnection from the job for which it was testing, read:

> The saying "Straight trees are the first to be felled" means most nearly
> A) Honest effort is always rewarded.
> B) The best are the first chosen.
> C) Ill luck passes no one by.
> D) The highest in rank have farthest to fall.
> E) The stubborn are soon broken.

and

> "Although the types of buildings in ghetto areas vary from the one-story shack to the large tenement building, they are alike in that they are all drab, unsanitary, in disrepair and often structurally unsound." The quotation best supports the statement that all buildings in ghetto areas are
> A) overcrowded
> B) undesirable as living quarters
> C) well-constructed
> D) about to be torn down
> E) seldom inspected

It is hard to imagine how these questions would be helpful in selecting police officers. The plaintiffs argued that using a test with no clear relationship to the job at hand and with such starkly disproportionate outcomes amounted to racial discrimination. The Supreme Court disagreed.

The harms suffered and stigma endured by the victims of racial inequality exist regardless of motive. Yet despite acknowledging that there was no proof that an applicant's score on Test 21 predicted job performance, in a 7–2 decision written by Justice Byron White, the court held that laws that appear neutral on their face or government policies that disproportionately harm Black people do not violate the Constitution's Equal Protection Clause no matter how stark the outcome. A facially neutral law is only invalid if the plaintiff can prove that a government actor specifically intended to discriminate against a person because of their race and that the disparate impact is the direct result of that discriminatory intent. The court reasoned that the Equal Protection Clause protects the rights of *individuals* against racial discrimination. Because the existence of racially disproportionate outcomes does not prove that any *individual* was the victim of racial discrimination, there was no constitutional violation.

If an exam that consistently eliminated nearly 60 percent of Black applicants was not sufficient evidence of discrimination, even when there was no evidence that the exam was relevant to the job it was allegedly testing for, what hope was left? The court ignored the role of tests like Test 21 in America's evolving use of facially neutral "intelligence" tests to diminish the civil rights of Black people—like the use of literacy tests to deny Black people their right to vote or the use of IQ tests to advance the narrative of Black inferiority.

The court's intent standard put a nearly insurmountable burden on the people least likely to have access to the evidence to prove intent. Government actors know that racial discrimination is illegal and know how to disguise any nefarious motives. It is not a difficult task, and smoking gun evidence is rare. Unearthing evidence of improper motives is extremely challenging.

Not only that, but government decision-making is complex. Rarely is there one actor doing the deciding. Instead, legislative bodies, consultants, regulators, community organizations, business leaders, and elected officials, with interests that at times overlap and at times are in conflict, engage together over time to shape public policy. What does it mean to require specific racial intent by a government actor in a world where decisions are driven by a broad set of actors with myriad intentions? When seeking to root out racial animus, courts can easily be overwhelmed by the chorus of other factors alleged to be at play. And this near-impossible challenge is exacerbated by the wide deference that courts give to any non-discriminatory justification presented for a decision that appears neutral on its face, despite its discriminatory impact.

An intent framework may have made sense in the context of laws that explicitly required Black people to sit at the back of the bus, outlawed racially integrated schools, explicitly denied mortgages to Black people, or mandated racial zoning. In these cases, there was no need to search in the legislative records for proof of racial animus. The racist intent was written into the text of the laws themselves. When a government policy explicitly directs officials not to provide mortgages to people in Black neighborhoods, there is little more to be said.

But by 1976, with the aid of the Supreme Court, most facially discriminatory laws had already been struck down. Public officials knew that future laws would have to at least appear to be racially neutral. With *Washington v. Davis*, the Supreme Court made clear that it would not be in the business of challenging systemic or structural racial discrimination or even intentional discrimination hiding behind a mask of race neutrality. There would be no pressure on lawmakers to treat Black people equally. No pressure to respect Black communities in the way government might respect white communities. No pressure to protect Black communities the way government might protect white communities. The fixation on traditional notions of intent is especially problematic when considering the evolving nature of racial bias. The focus on intent presumes that by eliminating the aberrant behavior of a few "bad apples," we are rooting out and eliminating bias within our systems.

Today, for the most part, racism is not Bull Connor siccing his dogs on Black children seeking to integrate public schools; a sign posted on a restaurant door saying, "No Blacks Allowed"; or a map clearly delineating where Black people are or are not allowed to live. This understanding of racism—as the actions of individual racist people acting openly and without shame—overlooks the many other, more insidious manifestations of racial animus. Our systems of separation and oppression have been so durable because they are malleable; they evolve and adapt. As we saw earlier in the book, when looking at the history of racial zoning laws, each legal challenge gives the agents of oppression better guidance on how government actors and private citizens can adapt to evade the law's reach.

There is no question that *intentional* racial discrimination permeated decisions around transportation infrastructure in Nashville and other communities and that it continues to do so. But explicitly racially motivated decisions alone did not lead to the systemic devastation of Black communities or the systemic exclusion of Black people. What began as forthright acts of racial discrimination, publicly acknowledged and praised by public officials, have evolved into facially race-neutral policies that continue to have a racially disproportionate impact, in part because they are implemented in the wake of a long history of intentional discrimination. The racism of the current generation, though less explicit than that of prior generations, effectively compounds the accomplishments of its forebears.

Courts hearing challenges to racially discriminatory infrastructure projects continue to look for bad apples and smoking guns. Their refusal to move beyond the traditional vision of individual perpetrators and victims means that real change will be difficult.

The flaw inherent in *Washington v. Davis* has spread beyond the confines of the Constitution and into Title VI of the Civil Rights Act of 1964. Title VI states that "no person in the United States shall, on the ground of race, color, or national origin, be excluded from participation in, be denied the benefits of, or be subjected to discrimination under any program or activity receiving Federal financial assistance." Title VI has a very wide reach. It can be enforced not only in the court system but in administrative agencies. Given the scope of federal funding, it can be used to attack bias just about everywhere. And while it can be used to challenge intentional racism, federal regulations adopted under Title VI also prohibit decisions that *result* in significant racial disparities, regardless of discriminatory intent.

For these reasons, scholars have noted Title VI's potential to be the nation's "most powerful civil rights statute," and it has been called "the sleeping giant." Yet the federal courts have limited Title VI's potential by ruling that it is coextensive with the Equal Protection Clause—and therefore allows private citizens to file Title VI claims in court only where there is proof of intentional discrimination. The Supreme Court has ruled that administrative complaints to federal agencies like the Federal Highway Administration (FHWA) are the only means to enforce Title VI's disparate impact regulations, cutting off the federal courts as an avenue for relief.

Because many large highway, road, and other infrastructure construction projects receive federal funding, Title VI has been used to challenge a host of transportation decisions using both intentional discrimination and disparate impact theories. Many of these Title VI challenges have been unsuccessful, with courts and administrative decision makers repeatedly concluding that evidence of racial considerations was insufficient to prove intentional discrimination, despite substantial circumstantial evidence. Furthermore, administrative decision makers have been reluctant to reject public actions under a disparate impact theory even when presented with clear evidence. As we have seen, it was not until Beavercreek, Ohio, in 2013—nearly fifty years after the adoption of Title VI—that the FHWA found a municipality to be in violation of Title VI's disparate impact provisions.

Another case from Ohio is illuminating. In *Coalition of Concerned Citizens Against I-670 v. Damian*, decided in 1984, a group of citizens filed a Title VI challenge to a proposed six-lane extension of I-670 in Columbus. The case was filed in district court; it was not until 2001 that the Supreme Court barred plaintiffs from enforcing Title VI's disparate impact regulations in federal court. The I-670 project was planned to run through a predominantly Black community and would displace a significant portion of its population. The plaintiffs argued that the I-670 extension would violate Title VI because of its disparate impact on the city's Black population. But the court decided in favor of the defendants because they had also shown "legitimate nondiscriminatory justifications" for their decision to follow that particular route.

The judge acknowledged the clear disparate impact, stating that

> There is no dispute that parts of I-670 would travel through neighbor-
> hoods that range from 50% to over 90% racial minorities. Further, of
> the 355 persons displaced by the construction of I-670, 260 or nearly
> 75% are members of racial minorities. There is also ample evidence to
> support a finding that the disruptions and negative impacts of high-
> way construction and after the highway is operating will fall primar-
> ily upon neighborhoods that are mostly comprised of minorities.

Still, in the end, the court concluded that the defendants met their burden under Title VI. The judge ruled that the "defendants are not per se
prohibited from locating a highway where it will have differential impacts
upon minorities. Rather, Title VI prohibits taking actions with differential
impacts without adequate justification." The court found that justification.

Acknowledging that "it is true that all of the *reasonable* alternatives for
the location of I-670 had moderate or high negative impact upon racial
minorities" (my emphasis), the court found that the decision makers
avoided other routes that would have caused even greater harm to Black
residents. It may have been true that the selected route was less harmful than others the defendants considered, but it was also true that *every*
route that they seriously considered went through a Black community. The
fact that the city chose one of the least harmful of these routes perversely
became evidence of the city's magnanimousness.

BY THE EARLY 1960S, MANY AMERICANS BEGAN TO PUSH BACK AGAINST THE
harms of highway construction. They questioned whether the benefits
outweighed the environmental damage they caused and the destruction of parks, historic sites, and entire communities. As the construction
of the interstate highway system continued in the late 1960s and early
1970s, "freeway revolts"—organized efforts to slow the pace of highway
development—began to spread. These protests ultimately led many states
to abandon plans to build highways through parks, including in Overton
Park in Memphis, Fairmont Park in Philadelphia, and the waterfront in

San Francisco. They were also successful in protecting historic neighborhoods in Baltimore, New Orleans, New York City, and Washington, DC.

But there was a compromise inherent in the revolts, a compromise that weakened them. The antihighway resistance efforts were often more successful when they linked their battles to environmental protection efforts and less successful when they raised issues of racial justice and equity. For example, in the Overton Park neighborhood in Memphis, the freeway revolt focused on the environmental costs of building a planned highway. After over a decade of fighting back against local, state, and federal efforts to route I-40 through their park, a group of citizen activists called the Citizens to Preserve Overton Park were able to use environmental protection tools to defeat the freeway. As we've seen, a few hours away, in Nashville, the Nashville I-40 Steering Committee was not successful with their challenge, which was based on discrimination against the Black community.

In response to the freeway revolts, between 1962 and 1970 Congress enacted a range of legislation to moderate the impact of highway construction. These laws mostly responded to environmental concerns and did not directly address the destruction of Black communities or other communities of color. This new legislation required regional transportation planning for transportation projects that received federal aid; sought to protect parks, historic districts, and other environmentally sensitive places; and required governments to secure new housing for people displaced by road construction.

Concern for preserving historic sites and neighborhoods was the primary motivation behind most of the legislation. In an April 1966 speech, Pennsylvania senator Joseph S. Clark said: "It is time that Congress took a look at the highway program, because it is presently being operated by barbarians, and we ought to have some civilized understanding of just what we do to spots of historic interest and great beauty by the building of eight-lane highways through the middle of our cities." Similarly, after discovering that a highway was planned through Brackenridge Park in San Antonio, Texas, an outraged Senator Ralph Yarborough led the effort to include, in the Federal-Aid Highway Act of 1966, a prohibition on construction of "federally assisted highways through parks and historic sites unless all possible alternatives had been considered." It came to be known as the Yarborough Amendment.

Although these statutes were and remain helpful in constraining high-way builders, the laws stopped far short of remedying racial disparities, restricting the placement of highways in Black communities, or offering tools to challenge racial disparities in transportation infrastructure deci-sions. That was not, after all, their intent—despite widespread activism at the time not only by environmental groups but by Black communities themselves. Although some of the legislation, including the Uniform Relo-cation Act of 1970, required states to aid the relocation of families dis-placed by highway development, this law did not take affirmative steps to halt the destruction of Black communities in the way it did the destruction of parks and historic districts. It may have become harder and more costly for highway departments to destroy homes without offering any relocation assistance, but those homes could still be destroyed. Furthermore, reloca-tion assistance for displaced residents did not address the harms caused to displaced businesses, churches, and other community institutions, let alone the people who rely on them. Finally, these laws also bumped up against the existing realities of discrimination. States may be required to provide funding for relocation, but that assistance is of limited help if there is a shortage of housing in the community, or if racial discrimination keeps displaced Black families out of their preferred neighborhoods. Their lives are still disrupted, and their connections to important community institutions, work, school, and networks are still broken.

The laws enacted after the freeway revolts also failed to resolve how officials should balance competing interests in transportation policy, other than to make clear that environmental concerns would be paramount. Even with the growing awareness of the damage that highways were inflict-ing on communities of color, the antihighway discourse was driven by a complex array of concerns. Citizens, consumers, and community groups challenged transportation policy on a wide variety of grounds, including highway safety, roadside beautification, environmental protection, his-toric district preservation, neighborhood integrity, protection of parks, financial responsibility, pedestrian safety, and speed regulation. These competing pressures make it hard to keep racial justice considerations at the forefront. Indeed, racial justice and environmental considerations are sometimes in direct opposition: environmental protection is frequently used as a cudgel by suburban communities fighting housing development that has the potential to bring racial diversity to their communities.

Although not exclusively tied to transportation infrastructure, the environmental impact studies required under the National Environmental Policy Act of 1969 (NEPA) are a potentially useful tool for injecting racial equity considerations into the conversation. NEPA requires all federal agencies to identify and evaluate environmental impacts of major agency actions during their planning and decision-making process. But NEPA is not a fully effective tool for racial equity. Again, advocates for racial equity run up against the limitations of a law that provides some benefit, but that was not clearly designed for their cause.

NEPA, sometimes referred to as the Magna Carta of environmental legislation, laid the basis for a series of laws enacted in the 1970s in response to increasing public pressure on the federal government to address pollution, air quality, and other signs of environmental degradation. Because all projects funded with federal tax dollars fall under NEPA, it has a broad reach, and its mandates apply to many state and local government projects, including transportation infrastructure projects.

At the heart of the NEPA assessment process are detailed environmental impact statements (EISs). EISs are necessary whenever a major federal action is proposed that would significantly alter the quality of "the human environment." The analysis in the EIS must include the environmental effects of the proposed action, of reasonable alternatives to the action, and of taking no action. Nothing in the statute, however, prevents the agency from taking the desired action, even when a serious environmental impact is identified.

Congress's goal in requiring EISs was not only to ensure that agencies would consider the effects of their decision-making on the human environment, but to make sure that larger groups of people could play a meaningful role in making and implementing decisions that have an environmental impact. NEPA's regulations make clear that effects on the human environment include "ecological, . . . aesthetic, historic, cultural, economic, social, or health, whether direct, indirect, or cumulative." As further clarified, "when an environmental impact statement is prepared and economic or social and natural or physical environmental effects are interrelated, then the environmental impact statement will discuss all of these effects on the human environment." Although race is not explicitly mentioned in the list of considerations, one could argue, as the FHWA did in its 2011 Guidance on Environment Justice and NEPA, that examining "social" effects requires "explicit consideration of potential effects on minority and low-income populations."

On their face, NEPA and its implementing regulations could provide a mechanism for examining the racially disparate impact of transportation projects. Social justice advocates have seized on this potential and used NEPA to launch challenges to infrastructure projects. They have met with mixed success. For example, in 2013, a federal district court decided the case *Milwaukee Inner-City Congregations Allied for Hope (MICAH) v. Gottlieb*, in which plaintiffs representing inner-city Milwaukee residents challenged the FHWA's and the Wisconsin Department of Transportation's (WisDOT's) planned improvements to a highway interchange. Invoking NEPA, plaintiffs alleged that the agencies failed to adequately consider several kinds of environmental impacts, including the social and economic impacts on inner-city residents of expanding highway capacity while transit capacity was declining and the cumulative impact of encouraging suburban sprawl. The plaintiffs also alleged that FHWA and WisDOT failed to adequately explore expanding the Milwaukee public transportation systems as an alternative to expanding the highway.

In a decision on a motion to preliminarily halt the construction, the district court held that the plaintiffs were unlikely to succeed because there was evidence that the FHWA and WisDOT did consider that alternative. Unlike with most other decisions challenging EISs, however, the district court found that the agencies' EIS was likely deficient because they failed to adequately explore the project's impact on suburban sprawl. Although the opinion echoes Supreme Court precedent holding that "NEPA merely prohibits uninformed—rather than unwise—agency action," the district court did endorse a very expansive understanding of NEPA's reach. The interpretation opens the door for courts to consider a broad range of social impacts—including the racial impacts of transportation infrastructure decisions.

The Supreme Court's interpretations of NEPA have not been so expansive. The court has repeatedly interpreted NEPA in a way that maintains its vast reach but limits its substantive power. Again, the statute itself does not include language that can stop a project from moving forward. And the court has effectively confirmed that NEPA's requirements are procedural only: it does not require federal agencies to promote environmental goals. Once an agency has conducted a NEPA assessment, the agency's substantive decisions are rarely, if ever, overturned. Indeed, largely due to the Supreme Court's narrow interpretations, NEPA has been called both "the most successful environmental law in the world and the most disappointing."

A critical case in understanding the limits of NEPA is the 1980 case *Strycker's Bay Neighborhood Council, Inc. v. Karlen*, where the Supreme Court heard a NEPA challenge to the placement of low-income housing in New York City. The federal court of appeals had held that the Department of Housing and Urban Development (HUD) violated NEPA when it considered but dismissed alternative sites for low-income housing projects. HUD conceded that while there were possible alternative sites that would reduce the concentration of low-income housing, it had rejected these alternatives because switching to a different site would delay the project for two years or more. The United States Court of Appeals for the Second Circuit determined that concentrating low-income housing projects within one neighborhood created significant "social environmental impacts." The appeals court sent the case back to the trial court and ordered HUD to find a way to meet New York City's affordable housing needs without such concentration.

The Supreme Court agreed to review the case and reversed the lower court's decision. Significantly, the Supreme Court did not say it was inappropriate to consider the concentration of low-income housing as a relevant impact under NEPA, nor did it say it was inappropriate to explore whether reasonable alternative sites were available. But these are substantive questions: NEPA's demands are procedural. The court ruled that NEPA did not *require* HUD to weigh environmental concerns over other reasonable considerations, such as the time and cost to complete the project. Instead, "once an agency has made a decision subject to NEPA's procedural requirements, the only role for a court is to ensure that the agency has considered the environmental consequences."

HISTORICALLY, THE ENEMIES OF RACIAL JUSTICE HAVE HAD MANY TOOLS at their disposal, including legal tools. As those legal tools became less potent with the advance of court decisions like *Brown v. Board of Education* and legislation like the Civil Rights Act of 1964—legal victories often bought with the blood of everyday Americans during the civil rights movement era and after—the enemies of racial justice have innovated over the decades to maintain racial inequality in the face of that progress. As this book has striven to demonstrate, one of the most effective innovations has been the use of the physical environment—highways, roads, sidewalks, and public transportation—to solidify boundaries that laws have made more porous. As racial justice makes advances, the forces of retrenchment find new ways to pull us back. The key to real progress is to take two steps forward for every one we are pushed back.

This war plays out in how courts interpret those very laws that were designed to achieve racial justice. Many other scholars have written about the concerted and largely successful campaign to limit the racial justice impact of the Constitution and civil rights laws. As we have seen in this chapter, the federal judiciary's narrow reading of these laws has limited their potential to defend Black homeowners, commuters, pedestrians, and community members as they seek to protect their neighborhoods, their families, and their very lives from America's history of racism in transportation infrastructure. It should not be surprising that NEPA, as interpreted by the Supreme Court, has not lived up to its bold *intended* promise to inject environmental considerations into public decision-making, much less its equally bold, though *unintended*, promise as a tool to center racial justice in public decision-making.

But NEPA nevertheless illustrates the potential of a legal framework that forces public agencies to focus on racial justice. Though very far from perfect, and far too deferential to government actors, NEPA's EIS requirement does not ask plaintiffs to mount a quixotic quest for evidence of bad actors who are intentionally out to destroy the so-called human environment. Instead, it places the burden on government actors to analyze the environmental impacts of their decision-making, and to do so in the earliest stages of the process, publicly and transparently, before harmful decisions have the chance to gain momentum. NEPA's key shortcoming is that while it requires governments to consider the environmental impacts of development, it requires courts to defer to those governments even when they make the wrong decisions.

We need new legal tools to overcome the limitations of the discriminatory intent framework evident in decisions like *Washington v. Davis*. A framework similar to NEPA's EIS, but one that foregrounds racial justice considerations and avoids its shortcomings, suggests a path forward. We need a framework for evaluating transportation projects that requires government agencies not only to engage the public and evaluate racial impacts early in their decision-making processes, but *to make different decisions* when their evaluation shows that Black communities face devastating, disproportionate, and avoidable harms. Such a legal framework would help Americans who are seeking to defend what they have left and reclaim what they have lost.

So what, exactly, is the next step?

Chapter 8

The Goal Is Justice

A mural covering Detroit's Eight Mile Wall.

On a recent trip to Indianapolis, Indiana, I spent time with Paula Brooks, a local community organizer. For several years, Brooks has been working with a coalition to guide the reconstruction of the decaying portions of I-65 and I-70 that go through downtown Indianapolis. The arrival of the highways forever changed her childhood neighborhood. Now, she wants to make sure that the sins of the past are not repeated when the highways are rebuilt.

During one of our conversations, I asked Brooks what she was fighting for. What should the future look like for communities such as hers, damaged by the decisions of policymakers who, at best, ignored the effects of their decisions on Black communities, and at worst, actively worked to harm those communities? She answered, "the goal is justice, which means reparations." Brooks appreciates that a growing number of people understand how racism guided the building of the interstate highway system, including the stretches that ran through Indianapolis. As she explained, "until there is some recognition of what happened, the community and neighborhood can never prosper." But she also knows that it is not enough just to understand that history. "We are a community. We are here. We never went anywhere," she said. "The people in this community need remedies that help them. People engaged in new highway projects need to deal with the people who were here then and are still here. What can we do for them? Invest in the community for them. Help return their community to a place where other people want to come back and raise their kids. Help recreate their community. They don't want another museum or monument. We are still alive. The community is still alive. For now."

Indeed, all Americans have a responsibility to bring justice—racial justice, spatial justice, climate justice, and other forms of environmental justice—to the nation's transportation system. Today, more and more people are having open and direct conversations about the complex role of race in American society. More and more people understand how this country created a system in which wealth, opportunity, education, health, and safety were and are inequitably distributed on the basis of race. We have a better collective understanding of the ways that racial inequality and white supremacy have been embedded into our laws, policies, institutions, physical environment, narratives, and cultural norms—we have a better collective understanding, that is, of the *infrastructure* of racial inequality.

Many highways, roadways, tunnels, subways, and bridges across the country are in dire need of repair or replacement. In a press release celebrating passage of the Bipartisan Infrastructure Act, the White House pointed out that "1 in 5 miles of highways and major roads, and 45,000 bridges, are in poor condition," and noted a "multi-billion dollar repair backlog" in the nation's public transportation infrastructure, including tens of thousands of buses and rail cars needing repair and thousands of miles of track and power systems that need to be replaced.

Many of the segments of the interstate highway system that are past or approaching the end of their useful lives are in urban neighborhoods, surrounded by communities of color that are still fighting to overcome the harms caused when those highways were originally built. Activists are rightly demanding that transportation agencies rebuild our infrastructure differently this time around. But there is a serious risk that those decision makers, even when well-meaning, will only reproduce and expand the harms of the past.

The country has a rare opportunity to support people like Paula Brooks who are seeking justice for their families and communities. As she put it, we have a chance to return these communities to their former vibrancy, to become places where people want to live, to come back to, and to raise their children. But we have not learned the necessary lessons. Too often, government actors continue to embark on new transportation infrastructure projects that are disproportionately hurting Black communities. Consider recent developments in Houston, Texas. In 2021, the Federal Highway Administration used its power under Title VI of the Civil Rights Act of 1964—which gives the FHWA authority to withdraw all federal funding for a project—to temporarily halt the expansion of Interstate 45 in the city. The $9 billion project was slated to displace an overwhelmingly Black and Brown community, including an estimated 1,300 homes and businesses as well as schools and houses of worship, and did not include plans to expand public transportation. According to local leaders, it would also increase pollution and flooding for those who remained. But in March 2023, after a two-year investigation, the FHWA allowed the project to proceed after the state promised that it would provide relocation assistance and build housing for those who lost their homes and also improve drainage in the area. The Texas Department of Transportation also agreed to "evaluat[e] reasonable opportunities to reduce the project footprint in ways that would not compromise the integrity and functionality of the purpose and need of the" expansion. Texas does not have a robust history of voluntarily respecting the rights and interests of Black communities when left to its own devices—to put it mildly. So, although many local Black leaders praised the resolution, promises of mitigation and evaluation do not inspire confidence. The FHWA's intervention, ultimately, will not keep the bulldozers away from Black homes and businesses near downtown Houston.

In the history of the United States, building transportation infrastructure is, and always has been, a political act. And over time, it has been deployed in service of shifting political and economic goals. Starting in the 1820s it was built to bring goods to market. In the 1930s, it was a jobs creation program. And in the 1950s and 1960s, it was focused on moving people, and particularly white people, more quickly and more safely between urban centers and residential suburbs, as well as on connecting distant states and cities to one another. During the postwar period of transformative investment in the new interstate highway system, a battle took place over the new vision for transportation infrastructure. Robert Moses's approach—building roads through urban centers without any regard for the people who lived there—won an overwhelming victory.

We are at the precipice of a new era, a new political economy of transportation infrastructure. Across the country, urban downtowns are experiencing a renaissance, not only as places to work but as places to live. The COVID-19 pandemic has threatened many of those downtowns as fewer people regularly commute to work in central business districts. Big box retail and e-commerce have upended how people get their daily necessities and how those things get to customers. At the same time, Black Lives Matter and the movement for environmental justice are reshaping the discourse. The idea of what transportation infrastructure is, and whom it is for, is once again open for debate.

Climate change makes demands for justice even more urgent. Around the country, Black people were forced to build their homes in low-lying, flood-prone areas because racial zoning and restrictive covenants relegated them to these less desirable, higher-risk places. Eventually, highways were built around and through many of these communities. When the impact of climate change is layered over this spatial racism, an increasing number of Black communities will find themselves literally under water.

Shiloh is a historic Black community in Elba, Alabama. For more than 150 years, families in Shiloh have passed their homes down from generation to generation. But they worry the community will not survive much longer. In 2018, US Route 84—until then largely a simple dirt road leading into Shiloh—was expanded from two lanes to an elevated, four-lane thoroughfare, creating runoff that collected in Shiloh. Since then, residents have witnessed the progressive erosion of their community with each rainstorm. Floodwaters fill residents' homes, some of which are sinking. The deterioration has only hastened as Shiloh experiences more frequent and more intense rainstorms and chronic localized flooding. One resident said, "Shiloh today is just washing away."

The original architects of the country's transportation infrastructure were often motivated by racism. Today, Black lives, communities, and homes continue to be assigned less value than white lives, communities, and homes. Race remains a powerful and frequently used tool to sort physical space, guide public policies, and distribute public benefits and burdens. So there is a real risk that federal, state, and local policymakers will rebuild the nation's infrastructure at the expense of poor communities of color.

Residents are rightfully worried that they will lose their homes, either behind the force of a bulldozer or because they will not be able to afford rising rents or taxes. They are worried about gentrification and displacement. They worry that their communities will be excluded from the jobs and wealth that infrastructure creates but will disproportionately suffer the environmental harms that infrastructure often causes. They are worried that new highways and roads will be built without community knowledge and input. They worry that they will lose the communities they have created and that they will never have the opportunity to rebuild what they have lost.

The language used by public officials today is often reminiscent of the arguments used to support the initial highway and road construction decades ago, when "slum " and "urban renewal" were protective cloaks. Now, the supposedly race-neutral and seemingly universally beneficial goals of "improving transportation," "rebuilding infrastructure," and "spurring economic investment" can lull communities into trusting the good faith of the public officials who spout such language. But these catchphrases are imbued with race and class judgments. They obscure the effects that transportation infrastructure projects can have on long-term residents by further destabilizing communities and forcing out residents after they have spent decades rebuilding.

THE LATE HISTORIAN MANNING MARABLE POSITED THAT "THE MOST striking fact about American economic history and politics is the brutal and systemic underdevelopment of Black people." According to his theory, Black people "have never been equal partners in the American Social Contract, because [our] system exists not to develop, but to *underdevelop* Black people." Black people and Black communities have been intentionally sacrificed to feed America's growth and expansion. Ultimately, Manning argued, the oppression of Black America is the driving force behind the development of the United States.

The nation's transportation system, like other aspects of American life, has been deployed to maximize the oppression of Black America while accelerating the accumulation of political and economic power in white communities. Black communities are disproportionately exploited economically, marginalized socially, and disfranchised politically. This *must* change. Moving forward, transportation infrastructure and policy should be a catalyst for rebuilding Black communities rather than destroying them. That means transforming how everyone involved in reimagining our transportation system—from federal, state, and local government officials to city planners, architects, and builders—values Black lives and communities. We need a new national framework for transportation infrastructure, one centered on racial equity.

Rebuilding while centering racial equity requires more than removing physical dividers between communities. It requires us to help underdeveloped communities flourish. Transportation projects should include quality jobs for residents that provide benefits, living wages, and opportunities to advance. New projects should be tied to housing policies that ensure homeowners are not driven out by rising tax rates and renters are not driven out by rising rents. New projects should be combined with affordable housing development. For example, concentrating housing near redeveloped public transportation hubs can reduce commute times, increase demand for mass transit, and improve the environment by reducing motor vehicle traffic. Transportation projects should include aggressive goals for local small businesses, minority-owned businesses, and women-owned businesses to participate as contractors and subcontractors, helping community members build wealth. Every community has different needs, and each should be deeply engaged in deciding what it needs to thrive.

A new framework for racial equity in transportation infrastructure must involve massive changes in how government officials, policymakers, and urban planners treat predominantly Black communities. To this day, Black communities are sacrifice zones, forced to house the things no one else wants but that we all need. Too many Black communities are still considered to be the path of least resistance. When this is your lens, when Black homes are worth less than white homes, when Black pain is felt less than white pain, destructive decisions can seem rational. The result is that the benefits of transportation infrastructure are dispersed, while the harms are concentrated in communities of color. And it all seems so natural, so efficient, and so fair.

———

A TRULY REPARATIVE FRAMEWORK, AS SO MANY COMMUNITY ACTIVISTS and residents like Brooks have demanded, would reverse the decades of disinvestment and theft. It would help people who were forced out of their communities, whether through condemnation or eminent domain or because of gentrification, to return and receive some compensation for their loss. Several communities around the United States have adopted or are exploring programs that would do just that.

A prime example is the "Preference Policy" of Portland, Oregon. This policy provides housing assistance and incentives to people with generational ties to the city's historically Black communities of North and Northeast Portland (N/NE Portland). Decades of displacement caused by urban renewal projects including highway, stadium, and transportation development, as well as gentrification, have caused N/NE Portland, once home to most Black Oregonians and long the center of Black Portland life, to lose two-thirds of its Black residents between the 1950s and 2010. Portland no longer has any majority-Black neighborhoods.

The Preference Policy was born of protest. A community group, the Portland African American Leadership Forum (now known as Imagine Black), advocated for increased affordable housing opportunities in the neighborhood after the city sold a publicly owned site to a private developer at 80 percent less than market value, even though no affordable housing or economic development opportunities for local residents were included as part of the deal. The developer planned to bring a Trader Joe's to the gentrified neighborhood. The Preference Policy is one result of the Forum's advocacy.

As described by Portland officials, the Preference Policy "is an effort to address the harmful impacts of urban renewal by giving priority [housing] placement to applicants who were displaced, are at risk of displacement, or who are descendants of households that were displaced due to urban renewal in North and Northeast Portland." Although the program is not restricted to Black people, the city believes that by focusing on "marginalized communities with historic ties" to these neighborhoods, the mostly Black families who were displaced will now be able to return.

Applicants for the preference program are assigned "points" according to their historical ties to the community and whether their current or former address falls within one of the identified areas "where City plans had a destabilizing effect on long-term residents." Preference for housing and financial support is given to people who can prove that they, their parents, or their grandparents lived in the affected neighborhoods. Furthermore, some addresses within those neighborhoods get top priority because the actions that displaced those particular residents are considered especially egregious. These addresses include the roughly three hundred homes torn down in the 1970s when the city expanded Legacy Emanuel Medical Center, as well as the homes lost amid the waves of displacement caused by the building of the Memorial Coliseum in 1956 and Interstate 5 in 1966.

The redress of current and former residents takes many forms, including affordable rental housing, zero-interest home loans, and down payment assistance for first-time homebuyers. The goal is to bring people back to their community and help them rebuild their lives as new homeowners or renters. Portland's program is not perfect. For one thing, it is likely not large enough to meet the need. As of 2021, 5,700 people had applied for 531 rental homes. Residents report experiencing racial prejudice from newer white residents as they use parks and other neighborhood amenities that had been gathering places for the Black community just a few decades ago. Others expressed economic stress due to the lack of employment opportunities and high prices at stores in the gentrified area.

But despite these challenges, the Preference Policy is making a difference for many. A 2021 evaluation of the first five years of the program found Portland had provided home repair grants to 680 homeowners and supported 100 first-time homebuyers. The study found that the program was serving the people it intended to help—people with direct ties to N/NE Portland—and those residents expressed their approval. As one returning resident said, "The history of this neighborhood matters to me." Even if it isn't perfect, Portland's Preference Policy offers a powerful model for other communities seeking to repair the harms of the past and build more equitable communities in the future.

Portland's program navigates around some of the hurdles that make redress for harmed communities vulnerable to legal challenges. The United States Supreme Court has made a long-standing, though historically misguided, reading of the Equal Protection Clause as requiring colorblindness. Because Portland's program aids the predominantly Black communities that were harmed through infrastructure projects, detractors may challenge it as a legally prohibited race-conscious measure. However, the Equal Protection Clause was not enacted to implement some general principle of racial neutrality. It was designed to eradicate slavery and its vestiges and challenge the racial subjugation of the people whose lives were destroyed. The court has also restricted efforts to redress what it has called societal discrimination. No doubt, these theories will continue to guide the court's jurisprudence for many years to come. In any case, Portland's program is not about correcting generalized harm to Black people—it is about providing support to those who are directly tied to the communities that were directly harmed by government actions. Such a policy should survive even the court's wrongheaded jurisprudence on race-conscious measures.

MANY PEOPLE IN POSITIONS OF POWER WHO UNDERSTAND THE STEPS THEY should take to minimize racialized harm will nonetheless fail to take them, not necessarily out of malice, but because taking another path is easier, or cheaper, or faster. And it is true that government actors often have the "efficiency" argument on their side. It can be faster and cheaper to build when you do not have to account for some peoples' rights and interests, or even answer their questions. And "faster and cheaper" have significant appeal when a bridge or highway is crumbling. But faster and cheaper does not always mean better, and rarely does it mean fairer or more just. That is especially true when the people whose rights and interests you ignore are those with the least power.

Decision makers do not always do the right thing, at least not voluntarily. Fortunately, advocates have tools to compel them. As we have seen, civil rights laws and protections leave much to be desired when it comes to the unique challenges presented by transportation policies and infrastructure. The laws on the books were not specifically designed to address how race manifests in complex transportation policy decisions, and the federal courts' interpretations of those laws have made the challenge more difficult.

Still, while we work to create new tools—by electing public officials committed to racial justice, advocating for better laws, and strategizing for a reformed racial justice jurisprudence that breaks free of the Supreme Court's denuding of our most powerful civil rights laws—we must at the same time make the most of the tools we currently have. Legal scholar Dan Farbman has shown how abolitionist lawyers used the reviled Fugitive Slave Law of 1850 to *resist* slavery, to help free enslaved people, and to aid the abolition movement. Nineteenth-century lawyers worked within an avowedly racist legal system that was designed to protect white supremacy. They employed the limited procedural tools of that law—such as requesting continuances or trying to move the alleged fugitives from federal to state custody where it would be easier to escape—to dismantle the operation of that law itself, protect individual clients, and build political opposition to slavery.

Like those abolitionist lawyers who resisted slavery by using one of the tools of the enslavers they most hated, civil rights advocates today will need to be creative in adapting civil rights laws to the challenges of the moment. This is no easy task, given a federal judiciary that is often hostile to the expansion of civil rights protections.

The Fourteenth Amendment, and its Equal Protection Clause, was adopted by Congress after the Civil War, one of three so-called Reconstruction Amendments focused on establishing the civil, economic, and political rights of the formerly enslaved. As many scholars have demonstrated, the goal of the Equal Protection Clause was not to prohibit laws that treated Black and white people differently on account of their race. Indeed, the historical record shows that Congress intended no such thing. Instead, its purpose was to empower Congress to pass laws that would end the racial subjugation of Black Americans, something that could not be done without consciousness of race. Yet the Supreme Court has long interpreted the Equal Protection Clause to embody a principle of colorblindness that holds all racially conscious laws suspect, even when they are aimed *against* racial subjugation.

The court's insistence on a colorblind jurisprudence—in a world that is anything but colorblind—is one of many limitations of our current laws. Many public officials happily cloak themselves in the principle of color-blindness because it allows them to avoid difficult discussions about the role of race in our society and efforts to address stark racial disparities.

If we are to achieve a transportation infrastructure policy grounded in racial equity, decision makers cannot close their eyes to the realities of racism. Government entities must be able to directly and meaningfully address racial inequality. Our public policy must first acknowledge the existence or racism, and then move beyond hunts for cartoonish individual bad actors when the sources of racism are much more pervasive and com-plex. Analysis of racial impacts must happen earlier in decision-making processes, well before plans are written in stone—or roads are paved in asphalt. And we need to put the "burden of proof" on the right people— the government actors who are closest to the decision-making and have the greatest power to drive it, rather than on the private citizens who are forced to react to their decisions.

Fortunately, the law gives us a model that does just that. The Voting Rights Act of 1965 (VRA) is widely recognized as the most successful piece of legislation to come from the civil rights movement. Section 5—known as the preclearance requirement—mandates that all or part of fifteen juris-dictions covered under section 4b of the Act submit all proposed voting changes to the United States Department of Justice or the federal court of appeals for the District of Columbia for preclearance before they can go into effect. The jurisdictions covered by Section 5 include states, counties, cities, and towns with a history of the most entrenched racial discrimi-nation in voting. And when Section 5 requires jurisdictions to preclear all proposed voting changes, it really does mean *all*. Every polling place change, every annexation, every redistricting plan, and every voter identi-fication requirement must be preapproved by the federal court of appeals for DC or the Justice Department.

Section 5 correctly placed the burden on the government to establish that the proposed change was nondiscriminatory rather than requiring voters—many of whom were being discriminated against—to challenge the change after the fact. And it does not require voters to prove that some nefarious person engineered the change because of racist intent; voting changes with discriminatory *impact* are precluded even in the absence of discriminatory *intent*. Section 5 also helped empower communities to fight discriminatory voting practices and procedures by sharing information critical to self-advocacy. Until the Supreme Court hobbled Section 5 in the 2010 case *Shelby County v. Holder*, it had genuinely helped to make our democracy more racially inclusive.

Section 5 applies specifically to voting, but it has applications in other areas, including transportation. Racial Equity Impact Assessments or studies (REISs) are a cousin of Section 5 and of the Environmental Impact Studies (EISs) created by the National Environmental Policy Act. REISs have demonstrated extraordinary potential to center racial and cultural equity in challenges to spatial inequality. The result can be a shift in the culture and design of decision-making. But this path is not without risks.

An REIS should operate like an EIS but be focused on racial impact rather environmental impact. But to be effective, an REIS should require more than process. Before any state or locality proposes a transportation infrastructure plan, such as building a new road or designing a public bus route, it should be required to complete an REIS and affirm that the proposal will not disproportionately burden communities of color. Substantively, an REIS should analyze how racial groups will be affected by an infrastructure development project; consider how past, present, and proposed systems and procedures contribute to racial inequality; and evaluate both the current and historical distribution of the benefits and burdens of transportation projects in that community. Procedurally, an REIS asks these questions from the very first stages of the project and engages a broad swath of community members in considering them.

These studies would force us to grapple with the historical harms discussed in this book. Communities would be compelled to define what equity means, how it can be measured, and what it will require of government, communities, and individuals. REISs can help move decision makers beyond their traditional focus on intentional racial bias by discrete actors to a more accurate focus on identifying, alleviating, eliminating, and overcoming the sources of structural racial inequality. Moreover, racial equity impact studies can unearth the sources of cumulative racial disadvantage across domains that are often dismissed or ignored. When adopted by state and local governments, REISs can be powerful tools for racial equity.

Some policymakers and advocates have embraced the broad concept of REISs in various fields. The push began in the criminal legal sphere, where there are staggering racial disparities. In response to a study indicating that it led the country in disproportionately imprisoning Black people, in 2008 Iowa became the first state to require a racial impact statement for any proposed legislation that affects sentencing, probation, or parole policies. Recognizing that criminal legal system policies are often neutral on their face but have adverse impacts on communities of color, and that these disparate impacts could be more effectively addressed prior to adoption of new laws and policies, several states, including Connecticut, Maryland, New Jersey, Oregon, and Virginia, have followed Iowa's lead by adopting mandatory or voluntary racial impact statements for laws relating to criminal justice.

Racial impact studies have spread beyond the criminal legal system. The federal government requires some funding recipients to assess how their programs and policies affect people of color, including public transportation policies. There is also a growing body of statewide legislative mandates and local ordinances requiring policymakers to carry out such studies.

Requiring state governments to conduct an REIS for every transportation infrastructure project would allow us to rebuild America's aging infrastructure while also promoting racial equity. It could help states and localities unearth the deep structure of inequality and consider how proposed projects will shape spatial equity, racial segregation, concentrated poverty, economic opportunity and investment, quality education, affordable housing, and health outcomes. With an REIS requirement, policymakers would have access to the information they need to promote fairness and equity. Importantly, an REIS requirement could also open community-wide conversations about the reality of racial inequality in every city and town that is rebuilding a bridge, repaving a road, or expanding a transit line. As in perhaps every other period in American history, ours is witnessing a backlash to honest conversations about the role of race and racism in our society. REISs could create spaces where those conversations *have to* take place.

Although REISs hold promise, as they stand now, they are not a panacea. Some critique REISs on the grounds that they can amount to nothing more than a certification requirement. If relevant agencies are not forced to take concrete steps to mitigate the harms to marginalized communities of color identified through the study process, much of the transformational potential is lost. Effective REISs require built-in, automatic enforcement mechanisms.

Another critique is that REISs add additional bureaucratic hurdles, adding costs and time, to much needed development projects. This is a valid concern. Process can be a powerful tool of NIMBYism. Effective REISs should ensure that the review processes they require are meaningful without being open-ended. We do not have to choose between racial justice and critical infrastructure.

Others critique REISs for potentially requiring only performative community engagement. Just as a federal court allowed public officials seeking to build I-40 through Black communities in Nashville to check the community participation box despite minimal community engagement, some states and localities allow the REIS box to be checked without any input from those most affected. Too often, public engagement efforts by governments privilege communities that already have political power and are used to being heard. For example, community meetings are scheduled during the day when only white-collar workers have the flexibility to attend, they are not advertised in every neighborhood, or they are held in spaces where not everyone feels welcome. REISs must do more than require transportation officials to listen to community concerns. They must require decision makers to meaningfully share power with community members. Historically marginalized communities must have a real seat at the table. REISs should point to the ideal of collaborative government.

ONE OF THE COUNTRY'S MANY AGING HIGHWAY SEGMENTS IS ONE WE HAVE already examined, in Indianapolis. In 2017, the Indiana Department of Transportation (INDOT) announced plans to rebuild the Inner Loop, the area in downtown Indianapolis where I-65 and I-70 come together. The original Inner Loop was completed in 1975. By the time it was completed, it had displaced more than 17,000 residents and demolished 8,000 buildings. Thirty churches were razed, with more left to wither and die. INDOT's original plans for the redevelopment of the Inner Loop called for adding more lanes and building twenty-to-thirty-foot embankment walls, further encasing the predominantly Black neighborhoods that lined the highway.

The Rethink Coalition was founded as a grassroots nonprofit organization dedicated to bringing community, civic, and business leaders together to help shape the direction of the Inner Loop project. Rethink recognized that the reconstruction of I-65 and I-70 would determine life in Indianapolis for the next fifty years. One of their tag lines is: "Today is our chance to make a better tomorrow for Indianapolis." The members of Rethink saw that even though the rebuilding of the Inner Loop posed a real threat, it was also a rare opportunity to reconnect communities, improve the lives of residents, and bring about some measure of justice in a city that had been victimized by prior development. The goal, they realized, was not to rebuild the Inner Loop, but to rebuild a vibrant and unified community with all members contributing to that vision of the future. So, Rethink stepped in to do what its members thought INDOT should have been doing already.

In the beginning, their efforts to influence the highway project raised opposition. No group is a monolith. Many older community leaders grew up with the highway and were repeatedly told the lore that the highway was essential to the city's economic vitality. Eventually, they internalized that message and returned to it when faced with a new highway project. The Inner Loop was all they knew, and there was no will to challenge it. The tide shifted when, as part of Rethink's campaign, a community member created visual depictions of what the highway expansion project would mean to those who lived near it. It made clear that the redevelopment of the Inner Loop risked subjecting another generation of Indianapolis residents to the ravages of highway development. As Brenda Freije, Rethink's president and CEO, said, "a picture is worth 1,000 words and even more when they are engineering words."

Rethink has continued to use visual and narrative aids, including photographs, renderings, and maps, to help translate the technical details of the highway project for residents. They have enlisted planning professionals who live in the community to help prepare their neighbors to participate in public meetings. They have hosted gatherings at community institutions where residents feel more welcome than they might in a government office far from home. And they are enlisting local historians and longtime community members to make sure that everyone understands the history and context of transportation infrastructure in Indianapolis.

Rethink was able to get the community a seat at the table with INDOT and other policymakers, who now treat the organization as an integral part of the conversation about the future of the Inner Loop. For example, in 2021 Rethink released a design study with the Indianapolis Chamber of Commerce on the future of the Inner Loop and was a successful co-applicant with the City of Indianapolis and INDOT on a United States Department of Transportation planning grant. Rethink is also focused on fighting displacement and protecting access to safe and affordable housing. They are exploring the development of a community land trust to hold land on behalf of its residents and protect their assets from skyrocketing property taxes. Those who live near the Inner Loop are tired of passing on stories about better days in the past; they want to pass on their homes and their wealth.

At the same time, Rethink is realistic about the nature of big transformational projects like rebuilding the Inner Loop. The coalition understands that it needs to operate within the framework set by the state. And it knows that the community needs to articulate its demands using language that the legislature understands. Yes, members of Rethink believe that replacing the elevated highway with a recessed one would do justice to the community, and they are focused on social equity and neighborhood connectivity; they have made that message clear. But when they communicate with legislators, they also speak about increasing public safety, improving the environment, decreasing noise and air pollution, and saving money. Rethink is planning for the long term. They are working to build knowledge within the community to prepare its members to engage not only with the Inner Loop project, but also to develop the community's capacity to influence future projects.

Many government officials, especially within INDOT, have been responsive. The INDOT officials working on this particular project have changed the way they speak about transportation infrastructure and demonstrated openness to a broader range of concerns. They appear to recognize that the highway is not just about moving cars and trucks.

INDOT's ProPEL Indy initiative provides a glimpse into that evolution. ProPEL Indy is a self-described collaborative initiative intended to engage Indianapolis residents in reenvisioning the state's urban interstates and to shape transportation infrastructure projects over the next twenty years. Its aim is to bring in community voices long before any plans have been developed. INDOT speaks about the importance of blending transportation needs and other community goals, and clarifies that transportation infrastructure is about "more than just roads; it's a pathway to economic growth, quality of life, mobility, and equity for all." So far, residents and community leaders are encouraged by the new mode of engagement. That said, the ProPEL Indy initiative will come to a close in the second half of 2025, and only after that will anyone see what it will mean for future projects when the bulldozers actually arrive.

Maybe what Rethink is doing will make a meaningful difference for the community. Maybe, in the end, the usual forces will reassert themselves, or the progress evident in Indianapolis will not spread to other projects there or in other parts of the state, or to other parts of the country. But Rethink is trying.

Traditional community engagement techniques, such as those spawned by the 1956 Federal-Aid Highway Act, which required public notification but not meaningful involvement, did not serve marginalized communities well. At the time, most employees of the Bureaus of Public Roads and many departments of transportation were white men. Their backgrounds and experiences helped to determine approaches to public involvement that remain in place to this day. Those approaches were designed for predominantly white, middle to upper income, English-speaking residents who were done with work by 5:00 p.m., had access to personal transportation, and did not need childcare to attend public hearings.

That is not the reality of many Americans today, and it is certainly not the reality of many people affected by massive, invasive transportation projects. Nor was it the reality of those affected in the 1950s. Part of moving toward a better model involves rooting out the assumptions built into the original one. And the people in the affected communities—even successful activists like those who make up Rethink—cannot alone be responsible for that change. It must come from all of us.

AS I WRITE THIS BOOK, I AM NOT SURE WHAT WILL HAPPEN IN INDIANAPO-lis, Indiana, in Conway, South Carolina, in Houston, Texas, or any of the other communities I visited that are fighting to right past wrongs and build better futures. The scope of the harm is daunting. In neighborhood after neighborhood, county after county, and state after state, the story is just about the same. Highways and bridges, roads and sidewalks, buses and trains have been used as tools to separate Black people from opportunity and to erase Black wealth and community while creating white wealth and community. As Jim Crow faltered and finally fell, transportation infrastructure stepped into its place.

We see the truth of this everywhere. I find it impossible to drive down a highway without thinking of the names of communities that were sacrificed for that privilege. Sugar Hill in California. The Hill District in Pittsburgh. Tulsa, Oklahoma; New York City; Hartford, Connecticut. When I tell people about my research, I am besieged with stories about what happened in their neighborhood—from Nashville to New Orleans, from Brooklyn to Berkeley. Transportation is everywhere, and so transportation racism is everywhere. Spatial inequality is so common, so ubiquitous, that change can seem an impossible task.

But if there is one truth that American history should tell us today, it is that the impossible is possible—from struggles against slavery and Jim Crow to the expansion of the right to vote, and beyond. We cannot go back in time and erase the damage that transportation infrastructure and policy has caused across generations. It is not as simple as stitching back together what was ripped apart. But we can build something new—more durable and more just than what came before. Then, perhaps, America's roads, trains, sidewalks, highways, and buses can fulfill their promise—serving not as barriers that oppress some of us and divide all of us, but as means of connection and empowerment for everyone.

Acknowledgments

My first and deepest thanks go to my family. To my parents, Paula and Delroy, I would be nowhere without your love and support. And to my siblings, Courtney and Danielle, thank you for everything, especially my amazing nieces and nephews. Thank you to my wonderful husband, Richard Buery. You read every draft, calmed every anxiety, and raised me up. Not everyone gets to have their spouse, best friend, and hero all in one person. I guess I am just lucky like that!

I am so grateful to Johanna Miller for inviting me to collaborate with her in supporting community organizations in Syracuse, New York, fighting for justice in the face of a highway redevelopment project. This was in many ways my introduction to what I have come to understand is a quintessential American story. Johanna, working with you and the Syracuse community was transformational. Since then, I have been blessed to be welcomed into so many communities to learn about their lives, join them in their fight, and hear their histories. I am so grateful to them, and inspired by their fights to bring justice, equity, and respect to their communities. To share one's story is a gift, particularly when the story is laced with so much love and so much pain. I especially want to thank Reverend Cedric Blain-Spain for making me feel like a member of the Sandridge community and Brenda Hacker Freije for being so generous with your time and knowledge.

In April 2021, I was interviewed on NPR about a law review article I wrote called "'White Men's Roads through Black Men's Homes': Advancing Racial Equity through Highway Reconstruction." Soon after, I received an email from editor Daniel Gerstle. After hearing me on the radio, he reached out because he thought there might be a book in me. I had not considered writing a book—I doubted I had the words and knew I did not have the time. But thank goodness Dan believed in me. Dan, I am so lucky that you emailed your way into my life. It has been my great fortune to work with such an extraordinary and experienced editor. Your deft questions, your pushing and prodding, and most importantly, your confidence in me throughout this process have made me a better writer and this a better book. And to my literary agent Wendy Strothman, my sincerest gratitude for your counsel and friendship throughout this process. Thank you for holding my hand through each stage of this project.

None of this book would be possible without the support of my New York University School of Law community. Thank you, NYU Law and Dean Troy McKenzie, for your generous institutional support, including through the Filomen D'Agostino and Max E. Greenberg Research Fund, and the excellent research assistance from our librarians, especially Sarah Jaramillo.

A veritable army of research assistants have supported me as I developed this book and represented community members seeking transportation justice: Anna Applebaum, Rachel Baker, Rochelle Ballantyne, Chloe Bartholomew, Al Brooks, Nelson Castano, Kenny Crouch, Nathan Cummings, Will Haskell, Camara Stokes Hudson, Kayla Hug, David Jacobs, Nathan Lee, Mariana Lopez, Max Markham, James Mayer, Deb Merino, Justin McCarroll, Dinesh McCoy, Veronica McLean, Nina McKay, Kevin Muench, Karina Shah, Rajan Srinivasan, Briana Thomas, David Tisel, Conor Vance, and Ashley Williams. They have all graduated and are out in the world, making me incredibly proud.

I could not imagine a more supportive community of friends and colleagues than the one I have at NYU Law. And a special thank-you to all of you who make NYU Law feel like home: Melissa Murray, Vincent Southerland, Leomaris Sanchez, Brittany Farr, Alexis Karteron, Daniel Harawa, and Richard Brooks. And to Tony Thompson, Kim Taylor-Thompson, and Randy Hertz, I would never have come to NYU had it not been for your encouragement, mentorship, and sponsorship. I do not have words to express what you all mean to me. So, I will just say thank you.

I teach a civil rights clinic. I work with students to represent people and communities in civil rights cases around the country. One of the joys of teaching is working with a new group of talented and passionate students every year. To my students: I learn more from you than I could ever teach. And when the world feels dark, your optimism gives me energy.

Research and writing can feel like such an isolating endeavor. To the women in my writing group, you have managed to bring community to this lonely process.

To my ride or dies—Maja Hazell, Diahann Billings-Burford, Becky Edwards, Mikeisha Anderson Jones, and Kenisha Farquharson—thank you for being so generous with your love and support; for being both personal cheerleaders and relentless nags. You can stop bothering me now. The book is done.

I get easily distracted writing at my desk. That is why I feel so lucky to have found interesting and welcoming places and spaces to bring this book to life. Thanks to everyone who opened space to me, including Heather Gerken and James Forman at Yale Law School, and the women of Easton's Nook. And special thanks go to Tony Marx and the New York Public Library's Center for Research in the Humanities for welcoming me to the Frederick Lewis Allen Room. I can't quite believe that I had the honor of writing large portions of this book in the same place where Robert Caro wrote much of *The Power Broker* and Betty Friedan spent two years writing *The Feminine Mystique*. That is pretty good company to be in! And the NYPL's librarians are magicians. There was never a source they couldn't procure or a question they could not answer.

Much of this book was written during summer vacations. It was never easy to be at a laptop while my family was at the beach. Thank you to our housemates and friends Joshua Wright, Eliza Leighton, Matthew Klein, Alyssa Casden, Aviva, Isaac, Maya, Vivian, and Mari for keeping my family company during the days and keeping me entertained during the evenings.

To the heroes who moved mountains to ensure I had the time and capacity to write: Damaris Marrero, Lisa Evans-Graham, and Andrew Domingue. Thank you for doing the miraculous work of defending my time for writing (including from myself) and for saying no when I did not know how to.

So many friends and colleagues helped me to explore the ideas that found their way into this book. Thank you, Annette Gordon-Reed, Barry Friedman, Noah Rosenblum, and Teal Arcadi for the generative conversations. A special thank-you to my co-professor Joseph Schottenfeld. I am a better advocate because of my time working with you.

To my American Civil Liberties Union family: It is the honor of a lifetime to help lead an organization that is so critical to the American experiment. During these perilous times for our democracy, your brilliance and fortitude give me faith in the future. So, to our members, our staff, and our leadership, thank you. Anthony Romero, you are more than a friend and a colleague. You are family.

And finally, to my beautiful sons, Ellis and Ethan. Everything I do, I do because I want to leave you a world better than the one I found. I love you more.

Selected Sources

Books, Chapters, and Manuscripts

Allen, Ivan, Jr., and Paul Hemphill. *Mayor: Notes on the Sixties.* Simon & Schuster, 1971.

Asch, Chris Meyers, and George Derek Musgrove. *Chocolate City: A History of Race and Democracy in the Nation's Capital.* University of North Carolina Press, 2017.

Barkow, Rachel E. *Prisoners of Politics: Breaking the Cycle of Mass Incarceration.* Belknap Press of Harvard University Press, 2019.

Bayor, Ronald H. "Racism as Public Policy in America's Cities in the Twentieth Century." In *Crossing Boundaries: The Exclusion and Inclusion of Minorities in Germany and the United States,* edited by Larry Eugene Jones. Berghahn Books, 2001.

Bell, Derrick. *Faces at the Bottom of the Well: The Permanence of Racism.* Basic Books, 1992.

——. *Silent Covenants:* Brown v. Board of Education *and the Unfulfilled Hopes for Racial Reform.* Oxford University Press, 2005.

Blackmon, Douglas A. *Slavery by Another Name: The Re-Enslavement of Black Americans from the Civil War to World War II.* Doubleday, 2008.

Blumenberg, Evelyn. "Social Equity and Urban Transportation." In *The Geography of Urban Transportation,* 4th ed., edited by Genevieve Giuliano and Susan Hanson, 333–354. Guilford Press, 2017.

Books, Richard R. W., and Carol M. Rose. *Saving the Neighborhood: Racially Restrictive Covenants, Law, and Social Norms.* Harvard University Press, 2013.

Borzo, Greg. *The Chicago "L."* Arcadia Publishing, 2007.

Caro, Robert A. *The Power Broker: Robert Moses and the Fall of New York.* Vintage Books, 1974.

Christian, Charles M., and Sari J. Bennet. *Black Saga: The African American Experience: A Chronology.* Houghton Mifflin, 1998.

City of Atlanta. *Ordinance Book,* 11:391–93. City of Atlanta, June 17, 1913.

Cohen, Lizabeth. *Saving America's Cities: Ed Logue and the Struggle to Renew Urban America in the Suburban Age.* Farrar, Straus and Giroux, 2019.

Connerly, Charles E. *The Most Segregated City in America: City Planning and Civil Rights in Birmingham, 1920–1980.* University of Virginia Press, 2005.

Davis, Sidney. "Race and the Politics of Transportation in Atlanta." In *Just Transportation: Dismantling Race and Class Barriers to Mobility,* edited by Robert D. Bullard and Glenn S. Johnson, 84–96. New Society Publishers, 1997.

Day, John Kyle. *The Southern Manifesto: Massive Resistance and the Fight to Preserve Segregation.* University Press of Mississippi, 2014.

Doyle, Bertram Wilbur. *The Etiquette of Race Relations in the South: A Study in Social Control.* University of Chicago Press, 1937.

Du Bois, W. E. B. *The Souls of Black Folk.* A. C. McClurg, 1903.

Foner, Eric. *Nothing but Freedom: Emancipation and Its Legacy.* Louisiana State University Press, 2007.

Fotsch, Paul Mason. *Watching the Traffic Go By: Transportation and Isolation in Urban America.* University of Texas Press, 2007.

Freilla, Omar. "Burying Robert Moses's Legacy in New York City." In *Highway Robbery: Transportation Racism and New Routes to Equity*, edited by Robert D. Bullard, Glenn S. Johnson, and Angel O. Torres, 75–96. South End Press, 2004.

Frug, Gerald E. *City Making: Building Communities without Building Walls*. Princeton University Press, 1999.

Goodell, William. *The American Slave Code in Theory and Practice*. New York: American and Foreign Anti-Slavery Society, 1853.

Greenberg, Jack. *Crusaders in the Courts: How a Dedicated Band of Lawyers Fought for the Civil Rights Revolution*. Basic Books, 1994.

Hadden, Sally E. *Slave Patrols: Law and Violence in Virginia and the Carolinas*. Harvard University Press, 2001.

Hanchett, Thomas W. *Sorting Out the New South City: Race, Class, and Urban Development in Charlotte, 1875–1975*. University of North Carolina Press, 1998.

Hébert, Richard. *Highways to Nowhere: The Politics of City Transportation*. Bobbs-Merrill, 1972.

Higginbotham, Leon A., Jr. *In the Matter of Color: Race and the American Legal Process*. Oxford University Press, 1978.

Houston, Benjamin. *The Nashville Way: Racial Etiquette and the Struggle for Social Justice in a Southern City*. University of Georgia Press, 2012.

Hunter, Tera. *To 'Joy My Freedom: Southern Black Women's Lives and Labors after the Civil War*. Harvard University Press, 1998.

Hyatt, Susan B. *The Neighborhood of Saturdays: Memories of a Multi-Ethnic Community on Indianapolis' South Side*. Dog Ear Publishing, 2012.

Jackson, Kenneth T. *The Ku Klux Klan in the City, 1915–1930*. Oxford University Press, 1967.

Jackson, Mandi Isaacs. *Model City Blues: Urban Space and Organized Resistance in New Haven*. Temple University Press, 2010.

James, Rawn, Jr. *Root and Branch: Charles Hamilton Houston, Thurgood Marshall, and the Struggle to End Segregation*. Bloomsbury Press, 2010.

Kelley, Blair L. M. *Right to Ride: Streetcar Boycotts and African American Citizenship in the Era of Plessy v. Ferguson*. University of North Carolina Press, 2010.

Kluger, Richard. *Simple Justice: The History of* Brown v. Board of Education *and Black America's Struggle for Equality*. Vintage Books, 2004.

Kruse, Kevin M. *White Flight: Atlanta and the Making of Modern Conservatism*. 1st ed. Princeton University Press, 2005.

Lebsock, Suzanne. *The Free Women of Petersburg: Status and Culture in a Southern Town, 1784–1860*. W. W. Norton, 1984.

Lee, Helen Shores, and Barbara Sylvia Shores, with Denise George. *The Gentle Giant of Dynamite Hill: The Untold Story of Arthur Shores and His Family's Fight for Civil Rights*. Zondervan, 2012.

Lewis, John. Foreword to *Highway Robbery: Transportation Racism and New Routes to Equity*, edited by Robert D. Bullard, Glenn S. Johnson, and Angel O. Torres, iii–v. South End Press, 2004.

Lewis, Tom. *Divided Highways: Building the Interstate Highways, Transforming American Life*. Cornell University Press, 2013.

Litwack, Leon. *Been in the Storm So Long: The Aftermath of Slavery*. 1st ed. Alfred A. Knopf, 1979.

Loewen, James W. *Sundown Towns: A Hidden Dimension of American Racism*. New Press, 2005.

Logan, John R., and Harvey L. Molotch. *Urban Fortunes: The Political Economy of Place*. 20th ed. University of California Press, 2007.

Loukaitou-Sideris, Anastasia, and Renia Ehrenfeucht. *Sidewalks: Conflict and Negotiation over Public Space*. MIT Press, 2023.

Lovett, Bobby L. *The Civil Rights Movement in Tennessee: A Narrative History*. University of Tennessee Press, 2005.

Lucas, Karen, ed. *Running on Empty: Transport, Social Exclusion and Environmental Justice*. Policy Press, 2004.

Luxenberg, Steve. *Separate: The Story of* Plessy v. Ferguson, *and America's Journey from Slavery to Segregation.* W. W. Norton, 2019.

Marable, Manning. *How Capitalism Underdeveloped Black America: Problems in Race, Political Economy, and Society.* Haymarket Books, 2015.

Massey, Douglas S., and Brandon Wagner. "Segregation, Stigma, and Stratification: A Biosocial Model." In *The Oxford Handbook of Stigma, Discrimination, and Health,* edited by Brenda Major, John F. Dovidio, and Bruce G. Link, 147–62. Oxford University Press, 2018.

Mohl, Raymond A. "Planned Destruction: The Interstates and Central City Housing." In *From Tenements to the Taylor Homes,* edited by John F. Bauman, Roger Biles, and Kristin M. Szylvian, 226–45. Pennsylvania State University Press, 2000.

———. "Race and Space in the Modern City: Interstate-95 and the Black Community in Miami." In *Urban Policy in Twentieth-Century America,* edited by Arnold R. Hirsch and Raymond A. Mohl, 100–58. Rutgers University Press, 1993).

Myrdal, Gunnar. *An American Dilemma: The Negro Problem and Modern Democracy.* Harper & Row, 1944.

Ogletree, Charles J., Jr. *All Deliberate Speed: Reflections on the First Half-Century of Brown v. Board of Education.* W. W. Norton, 2004.

Pearson, Charles Chilton. *The Readjuster Movement in Virginia.* Yale University Press, 1917.

Pryor, Elizabeth Stordeur. *Colored Travelers: Mobility and the Fight for Citizenship Before the Civil War.* University of North Carolina Press, 2016.

Rae, Douglas W. *City: Urbanism and Its End.* Yale University Press, 2003.

Ross, Benjamin. *Dead End: Suburban Sprawl and the Rebirth of American Urbanism.* Oxford University Press, 2014.

Rothstein, Richard. *The Color of Law: The Forgotten History of How Our Government Segregated America.* Liveright, 2017.

Schmitt, Angie. *Right of Way: Race, Class, and the Silent Epidemic of Pedestrian Deaths in America.* Island Press, 2020.

Seley, John E. *The Politics of Public-Facility Planning.* Lexington Books, 1983.

Seo, Sarah A. *Policing the Open Road: How Cars Transformed American Freedom.* Harvard University Press, 2019.

Sharkey, Patrick. *Stuck in Place: Urban Neighborhoods and the End of Progress Toward Racial Equality.* University of Chicago Press, 2013.

Silverstein, Shel. "Where the Sidewalk Ends." In *Where the Sidewalk Ends: Poems and Drawings of Shel Silverstein,* 64. Harper & Row, 1974.

Wade, Richard C. *Slavery in the Cities: The South 1820–1860.* Oxford University Press, 1967.

Wiese, Andrew. *Places of Their Own: African American Suburbanization in the Twentieth Century.* University of Chicago Press, 2004.

Wilkerson, Isabel. *The Warmth of Other Suns: The Epic Story of America's Great Migration.* Random House, 2010.

Williams, Heather A. *Help Me to Find My People: The African American Search for Family Lost in Slavery.* University of North Carolina Press, 2012.

Woodward, C. Vann. *The Strange Career of Jim Crow.* Oxford University Press, 1974.

Wright, George C. *Life Behind a Veil: Blacks in Louisville Kentucky, 1865–1930.* Louisiana State University Press, 1985.

Young, Coleman, and Lonnie Wheeler. *Hard Stuff: The Autobiography of Coleman Young.* Viking, 1994.

Zielinkski, Kimberly, ed. *Children of Rondo: Transcriptions of Rondo Oral History Interviews.* Hamline University Press, 2006.

Zuzak, Charles A. *Beyond the Ballot: Citizen Participation in Metropolitan Nashville,* 30–31. With contributions by Kenneth E. McNeil, Frederic Bergerson, and Nashville Urban Observatory. University of Tennessee Press, 1971.

Scholarly Articles

Alderman, Derek H. "Street Names as Memorial Arenas: The Reputational Politics of Commemorating Martin Luther King Jr. in a Georgia County." *Historical Geography* 30 (2002): 99–120.

Alfieri, Anthony V. "Black, Poor, and Gone: Civil Rights Law's Inner-City Crisis." *Harvard Civil Rights-Civil Liberties Law Review* 54, no. 2 (2019): 629–702.

Archer, Deborah N. "How Racism Persists in Its Power." *Michigan Law Review* 120, no. 6 (2022): 957–69.

——. "Transportation Policy and the Underdevelopment of Black Communities." *Iowa Law Review* 106, no. 5 (2021): 2125–51.

——. "'White Men's Roads through Black Men's Homes': Advancing Racial Equity through Highway Reconstruction." *Vanderbilt Law Review* 73, no. 5 (2020): 1259–1330.

Audirac, Ivonne. "Shrinking Cities: An Unfit Term for American Urban Policy?" *Cities* 75 (May 2018): 12–19.

Austin, Regina. "'Not Just for the Fun of It!': Governmental Restraints on Black Leisure, Social Inequality, and the Privatization of Public Space." *Southern California Law Review* 71, no. 4 (1998): 667–714.

Barnett, Joseph. "Express Highway Planning in Metropolitan Areas." *Transactions of the American Society of Civil Engineers* 112, no. 1 (1947): 636–94.

Bayor, Ronald. "Roads to Racial Segregation: Atlanta in the Twentieth Century." *Journal of Urban History* 15, no. 1 (1998): 3–21.

Beardsley, E. H. "Goodbye to Jim Crow: The Desegregation of Southern Hospitals. 1945–70." *Bulletin of the History of Medicine* 60, no. 3 (1986): 19.

Bell, Derrick. "The Racism Is Permanent Thesis: Courageous Revelation or Unconscious Denial of Racial Genocide." *Capital University Law Review* 22, no. 3 (1993): 571–87.

Bellis, Rayla, Becca Buthe, and Martina Guglielmone. "Dangerous by Design 2021." *Smart Growth America* (2021): 21. https://smartgrowthamerica.org/wp-content/uploads/2021/03/Dangerous-By-Design-2021-update.pdf.

Biles, Roger. "Expressways Before the Interstates: The Case of Detroit, 1945–1956." *Journal of Urban History* 40, no. 5 (2014): 843–54.

Biles, Roger, Raymond A. Mohl, and Mark H. Rose. "Revisiting the Urban Interstates: Politics, Policy, and Culture Since World War II." *Journal of Urban History* 40, no. 5 (2014): 827–30.

Bise, R. Devon, John C. Rodgers III, Michael A. Maguigan, Brian Beaulieu, William Keith, and Chanda L. Maguigan. "Sidewalks as Measures of Infrastructure Inequities." *Southeastern Geographer* 58, no. 1 (2018): 38–57.

Bonam, Courtney, Caitlyn Yantis, and Valerie Jones Taylor. "Invisible Middle-Class Black Space: Asymmetrical Person and Space Stereotyping at the Race–Class Nexus." *Group Processes and Intergroup Relations* 23, no. 1 (2018): 24–47.

Bullard, Robert D. "Addressing Urban Transportation Equity in the United States." *Fordham Urban Law Journal* 31, no. 5 (2003): 1183–1209.

Bullard, Robert D., Glenn S. Johnson, and Angel O. Torres. "Dismantling Transportation Apartheid in the United States Before and After Disasters Strike." *Human Rights* 34, no. 3 (2007): 2–6.

Chetty, Raj, and Nathaniel Hendren. "The Impacts of Neighborhoods on Intergenerational Mobility I: Childhood Exposure Effects." *Quarterly Journal of Economics* 133, no. 3 (2018): 1107–62.

Chetty, Raj, Nathaniel Hendren, and Lawrence F. Katz. "The Effects of Exposure to Better Neighborhoods on Children: New Evidence from the Moving to Opportunity Experiment." *American Economic Review* 106, no. 4 (2015): 855–902.

Chetty, Raj, Nathaniel Hendren, Patrick Kline, and Emmanuel Saez. "Where Is the Land of Opportunity? The Geography of Intergenerational Mobility in the United States." *Quarterly Journal of Economics* 129, no. 4 (2014): 1553–1623.

Chin, William Y. "Racial Cumulative Disadvantage: The Cumulative Effects of Racial Bias at Multiple Decision Points in the Criminal Justice System." *Wake Forest Journal of Law and Policy* 6, no. 2 (2016): 454.

Connerly, Charles E. "From Racial Zoning to Community Empowerment: The Interstate Highway System and the African American Community in Birmingham, Alabama." *Journal of Planning Education and Research* 22, no. 2 (2002): 99–114.

Conroy, Justin S. " 'Show Me Your Papers': Race and Street Encounters." *National Black Law Journal* 19, no. 2 (2007): 149–74.

Coughenour, Courtney, Sheila Clark, Ashok Singh, Eudora Claw, James Abelar, and Joshua Huebner. "Examining Racial Bias as a Potential Factor in Pedestrian Crashes." *Accident Analysis & Prevention* 98, no. 1 (2017): 96–100.

Cradock, Angie L., Philip J. Troped, Billy Fields, Steven J. Melly, Shannon V. Simms, Franz Gimmler, and Marianne Fowler. "Factors Associated with Federal Transportation Funding for Local Pedestrian and Bicycle Programming and Facilities." *Journal of Public Health Policy* 30, no. S1 (2009): S48.

Dailey, Jane. "Deference and Violence in the Postbellum Urban South: Manners and Massacres in Danville, Virginia." *Journal of Southern History* 63, no. 3 (1997): 553–90.

Davis, Angela J. "Prosecution and Race: The Power and Privilege of Discretion." *Fordham Law Review* 67, no. 1 (1998): 18.

Davis, Ronald L. F. "Racial Etiquette: The Racial Customs and Rules of Racial Behavior in Jim Crow America." https://web.archive.org/web/20040203140654/http:/www.jimcrowhistory.org/resources/lessonplans/hs_es_etiquette.htm.

Desmond, Matthew. "Severe Deprivation in America: An Introduction." *Russell Sage Foundation Journal of the Social Sciences* 1, no. 2 (2015): 1–11.

DiMento, Joseph F. C. "Stent (or Dagger?) in the Heart of Town: Urban Freeways in Syracuse, 1944–1967." *Journal of Planning History* 8, no. 2 (2009): 133–61.

Farbman, Daniel. "Resistance Lawyering." *California Law Review* 107, no. 6 (2019): 1877–1954.

Fotsch, Paul Mason. "Contesting Urban Freeway Stories: Racial Politics and the O.J. Chase." *Cultural Studies* 13, no. 1 (1999): 110–37.

Fox, James W., Jr. "Doctrinal Myths and the Management of Cognitive Dissonance: Race, Law, and the Supreme Court's Doctrinal Support of Jim Crow." *Stetson Law Review* 34, no. 2 (2005): 328–42.

Frug, Jerry. "Decentering Decentralization." *University of Chicago Law Review* 60, no. 2 (1993): 257.

Gans, David. " 'We Do Not Want to Be Hunted': The Right to Be Secure and Our Constitutional Story of Race and Policing." *Columbia Journal of Race and Law* 11, no. 2 (2021): 239–342.

Gillette, Clayton P. "Plebiscites, Participation, and Collective Action in Local Government Law." *Michigan Law Review* 86, no. 5 (1998): 930.

Goddard, Tara, Kimberly Barsamian Kahn, and Arlie Adkins. "Racial Bias in Driver Yielding Behavior at Crosswalks." *Transportation Research Part F: Traffic Psychology and Behavior* 33 (August 2015): 1–6.

Golub, Aaron. "Race, Space, and Struggles for Mobility: Transportation Impacts on African-Americans in San Francisco's East Bay." *Urban Geography* 34, no. 5 (August 2013): 699–728.

Guffey, Elizabeth. "Knowing Their Space: Signs of Jim Crow in the Segregated South." *Design Issues* 28, no. 2 (2012): 41–60.

Hall, Aaron. "Slaves of the State: Infrastructure and Governance through Slavery in the Antebellum South." *Journal of American History* 106, no. 1 (2019): 19–46.

Hammerschlag, Roel. "Legislating the Highway Act of 1956: Lessons for Climate Change Regulation." *Environs Environmental Law and Policy Journal* 31 (2007): 59–102.

Harris, Cheryl I. "Whiteness as Property." *Harvard Law Review* 106, no. 8 (1993): 1757.

Harris, J. William. "Etiquette, Lynching, and Racial Boundaries in Southern History: A Mississippi Example." *American Historical Review* 100, no. 2 (April 1995): 387–410.

Hasbrouck, Brandon. "The Antiracist Constitution." *Boston University Law Review* 102, no. 1 (2022): 87–165.

Haynes, Campbell. "One Mile North." *Belmont Law Review* 8, no. 1 (2020): 1–59.

Houck, Oliver A. "Is That All? A Review of *The National Environmental Policy Act, An Agenda for the Future* by Lynton Keith Caldwell." *Duke Environmental Law & Policy Forum* 11, no. 1 (2000): 173–91.

Johnson, Olatunde C. A. "Lawyering That Has No Name: Title VI and the Meaning of Private Enforcement." *Stanford Law Review* 66, no. 6 (2014): 1293–1332.

Kelley, Robin D. G. "'We Are Not What We Seem': Rethinking Black Working-Class Opposition in the Jim Crow South." *Journal of American History* 80, no. 1 (1993): 75–112.

Krawec, Nicholas D. "Constitutional Law—Racial Discrimination—Thirteenth Amendment." *Duquesne Law Review* 20, no. 1 (1981): 88.

Kuswa, Kevin Douglas. "Suburbification, Segregation, and the Consolidation of the Highway Machine." *Journal of Law in Society* 3 (2002): 31–66.

Lands, LeeAnn Bishop. "A Reprehensible and Unfriendly Act: Homeowners, Renters, and the Bid for Residential Segregation in Atlanta, 1900–1917." *Journal of Planning History* 3, no. 2 (2004): 83–115.

Lavine, Amy. "Urban Renewal and the Story of *Berman v. Parker*." *Urban Lawyer* 42, no. 2 (Spring 2010): 423–75.

Lawrence, Charles. "The Id, The Ego, and Equal Protection." *Stanford Law Review* 39, no. 2 (1987): 317.

Lenhardt, R. A. "Race Audits." *Hastings Law Journal* 62, no. 6 (2011): 1527–77.

Lowe, Kate. "Environmental Justice and Pedestrianism: Sidewalk Continuity, Race, and Poverty in New Orleans, Louisiana." *Transportation Research Record* 2598, no. 1 (January 2016): 119–23.

Maguire, Aideen, Declan French, and Dermot O'Reilly. "Residential Segregation, Dividing Walls and Mental Health: A Population-based Record Linkage Study." *Journal of Epidemiology and Community Health* 70, no. 9 (September 2016): 845–54.

Makarewicz, Carrie, Arlie Adkins, Charlotte Frei, and Audrey Wennink. "'A Little Bit Happy': How Performance Metrics Shortchange Pedestrian Infrastructure Funding." *Research in Transportation Business & Management* 29 (December 2018): 144–56.

Matthew, Dayna Bowen. "Equitable Community Development for Good Mental Health: A Discussion of Economic and Racial Equity in Housing." *Community Development Innovation Review* 13, no. 1 (2018): 61–67.

Mauer, Marc. "Racial Impact Statements: Changing Policies to Address Disparities." *Criminal Justice* 23, no. 4 (2009): 16–20.

McCammack, Brian. "'My God, They Must Have Riots on Those Things All the Time': African American Geographies and Bodies on Northern Urban Public Transportation, 1915–1940." *Journal of Social History* 43, no. 4 (2010): 973–88.

McFarlane, Audrey G. "Black Transit: When Public Transportation Decision-Making Leads to Negative Economic Development." *Iowa Law Review* 106, no. 5 (2021): 2369–96.

———. "Race, Space, and Place: The Geography of Economic Development." *San Diego Law Review* 36, no. 2 (1999): 295–354.

Mohl, Raymond A. "Citizen Activism and Freeway Revolts in Memphis and Nashville: The Road to Litigation." *Journal of Urban History* 40, no. 5 (2014): 870–93.

———. "The Interstates and the Cities: The U.S. Department of Transportation and the Freeway Revolt, 1966–1973." *Journal of Policy History* 20, no. 2 (2008): 194–226.

———. "Making the Second Ghetto in Metropolitan Miami, 1940–1960." *Journal of Urban History* 21, no. 3 (1995): 395–427.

Pollack, Michael. "Sidewalk Government." *Michigan Law Review* 122 (forthcoming): 7–9. https://papers.ssrn.com/sol3/papers.cfm?abstract_id=4198355.

powell, john a. "Dreaming of a Self Beyond Whiteness and Isolation." *Washington University Journal of Law and Policy* 18, no. 1 (2005): 13–45.

———. "Post-Racialism or Targeted Universalism?" *Denver Law Review* 86, no. 3 (2009): 785–806.

Power, Garrett. "Apartheid Baltimore Style: The Residential Segregation Ordinances of 1910–1913." *Maryland Law Review*, 42, no. 2 (1983): 310.

Rahman, K. Sabeel, and Jocelyn Simonson. "The Institutional Design of Community Control." *California Law Review* 108 (2020): 104–5.

Rajaee, Mozhgon, Brenda Echeverri, Zachary Zuchowicz, Kristen Wiltfang, and Jennifer F. Lucarelli. "Socioeconomic and Racial Disparities of Sidewalk Quality in a Traditional Rust Belt City." *SSM—Population Health* 16 (December 2021): 1–8.

Ray, Geoff. "LA Bus Riders' Union Rolls Over Transit Racism." *Race, Poverty & the Environment* 12, no. 1 (2005): 54.

Ringquist, Evan J., and David H. Clark. "Local Risks, States' Rights, and Federal Mandates: Remedying Environmental Inequities in the U.S. Federal System." *Publius* 29, no. 2 (1999): 87–89.

Rose, Mark H. "Reframing American Highway Politics, 1956–1995." *Journal of Planning History* 2, no. 3 (2003): 212–36.

Rose-Redwood, Reuben S. "From Number to Name: Symbolic Capital, Places of Memory and the Politics of Street Renaming in New York City." *Social and Cultural Geography* 9, no. 4 (2008): 431–52.

Sanchez, Thomas W., Rich Stolz, and Jacinta S. Ma. "Moving to Equity: Addressing Inequitable Effects of Transportation Policies on Minorities." A Joint Report of the Civil Rights Project at Harvard University and Center for Community Change (2003): 11.

Schindler, Sarah. "Architectural Exclusion: Discrimination and Segregation Through Physical Design of the Public Environment." *Yale Law Journal* 124, no. 6 (2015): 1934.

Simmons, Omari Scott. "Urban Removal: Reshaping Urban Landscapes Through a Responsive Communitarian Lens." *Cornell Journal of Law and Public Policy* 29, no. 4 (2020): 885–944.

Southerland, Vincent. "The Master's Tools and a Mission: Using Community Controls and Oversight Laws to Resist and Abolish Police Surveillance Technologies." *UCLA Law Review* 70 (2023): 2–90.

Sugrue, Thomas J. "Driving While Black: The Car and Race Relations in Modern America." *Automobile in American Life and Society* (2010).

Thomas, William G., III, Richard G. Healy, and Ian Cottingham. "Reconstructing African American Mobility after Emancipation, 1865–1867." *Social Science History* 41, no. 4 (2017): 673–704.

Thornbrough, Emma L. "Segregation in Indiana during the Klan Era of the 1920's." *Mississippi Valley History Review* 47, no. 4 (1961): 594–618.

Tiwari, Sweta, and Shrinidhi Ambinakudige. "Streetscapes and Stereotyping: Streets Named after Martin Luther King, Jr., and the Geographies of Racial Identity." *GeoJournal* 87 (2022): 921–34.

Troutt, David D. "Katrina's Window: Localism, Resegregation, and Equitable Regionalism." *Buffalo Law Review* 55, no. 4 (2008): 1109–90.

Tscheschlok, Eric. "Long Time Coming: Miami's Liberty City Riot in 1968." *Florida Historical Quarterly* 74, no. 4 (1996): 441–42.

Watras, Joseph. "The Racial Desegregation of Dayton, Ohio, Public Schools, 1966–2008." *Ohio History* 117 (2010): 93–107.

Newspaper and Other Articles

Abello, Oscar Perry. "Breaking Through and Breaking Down the Delmar Divide in St. Louis." *Next City*, August 19, 2019.

Ahmed, Beenish. "Historical Marker Commemorates Demolished Black Bottom Neighborhood in Detroit." *Michigan Public*, August 9, 2021.

Alam, Ehsan. "Before It Was Cut in Half by I-94, St. Paul's Rondo Was a Thriving African-American Cultural Center." *MinnPost*, June 19, 2017.

Anderson, Monica. "Who Relies on Public Transit in the U.S." *Pew Research Center*, April 7, 2016.

Azhar, Aman. "In Corpus Christi's Hillcrest Neighborhood, Black Residents Feel Like They Are Living in a 'Sacrifice Zone.'" *Inside Climate News*, July 4, 2021.

Badger, Emily. "The Inequality of Sidewalks." *Washington Post*, January 15, 2016.

——. "Why Are So Many More Pedestrians Dying in the U.S.?" Produced by Mooj Zadie and Clare Toeniskoetter. *Daily*, January 4, 2024. Podcast.

Badger, Emily, and Darla Cameron. "How Railroads, Highways and Other Man-Made Lines Racially Divide America's Cities." *Washington Post*, July 16, 2015.

Badger, Emily, Ben Blatt, and Josh Katz. "Why Are So Many American Pedestrians Dying at Night?" *The Upshot* (*New York Times* blog), December 11, 2023.

Balk, Gene. "Seattle Police Writing Fewer Jaywalking Tickets, but High Rate Still Issued to Black Pedestrians." *Seattle Times*, July 20, 2017.

Bass, Paul. "Crash Into a Kid? Still No Crime." *New Haven Independent*, August 24, 2018.

Bennet, Lerone Jr. "Southwest Citizens Group Discloses 'Barrier' Plans Endorsed by City Officials." *Atlanta Daily World*, October 14, 1952.

Bergal, Jenni. "Racial Justice, Pedestrian Safety Fuel Jaywalking Debate." *Stateline* (July 14, 2022).

Bernstein, Harry. "Protest March for Farm Labor Gets Under Way." *Los Angeles Times*, March 18, 1966.

BikeWalkKC (Kansas City, MO). "Decriminalizing Walking and Biking." Accessed February 24, 2024. https://bikewalkkc.org/advocacy/decriminalizing.

BikeWalkKC (Kansas City, MO). "Taking on Traffic Laws: A How-To Guide for Decriminalizing Mobility." Accessed February 24, 2024. https://bikewalkkc.org/takingontrafficlaws.

Birmingham Age-Herald. "Zoning Measure Will Carry Section for Separation of Races." January 8, 1923.

Birmingham News. "House in Zoning Dispute Blown Up." August 19, 1947.

Birmingham News. "Public Is Given Preview of Freeway Plans; Wins Protests, Praise." November 7, 1958.

Birmingham Reporter. "Mischievous, Harmful, and Useless Legislation." January 13, 1923.

Birmingham Reporter. "Negroes Make Appeal to City Commission for Relief Against Segregation Law in Zoning Act." January 20, 1923.

Bogel-Burroughs, Nicholas. "MTA Urged to Cut Service." *Baltimore Sun*, August 9, 2018.

Bogert, Carroll, and Lynnell Hancock. "Superpredator: The Media Myth That Demonized a Generation of Black Youth." *Marshall Project*, November 20, 2020.

Bograd, Sadie. "New Haven Gets Rolling on Pedestrian, Cycling and Transit Infrastructure." *Yale Daily News* (New Haven, CT), September 8, 2022.

Breen, Thomas. "Fatalities Mount on Death Blvd." *New Haven Independent*, January 6, 2021.

———. "Whalley Walked in The Dark (& Some Light)." *New Haven Independent*, February 26, 2020.

Byron, Aubrey. "In Much of Ferguson, Walking in the Street Remains the Only Option." *Strong Towns*, February 20, 2018.

Campbell, Colin. "Five Years Later, Many Across Baltimore Bitterly Lament Gov. Hogan's Decision to Kill the Red Line Light Rail." *Baltimore Sun*, September 11, 2020.

Cashin, Sheryll. "How Larry Hogan Kept Blacks in Baltimore Segregated and Poor." *Politico*, July 18, 2020.

Ceballos, Danica. "Is Jaywalking the New Stop-And-Frisk? De Blasio Pulls a Page from Giuliani's Playbook." *Observer* (New York), January 20, 2014.

Chan, Sewell. "Penalty for Fare Beating Rises to $100." *New York Times*, July 7, 2008.

Claxton, Kevin. "Californians Win the Freedom to Walk." *CalBike* (Sacramento, CA), October 1, 2022.

Clemons, Tracy. "Woman Files Suit Against City and Shreveport Police Officer." KSLA News 12 (Shreveport, LA), December 6, 2010.

Cobb, James C., and John C. Inscoe. "Georgia History." *New Georgia Encyclopedia*, last updated September 30, 2020.

Cohen, Josh. "Seattle Council Member Questions Jaywalking Law." *Next City*, August 3, 2017.

Columbus Ledger. "Supreme Court Decision in Montgomery Case Foretells the End of City Bus Services in Deep South Cities." November 14, 1956, 4.

Cook, Gareth. "The Economist Who Would Fix the American Dream." *Atlantic*, July 17, 2019.

Coolidge, Sharon, and Dan Horn. "Cincinnati Leaders to Apologize for Destruction of Black Neighborhood in 1950s." *Cincinnati Enquirer*, June 13, 2023.

Costello, Darcy. "After Last Saturday's Towson Mall Arrests, Baltimore County Officials Say They're Prepared to Prevent Similar Incidents." *Baltimore Sun*, February 25, 2022.

Crater, Paul. "Atlanta's Berlin Wall." *Atlanta Magazine*, December 1, 2011.

Cummins, Eleanor. "The Surprising Politics of Sidewalks." *Popular Science*, April 10, 2018.

Cwiek, Sarah. "Protesters Highlight Detroit Area's Racial Divide on Eight Mile Road." Michigan Public Radio (Ann Arbor, MI), June 17, 2020.

Davidson, Kyle. "More than 100 People March Down 8 Mile to Protest Racial Profiling." *Detroit Free Press*, June 5, 2021.

De Avila, Joseph. "Hartford Highlights a State's Divide." *Wall Street Journal* (Hartford, CT), September 30, 2012.

DiSalvo, Emily. "Greater Hartford's Race and Economic Disparities 'More Pronounced,' Report Shows." *Connecticut Insider* (Hartford, CT), March 16, 2023.

——. "How New Haven's Urban Renewal in the 1960s Continues to Influence the City." *Shorthand*. Accessed February 24, 2024. https://qujournalism.shorthandstories.com/new-haven-urban -renewal/index.html.

Dottle, Rachel, Laura Bliss, and Pablo Robles. "What It Looks Like to Reconnect Black Communities Torn Apart by Highways." *Bloomberg CityLab*, July 28, 2021.

Duncan, Ian. "Traffic Deaths Increased during the Pandemic. The Toll Fell More Heavily on Black Residents, Report Shows." *Washington Post*, June 22, 2021.

Elbert, Dave. "The Elbert Files: Racial Scar Left by Freeway." *Business Record*, June 25, 2020.

Eschner, Kat. "Three Ways the Interstate System Changed America." *Smithsonian Magazine*, June 29, 2017.

Esman, Marjorie R. "When 'Walking' Becomes a Criminal Act." *Louisiana Weekly*, September 8, 2014.

Estep, Tyler, and Amanda C. Coyne. "Gwinnett's MARTA Referendum Has Failed." *Atlanta Journal-Constitution*, March 19, 2019.

Fiery Cross (Indianapolis, IN). "Letters to the Editor." January 19, 1923, 2.

Frederick Douglass' Paper (Rochester, NY). May 13, 1852.

Fulwood, Sam III. "When Home Disappears." *Center for American Progress*, April 7, 2016.

Gardiner, Dustin. "California Will Decriminalize Jaywalking in the Street, at Least in Most Cases." *San Francisco Chronicle*, October 1, 2022.

Gellman, Lucy. "City Seeks to Make Boulevard Safer." *New Haven Independent*, July 11, 2017.

Glover, Maury. "How I-94 Ripped Apart the Rondo Neighborhood and One Group's Plan to Help Restore It." FOX Television Stations (Saint Paul, MN), February 15, 2021.

Godwin, Becca J. G. "Google Search Answered 'What Does MARTA Stand For' with Racist Joke." *Atlanta Journal-Constitution*, March 29, 2018.

Goldstein, Joseph, and Ashley Southall. "'I Got Tired of Hunting Black and Hispanic People.'" *New York Times*, June 17, 2020.

Gottfried, Mara H. "1,500 Protesters March from Capitol onto I-94 in St. Paul for about 1 Hour." *Twin Cities Pioneer Press*, May 31, 2020.

Gray, Noelle. "Detroit Marks Black Bottom Neighborhood Lost When I-375 Built." *Detroit News*, August 9, 2021.

Guse, Clayton. "Queens Councilman's Bill Would Decriminalize Jaywalking in NYC." *New York Daily News*, September 15, 2020.

Gutierrez, Melody. "Newsom Vetoes Jaywalking Bill Aimed at Easing Fines, Targeted Enforcement." *Los Angeles Times*, October 9, 2021.

Hale, Steven. "History Repeats Itself in North Nashville." *Nashville Scene*, June 7, 2018.

Hannagan, Charley. "Rethinking I-81: Eastern Suburbs Could See New Highway Names, Interchanges, Lanes." *Syracuse.com* (DeWitt, NY), November 16, 2016.

Harlan, Chico. "In St. Louis, Delmar Boulevard Is the Line that Divides a City by Race and Perspective." *Washington Post*, August 22, 2014.

Hilkevitch, Jon, and Mitch Smith. "CTA's New Weapon in Graffiti Battle: Suits Against Vandals, Parents." *Chicago Tribune*, April 24, 2014.

Holpuch, Amanda. "U.S. Pedestrian Deaths Are at Highest Level in 41 Years, Report Says." *New York Times*, June 27, 2023.

Howland, Lena. "'Freedom to Walk': Why One California Lawmaker Wants to Decriminalize Jaywalking." *abc10.com* (Sacramento, CA), March 6, 2021.

Indianapolis Recorder. "Vandals Throw a Bomb." July 23, 1927, 3.

Indianapolis Star. "Fences Isolate Colored Owner." July 16, 1920, 1.

Indianapolis Times. "Klan Gives Its Backing to Duvall." May 4, 1925, 1.

Irons, Meghan E. "Sidewalks Tell of Two Bostons." *Boston Globe*, March 4, 2018.

Jackson, Derrick Z. "Building Back Severed Communities." *American Prospect*, June 9, 2021.

Jackson, Emory. "Tip Off." *Birmingham Word*, August 12, 1949.

Jacobson, Stacy. "Who Pays to Repair Broken Memphis Sidewalks? You Do, City Says." *WREG.com*, September 26, 2022.

Johnson, Christopher. "The Epic of Collier Heights." *99% Invisible*, December 9, 2021.

Kendrick, Thomas R. "Selma Rights Activity Includes New Marches." *Washington Post,* March 20, 1965.

Knauss, Tim. "Report: Syracuse and Onondaga County Suffer from 'Hyper-Segregation.'" *Syracuse,* November 17, 2014.

Kofsky, Jared, Maia Rosenfeld, and Steve Osunsami. "Black Alabamans Say Highway Project Caused Major Flooding, Threatening Their Community." *ABC News,* October 31, 2023.

Kruse, Kevin M. "What Does a Traffic Jam in Atlanta Have to Do with Segregation? Quite a Lot." *New York Times Magazine,* August 14, 2019.

Kuntzman, Gersh. "'Jaywalking While Black': Final 2019 Numbers Show Race-Based NYPD Crackdown Continues." *Streetsblog NYC*, January 27, 2020.

Lau, Maya. "Echoes of Ferguson Visible in Shreveport." *Shreveport Times,* August 24, 2014.

Love, Hanna, and Jennifer S. Vey. "To Build Safe Streets, We Need to Address Racism in Urban Design." *Brookings Institution* (Washington, DC), August 28, 2019.

MacDonald, Thomas H. "The Case for Urban Expressways." *American City,* June 1947.

MacKenzie, Blake. "Race and Housing Series: Rondo and I-94—A Conversation with Nick Khaliq." *Twin Cities Habitat for Humanity,* February 14, 2020.

Mangla, Ravi. "The Secret History of Jaywalking: The Disturbing Reason It Was Outlawed—and Why We Should Lift the Ban." *Salon,* August 21, 2015.

Martin, Rachel. "Why Half of Nashville's Roads Still Don't Have Sidewalks." *Bloomberg,* January 6, 2017.

McCormick-Cavanagh, Conor. "Jaywalking Is Illegal in Denver. Is It Time to Change That Law?" *Westword* (Denver, CO), September 8, 2022.

McFetridge, Scott. "Sidewalks Become a Battlefield for Some Suburbs." *Detroit News,* November 20, 2016.

McGraw, Bill. "Bringing Detroit's Black Bottom Back to (Virtual) Life." *Detroit Free Press,* February 27, 2017.

Messerly, Megan, and Sean Golonka. "Right to Return, Minimum Wage Increase and Jaywalking Decriminalization among More than 200 Laws to Kick in Today." *Nevada Independent,* July 21, 2021.

Miami Herald. "What About the Negroes Uprooted by the Expressway?" March 4, 1957.

Miller, Johnny. "Roads to Nowhere: How Infrastructure Built on American Inequality." *Guardian,* February 21, 2018.

Mishra, Stuti. "Buttigieg Says America's Highways Are Racist and Infrastructure Bill Will Help Fix It." *Independent,* November 9, 2021.

Moses, Robert. "The New Super-Highways: Blessing or Blight?" *Harper's Magazine,* December 1956.

Mosqueda, Priscila. "A Neighborhood Apart." *Texas Observer* (Austin, TX), June 1, 2015.

Moxley, Elle. "How Kansas City's Complex Racial History Is Still Influencing Education Choices." NPR, May 9, 2018.

Mullins, Paul. "In the Shadow of the Interstate: Living with Highways." *Archaeology and Material Culture,* October 3, 2019.

——. "Racist Spite and Residential Segregation: Housing and the Color Line in Inter-War Indianapolis." *Archaeology and Material Culture,* January 20, 2019.

New Haven Independent. "Gabrielle Lee Buried." June 16, 2008.

New York Times. "Justices Say Closing Off Street Is Not a Violation of Civil Rights." April 21, 1983.

O'Neill, Madeleine. "Maryland Will Add Racial Impact Assessments to Key Pieces of Legislation." *USA Today* (Maryland), February 1, 2021.

Owens, Gwinn. "Down by the Station (But Not in Ruxton)." *Baltimore Sun,* May 14, 1992.

PBS. "Race and the Power of Illusion." Accessed February 24, 2024. https://www.pbs.org/race/000_General/000_00-Home.htm.

Perez, Jose. "Why Do Some Neighborhoods Have No Sidewalks?" *House Notebook,* February 28, 2021.

Powers, Colleen. "Roots of Rondo Honors a Neighborhood, Looks to the Future." *Creative Exchange*, March 8, 2017.

Reed, Lillian, and Yvonne Wenger. "Clashes with Teens Have Become a Polarizing Issue in Baltimore. As Adults Argue, Some Youth Feel Ignored." *Baltimore Sun*, May 30, 2019.

Riley, Betsy. "A Separate Peace: Collier Heights." *Atlanta Magazine*, April 30, 2010.

Roane, Kit R. "Police Balk at Crackdown on Jaywalkers by Giuliani." *New York Times*, February 8, 1998.

Roark, Laurie. "Mixed Signals: The Future of Pedestrian Safety in New Haven." *Yale Herald* (New Haven, CT), February 7, 2020.

Roberts, Gene. "Troopers Shove Group Resuming Meredith March." *New York Times*, June 8, 1966.

Roberts, Sam. "Metro Matters: Battle to Block the Re-naming of Fifth Avenue." *New York Times*, February 15, 1988, B1.

Robertson, Stanley G. "L.A. Confidential: Will New Freeway Affect Us?" *Los Angeles Sentinel*, October 27, 1966.

Robinson, Nathan J. "The Silent Epidemic of Pedestrian Deaths in America." *Current Affairs*, May 9, 2022.

Rosen, Rebecca J. "In Champaign-Urbana, Illinois, 89% of Those Arrested for Jaywalking Are Black." *Atlantic*, August 24, 2012.

Ross-Brown, Sam. "Transportation Secretary Foxx Moves to Heal Scars of Urban Renewal." *American Prospect*, September 30, 2016.

Rubinstein, Dana, and Emma G. Fitzsimmons. "New York Revives Its Alternate-Side Parking Ritual. Cue the Outrage." *New York Times*, April 19, 2022.

Sanders, Topher, Kate Rabinowitz, and Benjamin Conarck. "Walking While Black." *ProPublica*, November 16, 2017.

Scales, Rod. "Why Dallas Sidewalks Are in Such Bad Shape." *Dallas Morning News*, April 3, 2022.

Schmitt, Angie. "Building Highways Made Racial Segregation Worse. Can Removing Them Undo That Legacy?" *Streetsblog USA*, June 7, 2018.

———. "How 3 Communities Fought Discriminatory Transportation Policies." *Streetsblog USA*, July 3, 2014.

Semuels, Alana. "How to Decimate a City." *Atlantic*, November 20, 2015.

Shane, George. "Negroes Hit High Prices for Homes." *Des Moines Register*, May 27, 1959, 13.

Shreveport Times. "Cedric Murphy Talks About Getting a Ticket for Riding His Wheelchair on the Street." April 25, 2015.

Silberman, Steven. "Persistence Pays Off for King Committee." *Record*, October 9, 1988, A-64.

———. "Street for Dr. King Endorsed by Council." *Record*, November 3, 1987, B-3.

Spectrum News Staff. "Alternate Side Parking Fines Set at $65 Citywide." *Spectrum News* (New York), February 20, 2020.

Spiegel, Robert. "A Negro Family Moves In: Homes Put Up for Sale." *Des Moines Tribune*, June 25, 1956, 1, 6.

Steimer, Jacob. "Do You Live in One of Memphis' Blackest, Whitest or Most Segregated Neighborhoods? Read This Story to Find Out." *MLK50: Justice Through Journalism* (Memphis, TN), August 6, 2021.

Struck, Jules. "Forced to Live Here, Forced to Leave: The Twin Injustices of I-81 and the Demolition of the 15th Ward." *Syracuse.com*, July 13, 2022.

Susaneck, Adam Paul. "American Road Deaths Show an Alarming Racial Gap." *New York Times*, last updated September 6, 2023.

Tankersley, Jim, and Zolan Kanno-Youngs. "Biden Seeks to Use Infrastructure Plan to Address Racial Inequities." *New York Times*, April 1, 2021.

Theen, Andrew. "Gentrification: Can Portland Give Displaced Residents a Path Back?" *The Oregonian/ OregonLive*, December 23, 2015.

Thomas, Jacqueline Rabe. "Trinity College Students' Analysis Finds State Far from Promises Made to Desegregate Hartford Schools." *Connecticut Mirror*, May 15, 2022.

Thompson, Nigel. "Fighting the Police Stop Disparity: New Pilot de-Prioritizing Lowest-Level Offenses Comes to Northwest Philly." *Al Día News* (Philadelphia, PA), October 12, 2021.

Torres, Kristen. "Alternate Side Parking Fines Increasing to $65 Citywide Starting Feb. 20." *Brooklyn Post*, February 19, 2020.

Tuss, Adam. "Virginia Decriminalizes Jaywalking." NBC4 Washington, January 5, 2021.

US Environmental Protection Agency, "Summary of the National Environmental Policy Act." EPA. Accessed September 9, 2023. https://www.epa.gov/laws-regulations/summary-national-environmental-policy -act.

Vock, Daniel C. "Why Would You Have a Highway Run Through a City?" *Governing*, June 26, 2014.

Walsh, James. "Why Was I-94 Built Through St. Paul's Rondo Neighborhood?" *Star Tribune* (Saint Paul, MN), December 18, 2020.

Whiteman, Omer, and Protective League. "Letter to the Editor." *Indianapolis News*, February 9, 1926, 6.

Winerip, Michael. "A City Struggles Over an Honor for Dr. King." *New York Times*, January 19, 1988, B1.

Woods, Baynard. "Maryland Accused of Race Discrimination Over Scrapping of Baltimore Rail Project." *Guardian* (Baltimore, MD), December 23, 2015.

Yu, Isaac. "Where the Sidewalk Mends." *New Haven Independent*, May 14, 2021.

Yuen, Laura. "Central Corridor: In the Shadow of Rondo." MPR News (Saint Paul, MN), April 29, 2010.

Zaretsky, Mark. "New Haven's Most Accident-Prone Roads: UConn Data Shows the Hot Spots." *New Haven Register*, September 4, 2021.

Zipper, David. "The High Cost of Bad Sidewalks." *Bloomberg*, June 16, 2020.

Interviews and Conversations

All In Indiana. *The History and Culture of Indiana Avenue.* WFYI Indianapolis, Feb. 24, 2021.

Anderson, Marvin (Rondo, Detroit, MI, community member and community advocate). Conversation with author.

Baskerville-Burrows, Jennifer (Indianapolis, IN, community member and member, Rethink Coalition Board of Directors). Conversation with author.

Blain-Spain, Cedric (Conway, SC, community member, reverend, and community advocate). Conversation with author.

Blair, Oni (Houston, TX, community advocate). Conversation with author.

Brooks, Jonathan (Houston, TX, community advocate). Conversation with author.

Brooks, Judith (Syracuse, NY, community member). Conversation with author.

Brooks, Paula (Indianapolis, IN, community member and community organizer). Conversation with author.

Bundles, A'Lelia (great-great-granddaughter of Madame C. J. Walker and member, Rethink Coalition Board of Directors). Conversation with author.

Finkle, Lester (former Title VI program coordinator for the Federal Highway Administration). Conversation with author.

Franklin, John Whittington (former Tulsa, OK, community member). Conversation with author.

Freije, Brenda Hacker (Indianapolis, IN, community member and executive director, Rethink Coalition). Conversation with author.

Hughes, Taylor (Indianapolis, IN, community member and member, Rethink Coalition Board of Directors). Conversation with author.

Hyatt, Susan (Indiana community member, professor, Indianapolis historian). Conversation with author.

Isom, Chervis (former Birmingham, AL, community member). Conversation with author.

Jacobs, Ellis (attorney with Advocates for Basic Legal Equality, Inc., filed Title VI complaint on behalf of Leaders for Equality and Action in Dayton [LEAD]). Conversation with author.

Jordan, Bobbi-Ann Hemingway (Conway, SC, community member). Conversation with author.

Keeter, Susan (Syracuse, NY, community member). Conversation with author.

Laws, Irma Hemingway (Conway, SC, community member). Conversation with author.

Moore, Justin Garrett (grandson of Robert Edwards, former Indianapolis, IN, community member). Conversation with author.

Moreland, Ronnie (Dayton, OH, community activist and former president of Leaders for Equality and Action in Dayton [LEAD]). Conversation with author.

Mullins, Paul (former Indianapolis, IN, community member, professor, and Indianapolis historian). Conversation with author.

Pete, Miz (Indianapolis, IN, community member). Conversation with author.

Peterson, Traci Hinton (Syracuse, NY, community member). Conversation with author.

Richardson, Charlie (Indianapolis, IN, community member and cochair, Rethink Coalition Board of Directors). Conversation with author.

Ridley, Thomas (Indianapolis, IN, community member). Conversation with author.

Ridley-Merriweather, Kathi (Indianapolis, IN, community member). Conversation with author.

Ryan, Jordan (Indianapolis, IN, community member and architectural historian). Conversation with author.

Sigel, Ines (Houston, TX, community advocate). Conversation with author.

Thompson, Ernest (Newport News, VA, community member). Conversation with author.

Williams, Christine (Conway, SC, community member). Conversation with author.

Wilson, Cynthia (former Toledo, OH, community member). Conversation with author.

Wilson, James (former Toledo, OH, community member). Conversation with author.

Young, Andrea (Atlanta, GA, community advocate). Conversation with author.

Cases

Alexander v. Sandoval, 532 U.S. 275 (2001).

Balt. Gas & Elec. Co. v. Nat. Res. Def. Council, Inc., 462 U.S. 87, 97–98 (1983).

Berman v. Parker, 348 U.S. 26 (1954).

Brown v. Bd. of Educ., 347 U.S. 483 (1954).

Buchanan v. Warley, 245 U.S. 60 (1917).

The Civil Rights Cases, 109 U.S. 3, 22 (1883).

Coal. for Advancement of Reg'l Transp. v. Fed. Highway Admin., 959 F. Supp. 2d 982, 1021 (W.D. Ky. 2013), aff'd, 576 F. App'x 477 (6th Cir. 2014).

Coal. of Concerned Citizens Against I-670 v. Damian, 608 F. Supp. 110 (S.D. Ohio 1984).

Erie CPR v. Pa. Dep't of Transp., 343 F. Supp. 3d 531, 548 (W.D. Pa. 2018).

Harden v. City of Atlanta, 93 S.E. 338, 403 (Ga. 1917).

Indigenous Envtl. Network v. U.S. Dep't of State, 347 F. Supp. 3d 561 (D. Mont. 2018).

Karlen v. Harris, 590 F.2d 39 (2d Cir. 1978).

Memphis v. Greene, 451 U.S. 100 (1981).

Morgan v. Virginia, 328 U.S. 373 (1946).

Nashville I-40 Steering Comm. v. Ellington, 387 F.2d 179 (6th Cir. 1967).

Plessy v. Ferguson, 163 U.S. 537 (1896).

Robertson v. Methow Valley Citizens Council, 490 U.S. 332, 351 (1989).

Standing Rock Sioux Tribe v. U.S. Army Corps of Eng'rs, 301 F. Supp. 3d 50 (D.D.C. 2018).

Strycker's Bay Neighborhood Council, Inc. v. Karlen, 444 U.S. 223 (1980) (per curiam).

Town of Henrietta v. Dep't. of Envtl. Conservation, 430 N.Y.S.2d 440, 446 (App. Div. 1980).

Utahns for Better Transp. v. U.S. Dep't of Transp., 305 F.3d 1152 (10th Cir. 2002).

Washington v. Davis, 426 U.S. 229 (1976).

Women's Equity Action League v. Cavazos, 906 F.2d 742, 748 (D.C. Cir. 1990).

Litigation Documents

Brief for Plaintiff in Error at 29, Plessy v. Ferguson, 163 U.S. 537 (1896).

Brief for Respondents Ellington and Speight in Opposition, On Petition for a Writ of Certiorari to the United States Court of Appeals for the Sixth Circuit, Nashville I-40 Steering Comm. v. Ellington, 390 U.S. 921 (1968) (No. 995).

Complaint at ¶¶ 4–14, Kelly v. McKinney, No. 5:10-cv-01693-DEW-MLH (W.D. La. Nov. 8, 2010), ECF No. 1–3.

Complaint at 29–31, Erie CPR v. Pa. Dep't of Transp., 343 F. Supp. 3d 531 (W.D. Pa. 2018).

Complaint Filed under Title VI of the Civil Rights Act of 1964, Leaders for Equality and Action, Inc. (LEAD) v. City of Beavercreek (Aug. 10, 2011).

Complaint Pursuant to Title VI of the Civil Rights Act of 1964 at 11–12, Balt. Reg'l Initiative Developing Genuine Equal., Inc. v. Maryland (U.S. Dep't. of Transp. Departmental Off. C.R., Fed. Highway Admin. Off. C.R. 2015).

Fed. Highway Admin., Off. of C.R., Letter from Associate Administrator for Civil Rights, DOT #2012–0020 (June 26, 2013) (determination).

Fixing America's Surface Transportation (FAST) Act, Pub. L. No. 114–94, §§ 1101, 1104, 129 Stat. 1312, 1322–25, 1329–32 (2015).

Oral Findings of Fact and Conclusions of Law of District Court, Nashville I-40 Steering Comm. v. Ellington, No. 67–18288 (M.D. Tenn. Nov. 1st, 1967).

Petition for Writ of Certiorari, Nashville I-40 Steering Comm. v. Ellington, 390 U.S. 921 (No. 995).

U.S. Dep't. of Transp., Dismissal of Complaint DOT #2017–00387 (Aug. 28, 2018).

U.S. Dep't. of Transp., Dismissal of Complaint DOT #2018–0133 (June 13, 2018).

U.S. Dep't. of Transp., Dismissal of Complaint DOT #2018–0166 (Aug. 28, 2018).

U.S. Dep't. of Transp., Dismissal of Complaint DOT #2018–0235 (June 22, 2018).

U.S. Dep't. of Transp., FHWA Decision Letter (June 26, 2013).

U.S. Dep't. of Transp., Letter of Finding DOT #2015–0124 (Jan. 18, 2017).

U.S. Dep't. of Transp., Voluntary Resolution Agreement (Dec. 17, 2015).

Evans v. Tubbe

Amended Answer to First Amended Complaint, Evans v. Tubbe, No. TY–79–201-CA (E.D. Tex. Dec. 17, 1979).

Answer to Complaint, Evans v. Tubbe, No. TY–79–201-CA (E.D. Tex. June 25, 1979).

Civil Docket Continuation Sheet, Evans v. Tubbe, No. TY–79–201-CA (E.D. Tex. n.d.).

Complaint, Evans v. Tubbe, No. TY–79–201-CA (E.D. Tex. May 30, 1979).

Defendant's Requested Instruction No. 1, Evans v. Tubbe, No. TY–79–201-CA (E.D. Tex. May 13, 1982).

Defendant's Requested Instruction No. 2, Evans v. Tubbe, No. TY–79–201-CA (E.D. Tex. May 13, 1982).

Demand for Jury Trial, Evans v. Tubbe, No. TY–79–201-CA (E.D. Tex. June 14, 1979).

Deposition of Blanton L. Dickerson, Evans v. Tubbe, No. TY–79–201-CA (E.D. Tex. Feb. 2, 1981).

Deposition of Odie v. Evans, Evans v. Tubbe, No. TY–79–201-CA (E.D. Tex. Feb. 2, 1981).

First Amended Complaint, Evans v. Tubbe, No. TY–79–201-CA (E.D. Tex. Nov. 21, 1979).

Judgment, Evans v. Tubbe, No. 81–2072 (5th Cir. Oct. 7, 1981).

Judgment, Evans v. Tubbe, No. TY–79–201-CA (E.D. Tex. June 29, 1982).

Juror List, Evans v. Tubbe, No. TY–79–201-CA (E.D. Tex. May 10, 1982).

Motion in Limine, Evans v. Tubbe, No. TY–79–201-CA (E.D. Tex. Feb. 4, 1981).

Motion to Dismiss for Lack of Jurisdiction over Subject Matter, Evans v. Tubbe, No. TY–79–201-CA (E.D. Tex. Feb. 2, 1981).

Notice of Appeal, Evans v. Tubbe, No. TY–79–201-CA (E.D. Tex. Feb. 25, 1981).

Order, Evans v. Tubbe, No. TY–79–201-CA (E.D. Tex. Feb. 4, 1981).

Plaintiffs' Proposed Court's Instructions to the Jury, Evans v. Tubbe, No. TY–79–201-CA (E.D. Tex. Feb. 2, 1981).

Plaintiffs' Proposed Jury Instructions, Evans v. Tubbe, No. TY–79–201-CA (E.D. Tex. May 13, 1982).

Plaintiffs' Proposed Pre-Trial Order, Evans v. Tubbe, No. TY–79–201-CA (E.D. Tex. Feb. 1, 1982).

Plaintiffs' Proposed Pre-Trial Order, Evans v. Tubbe, No. TY–79–201-CA (E.D. Tex. May 13, 1982).

Proceedings, Evans v. Tubbe, No. TY–79–201-CA (E.D. Tex. Feb. 25, 1981).

Proceedings, Evans v. Tubbe, No. TY–79–201-CA (E.D. Tex. n.d.).

Proposed Pre-Trial Orders, Evans v. Tubbe, No. TY–79–201-CA (E.D. Tex. Feb. 4, 1981).

Verdict of the Jury, Evans v. Tubbe, No. TY–79–201-CA (E.D. Tex. May 14, 1982).

Jennings v. Patterson

Amended Complaint, Jennings v. Patterson, No. 894-E (M.D. Ala. n.d.).

Amended Complaint, Jennings v. Patterson, No. 894-E (M.D. Ala. Oct. 12, 1972).

Amended Judgment, Jennings v. Patterson, No. 894-E (M.D. Ala. Apr. 29, 1974).

Answer to Amended Complaint, Jennings v. Patterson, No. 894-E (M.D. Ala. Oct. 25, 1972).

Answer to Complaint, Jennings v. Patterson, No. 894-E (M.D. Ala. Mar. 15, 1972).

Answer to Complaint, Jennings v. Patterson, No. 894-E (M.D. Ala. Mar. 16, 1972).

Civil Docket, Jennings v. Patterson, No. 894-E (M.D. Ala. Feb. 28, 1973).

Complaint, Jennings v. Patterson, No. 894-E (M.D. Ala. Apr. 23, 1971).

Decree, Jennings v. Patterson, No. 894-E (M.D. Ala. Dec. 21, 1972).

Interrogatories to the Jury, Jennings v. Patterson, No. 894-E (M.D. Ala. Nov. 6, 1972).

Judgment, Jennings v. Patterson, 488 F.2d 436 (5th Cir. 1974) (No. 73–1541).

Letter from Chester Jennings to Hill, Jones & Farrington (Apr. 29, 1971), Jennings v. Patterson, No. 894-E (M.D. Ala. Apr. 29, 1971).

Letter from Fletcher Farrington to Robert E. Varner, Judge, U.S. District Court for the Middle District of Alabama (Nov. 9, 1972), Jennings v. Patterson, No. 894-E (M.D. Ala. Nov. 10, 1972).

Letter from Michael I. Kent to Hon. Robert E. Varner, Judge, U.S. District Court for the Middle District of Alabama (Apr. 29, 1974), Jennings v. Patterson, No. 894-E (M.D. Ala. Apr. 29, 1974).

Letter from Michael I. Kent to Hon. Robert E. Varner, Judge, U.S. District Court for the Middle District of Alabama (Apr. 29, 1974), Jennings v. Patterson, No. 894-E (M.D. Ala. Apr. 30, 1974).

Letter from Michael I. Kent to Hon. Robert E. Varner, Judge, U.S. District Court for the Middle District of Alabama (Oct. 18, 1972), Jennings v. Patterson, No. 894-E (M.D. Ala. Oct. 20, 1972).

Letter from Robert E. Varner, Judge, U.S. District Court for the Middle District of Alabama to Fletcher Farrington, Michael I. Kent, and Charles R. Adair, Jr. (Mar. 6, 1974), Jennings v. Patterson, No. 894-E (M.D. Ala. Mar. 6, 1974).

Letter from Robert E. Varner, Judge, U.S. District Court for the Middle District of Alabama to Michael I. Kent (May 3, 1974), Jennings v. Patterson, No. 894-E (M.D. Ala. May 3, 1974).

Motion for Leave to File Amended Complaint, Jennings v. Patterson, No. 894-E (M.D. Ala. Oct. 7, 1972).

Motion for Leave to File Second Amended Complaint, Jennings v. Patterson, No. 894-E (M.D. Ala. Oct. 26, 1972).

Motion to Alter Judgment, Jennings v. Patterson, No. 894-E (M.D. Ala. Jan. 2, 1973).

Motion to Dismiss, Jennings v. Patterson, No. 894-E (M.D. Ala. May 4, 1971).

Motion to Dismiss, Jennings v. Patterson, No. 894-E (M.D. Ala. May 6, 1971).

Motion to Modify Pre-Trial Order, Jennings v. Patterson, No. 894-E (M.D. Ala. Oct. 24, 1972).

Order, Jennings v. Patterson, No. 894-E (M.D. Ala. Apr. 22, 1974).

Order, Jennings v. Patterson, No. 894-E (M.D. Ala. Jan. 2, 1973).

Order, Jennings v. Patterson, No. 894-E (M.D. Ala. Jun. 8, 1971).

Plaintiffs' Pre-Trial Submission, Jennings v. Patterson, No. 894-E (M.D. Ala. n.d.).

Plaintiffs' Pre-Trial Memorandum, Jennings v. Patterson, No. 894-E (M.D. Ala. Nov. 1, 1972).

Satisfaction of Judgment for Costs, Jennings v. Patterson, No. 894-E (M.D. Ala. May 23, 1974).

Stipulation, Jennings v. Patterson, No. 894-E (M.D. Ala. Apr. 22, 1974).

Writ of Injunction, Jennings v. Patterson, No. 894-E (M.D. Ala. Apr. 22, 1974).

Steele v. City of Port Wentworth

Answer of the City of Port Wentworth, Georgia, Steele v. City of Port Wentworth, 2008 WL 717813 (S.D. Ga. Mar. 17, 2008) (No. CV405–135).

Complaint—Class Action, Steele v. City of Port Wentworth, 2008 WL 717813 (S.D. Ga. Mar. 17, 2008) (No. CV405–135).

Defendant's Brief in Support of Summary Judgment Motion, Steele v. City of Port Wentworth, 2008 WL 717813 (S.D. Ga. Mar. 17, 2008) (No. CV405–135).

Defendant's Reply to Plaintiffs Memorandum in Opposition to Defendant's Motion for Summary Judgment, Steele v. City of Port Wentworth, 2008 WL 717813 (S.D. Ga. Mar. 17, 2008) (No. CV405–135).

Memorandum of Understanding, Lawyers' Committee for Civil Rights Under Law (July 24, 2009).

Order on Special Master's Report on Petitioner's Motion for Partial Summary Judgment, City of Port Wentworth v. Steele, No. CV09–2440-FR (Super. Ct. E. Jud. Cir. Ga. Jan. 29, 2013).

Plaintiffs' Memorandum in Opposition to Defendant's Motion for Summary Judgment, Steele v. City of Port Wentworth, 2008 WL 717813 (S.D. Ga. Mar. 17, 2008) (No. CV405–135).

Report and Recommendation of the Special Master on Petitioner's Motion for Partial Summary Judgment, City of Port Wentworth v. Steele, No. CV09–2440-FR (Super. Ct. Chatham Cty. June 26, 2012).

Papers and Reports

An Analysis of Traffic Fatalities by Race and Ethnicity, 13. Washington, DC: Governors Highway Safety Association, June 2021.

A Citizen's Guide to NEPA: Having Your Voice Heard, 2. Council on Environmental Quality, 2007.

Anderson, Susan Willoughby. "The Part on Trial: The Sixteenth Street Baptist Church Bombing, Civil Rights Memory and the Remaking of Birmingham," 91. PhD diss., University of North Carolina at Chapel Hill, 2008.

Armstrong, Anthony, and Make Communities. *Deconstructing Segregation in Syracuse? The Fate of I-81 and the Future of One of New York State's Highest Poverty Communities*. Poverty and Race Research Action Council, 2018.

Brinckerhoff, Parsons, with Fitzgerald & Halliday, Inc. *Whalley Avenue Corridor Study*, 2–15. New Haven, CT: South Central Regional Council of Governments, December 2010.

Chicago Commission on Race Relations. *The Negro in Chicago: A Study of Race Relations and a Race Riot*. University of Chicago Press, 1922.

City of New Haven Complete Streets Design Manual. New Haven, CT: City of New Haven, September 7, 2010.

Citywide Active Transportation Plan, 17. New Haven, CT: Safe Routes for All New Haven, June 2022.

Clark, Hugh M., and CJI Research Corporation. *Who Rides Public Transportation*, 22. Washington, DC: American Public Transportation Association (2017).

Clarke, Gilmore D., and Michael Rapuano. *Report on the Inter-State Controlled-Access Highway System*. Davidson County, Tennessee, September 30, 1955 (on file with Metropolitan Nashville Planning Commission).

Dallas Sidewalk Master Plan: Final Report, 7. Dallas, TX: City of Dallas, June 2021.

De Leuw, Cather & Co. *Ensley-Pratt City Urban Renewal Study*. Chicago: August 1958.

de Moura, Maria Cecilia Pinto, and David Reichmuth. *Inequitable Exposure to Air Pollution from Vehicles in the Northeast and Mid-Atlantic*. Cambridge, MA: Union of Concerned Scientists, June 21, 2019.

Department of Justice Report Regarding the Criminal Investigation into the Shooting Death of Michael Brown by Ferguson, Missouri Police Officer Darren Wilson, 5–8. Washington, DC: US Department of Justice, March 4, 2015.

Eaton, Susan. *A Steady Habit of Segregation: The Origins and Continuing Harm of the Separate and Unequal Housing and Public Schools in Metropolitan Hartford, Connecticut*. NAACP Legal Defense and Educational Fund, Open Communities Alliance, Poverty & Race Research Action Council, and Sillerman Center at Brandeis University, 2020.

Environmental Justice: Guidance Under the National Environmental Policy Act, 9. Washington, DC: Council on Environmental Quality, 1997.

Finkle, Lester. *Beavercreek Investigative Report*. Washington, DC: US Department of Transportation, July 20, 2012.

Ford, Hubert James. "Interstate 40 Through North Nashville, Tennessee: A Case Study in Highway Location Decision Making," 34–36. Unpublished master's thesis, University of Tennessee, 1970.

Foxx, Anthony. *Beyond Traffic 2045*, 95. US. Department of Transportation, 2017.

Fullilove, Mindy Thompson. *Eminent Domain and African Americans: What Is the Price of the Commons?: Perspectives on Eminent Domain Abuse.* Institute for Justice, 2015.

Glassbrenner, Donna, Gabrielle Herbert, Leah Reish, Caitlin Webb, and Tonja Lindsey. *Evaluating Disparities in Traffic Fatalities by Race, Ethnicity, and Income*, Report No. DOT HS 813 188, at 21. Washington, DC: National Highway Traffic Safety Administration, September 2022.

Gutierrez, Roberto, et al. *Baltimore Metro: An Initiative and Outcome in Rapid Public Transportation*, 19. Johns Hopkins University, 1990.

Guzman, Gloria, and Melissa Kollar. *U.S. Census Bureau, Income in the United States: 2022*, Report No. P60-279, at 1. Washington, DC: US Census Bureau, September 12, 2023.

Journey to the Past. New York Transit Museum, December 2019.

Krolikowski, Aaron, and Sam Magavern. *Working Toward Equality, Updated: Race, Employment, and Public Transportation in Erie County.* Partnership for the Public Good, July 2017.

Love, Hanna, and Jennifer S. Vey. *To Build Safe Streets, We Need to Address Racism in Urban Design.* Washington, DC: Brookings Institute, August 28, 2019.

Melton, Courtnee. *How Transportation Impacts Public Health*, 2. Sycamore Institute, 2017.

Millsap, Adam A. *How the Gem City Lost Its Luster and How It Can Get It Back: A Case Study of Dayton, Ohio.* Fairfax, VA: Mercatus Center at George Mason University, January 16, 2018.

Mohl, Raymond A. *The Interstates and the Cities: Highways, Housing, and the Freeway Revolt.* Poverty & Race Research Action Council, Civil Rights Research, 2002.

Neff, John. *APTA Primer on Transit Funding: The Fixing America's Surface Transportation Act and Other Related Laws, FY 2016 Through 2020*, 14, 16. Washington, DC: American Public Transportation Association, 2016.

Neighborhood Residents and Youth. *Newhallville and Dixwell Neighborhood Community Index: A Project by Neighborhood Residents and Youth*, 43. New Haven, CT: DataHaven, August 2019.

Partnership Project, Grand Canyon Trust, and Environmental Law Institute. *NEPA Success Stories: Celebrating 40 Years of Transparency and Open Government.* Washington, DC: Environmental Law Institute, 2010.

Piper, Craig S. "The Civil Rights Movement in Starkville, Mississippi: A Local Struggle for Equality." Master's thesis, Mississippi State University, May 1993. ProQuest (1353409).

Pittsburgh, PA Demonstration Project: Lincoln and Frankstown Avenues. Washington, DC: Smart Growth America, July 29, 2019.

Posey, Kirby G. *Household Income in States and Metropolitan Areas: 2022*, Report No. ACSBR-017, at 3. Washington, DC: US Census Bureau, December 2023.

Purnell, Jason, Gabriela Camberos, and Robert Fields. *For the Sake of All*, 29. St. Louis: Washington University in St. Louis and Saint Louis University, 2014.

Ratcliffe, Caroline, Elaine Waxman, Cary Lou, Hannah Hassani, and Victoria Tran. *Disrupting Food Insecurity: Steps Communities Can Take*, 8, 12–13. Urban Institute, 2019.

Ringelstein, Kevin Lang. "Residential Segregation in Norfolk, Virginia: How the Federal Government Reinforced Racial Division in a Southern City, 1914–1959." Master's dissertation, Old Dominion University, December 2015. ProQuest (1605336).

Sanchez, Thomas W., Rich Stolz, and Jacinta S. Ma. *Moving to Equity: Addressing Inequitable Effects of Transportation Policies on Minorities.* Cambridge, MA: Civil Rights Project and Harvard University and Center for Community Change, 2003.

Sandt, Laura, Tabitha Combs, and Jesse Cohn. *Pursuing Equity in Pedestrian and Bicycle Planning*, 8. Chapel Hill, NC: Pedestrian & Bicycle Information Center, March 2016.

Transit Equity & Environmental Health in Baltimore City. Baltimore: Johns Hopkins Bloomberg School of Public Health and Baltimore Transit Equity Coalition, September 2021.

Underwriting Manual: The Underwriting and Valuation Procedure Under Title II of the National Housing Act. Washington, DC: Federal Housing Administration, February 1938.

US Department of Justice, Civil Rights Division. *Investigation of the Ferguson Police Department*, 4–5. Washington, DC: US Department of Justice, March 4, 2015.

Van Eyken, Chris. *Safety for All*. Transit Center, July 2021.

Venson, Ebony, Abigail Grimminger, and Stephen Kenny. *Dangerous by Design 2022*, 27, 30. Washington, DC: Smart Growth America, July 2022.

Whitten, Samuel. *The Atlanta Zone Plan: Report Outlining a Tentative Zone Plan for Atlanta, City of Atlanta City Planning Commission*. Atlanta: City of Atlanta City Planning Commission, 1922.

Other Sources

"1919: The Race Riot." Chicago Historical Homicide Project. Accessed February 24, 2024. https://homicide.northwestern.edu/crimes/raceriot/.

"2020 Decennial Census, table no. P1." US Census Bureau. Accessed February 24, 2024. https://data.census.gov/table/DECENNIALPL2020.P1?g=160XX00US0908000.

"AB403 Overview." Nevada Legislature. Accessed February 24, 2024. https://www.leg.state.nv.us/App/NELIS/REL/81st2021/Bill/8028/Overview.

American Community Survey. "2022 American Community Survey 5-Year Estimates, table no. S1901." US Census Bureau.

Barkow, Rachel E. *Statement of Rachel E. Barkow Before the United States Sentencing Commission*, 28. US Sentencing Commission. 2009.

Brown, Julia ("Aunt Sally"). "Ah Always Had a Hard Time." By Federal Writers' Project of the Works Progress Administration. *Slave Narratives: A Folk History of Slavery in the United States from Interviews with Former Slaves: Georgia Narratives, Adams-Furr*, vol. 4, no. 1 (1936–1938), 143.

Castro, Julián (Secretary, Department of Housing and Urban Development), John B. King Jr. (Secretary, Department of Education), and Anthony R. Foxx (Secretary, Department of Transportation). "Dear Colleague Letter: Regarding Mobility via Education and Socioeconomic Opportunity." Press release, June 3, 2016.

Claxton, Kevin. "Californians Win the Freedom to Walk!" CalBike, October 3, 2022.

Common Council of the City of Indianapolis, Indiana. "General Ordinance No. 15." Reprinted in *Journal of the Common Council of the City of Indianapolis, Indiana*, 53. Indianapolis, IN: Common Council of the City of Indianapolis, Indiana, March 15, 1926.

Eplan, Leon S. "Background Remarks before the Metropolitan Atlanta Conference on Equality of Opportunity in Housing," 5. May 29, 1968. Transcript available at Southern Regional Council Papers, 9:201:19, Woodruff Library, Atlanta University, Atlanta, GA.

"Frequently Asked Questions, Preference Policy." City of Portland. Accessed February 23, 2024. https://www.portland.gov/phb/nnehousing/preference-policy/faq.

Gratton, Charles. "Get Off the Sidewalk," in *Remembering Jim Crow: Bitter Times*. American Radio-Works. November 2001.

Griffith, D. W., dir. *The Birth of a Nation*. 1915; Kino Classics, 2011. DVD.

Hearings on Uniform Relocation Assistance and Land Acquisition Policies Before the House Commission on Public Works, 91st Cong. 502 (1970) (testimony of Yale Rabin).

Hughes, Franklin. "William Mahone." Jim Crow Museum, Ferris State University. September 2017.

"Jim Crow Laws." Martin Luther King, Jr. National Historical Park, National Park Service, US Department of the Interior.

Kirwan Institute for the Study of Race and Ethnicity. "Free to Ride: The Documentary." Ohio State University, 2014.

Kleinjung, Jennifer. "Rondo Neighborhood & I-94: Overview." Gale Family Library, Minnesota Historical Society.

Lee, Richard C. "Annual State of City Message to Board of Aldermen." February 4, 1957. Box 15, folder 2, MS 1970 of City and Regional Planning Collection, Manuscripts and Archives, Yale University Library.

Miscellaneous Reports and Lists Relating to Murders and Outrages, March 1867–November 1868. New Orleans: Bureau of Refugees, Freedmen and Abandoned Lands, March 9, 1867. Microfilm, Washington, DC: National Archives and Records Service, M1027, Roll 34, Records Relating to Murders and Outrages.

"Most to Least Segregated Cities." Othering and Belonging Institute.

Nelson, Robert K., LaDale Winling, Richard Marciano, and N. D. B. Connolly. "Mapping Inequality: Redlining in New Deal America." Mapping Inequality.

Petruzzello, Melissa. "Chicago Race Riot of 1919." *Encyclopaedia Britannica*. Last updated February 9, 2024. https://www.britannica.com/event/Chicago-Race-Riot-of-1919.

President's Advisory Committee on a National Highway Program. *Hearing Before the President's Advisory Committee on a National Highway Program*, 48 (October 7, 1954) (statement of Robert Moses, City Construction Co-ordinator of New York City).

"Registered Reports of Murders and Outrages, Sept. 1866–July 1867." In *Records of the Assistant Commissioner for the State of Texas Bureau of Refugees, Freedmen and Abandoned Lands 1865–1869*. Washington, DC: National Archives and Records Service, 1983. Microfilm, M821, Roll 32.

Retained Copy of Report Relative to Treatment of Freedmen Bureau Refugees, Freedmen and Abandoned Lands for Arkansas and Indian Territory. Little Rock, AR: Bureau of Refugees, Freedmen and Abandoned Lands, November 24, 1866. Microfilm, Washington DC: National Archives and Records Service, M979, Roll 52.

Sanders, Vikki, and Remember Rondo Committee. "Profile of a Visionary: Interview with Roger Anderson," in *Remember Rondo: A Tradition of Excellence*, 26–27. Bethel University, 1995.

Sanford, John W. A. *The Code of the City of Montgomery: Prepared in Pursuance of an Order of the City Council of Montgomery*. Gaines & Smith, 1861.

Seaberry, Camille. "Connecticut City Neighborhood Profiles." DataHaven. March 9, 2020.

"Sidewalk Replacement Program." City of Dallas. https://dallascityhall.com/departments/public-works/Pages/SidewalkReplacementProgram.aspx.

Tarter, Brent. "The Readjuster Party." Encyclopedia Virginia. Last updated September 22, 2023.

US Congress. Economic Research Service, US Department of Agriculture. *Access to Affordable and Nutritious Food: Measuring and Understanding Food Deserts and Their Consequences: Report to Congress*, 35 (2009).

US Department of Transportation, Federal Highway Administration. *Guidance on Environmental Justice and NEPA* (2011).

Congressional Record

Appendix. 84th Cong., 1st sess., *Congressional Record (Daily Edition)* 101, A219.

House Debated H.R. 7474. 84th Cong., 1st sess., Congressional Record (Daily Edition) 101 (1955), 9945.

House Rejected H.R. 7474 by Roll Call Vote. 84th Cong., 1st sess., Congressional Record (Daily Edition) 101 (July 27, 1955), 10121–10122.

Mr. Becker's Remarks on Need for Highway Legislation. 84th Cong., 1st sess., Congressional Record (Daily Edition) 101 (August 1, 1955), 10953.

Mr. Case's Proposal to Authorize an Expanded Highway Program by an Amendment to H.R. 6417. 84th Cong., 1st sess., Congressional Record (Daily Edition) 101 (July 29, 1955), 10468.

Mr. Case's Statement upon Introduction S. 1573. 84th Cong., 1st sess., Congressional Record (Daily Edition) 101 (March 28, 1955).

Mr. Mack's Remarks on Taxing Highway Users. 84th Cong., 1st sess., Congressional Record (Daily Edition) 101 (July 1, 1955), 8334.

Mr. McGregor's Remarks on Urgency of Highway Program. 84th Cong., 1st sess., Congressional Record (Daily Edition) 101 (March 28, 1955), 3293.

Mr. Robertson's Speech on Highway Refinancing by the Federal Government. 84th Cong., 1st sess., Congressional Record (Daily Edition) 101 (February 1, 1955), 887–91.

Mr. Sieminski's Remarks on Proposed Highway Legislation. 84th Cong., 1st sess., Congressional Record (Daily Edition) 101 (July 11, 1955), 8819–20.

Presidential Message on the Nation's Highway System. 84th Cong., 1st sess., Congressional Record (Daily Edition) 101 (February 22, 1955), 1606–7.

Remarks of Mr. Kerr and Mr. O'Mahoney on Proposed Highway Finance Corporation during Debate on Tax Rate Extension Act of 1955. 84th Cong., 1st sess., Congressional Record (Daily Edition) 101 (March 10, 1955), 2185–86.

Senate Debated S. 1048. 84th Cong., 1st sess., Congressional Record (Daily Edition) 101 (May 19, 1955), 5642.

Senate Passed S. 1048. 84th Cong., 1st sess., Congressional Record (Daily Edition) 101 (May 25, 1956), 6022.

US Congress. House. Amending and Supplementing the Federal-Aid Road Act, Approved July 11, 1916 (39 Stat. 355), as Amended and Supplemented, to Authorize Appropriations for Continuing the Construction of Highways: Report (to Accompany H.R. 7474). 84th Cong., 1st sess., 1955. H. Rep. 1336.

US Congress. House. Federal-Aid Highway and Highway Revenue Acts of 1956: Conference Report (to accompany H.R. 10660). 84th Cong., 2d sess., 1956. H. Rep. 2436.

US Congress. House. Federal Highway and Highway Revenue Acts of 1956: Report (to Accompany H.R. 10660). 84th Cong., 2d sess., 1956. H. Rep. 2022.

US Congress. House. Highway Revenue Act of 1956: Report (to Accompany H.R. 9075). 84th Cong., 2d sess., 1956. H. Rep. 1899.

US Congress. Senate. Federal-Aid Highway Act of 1955: Report (to Accompany S. 1048). 84th Cong., 1st sess., 1955. S. Rep. 350.

US Congress. Senate. Federal-Aid Highway Act of 1956: Report (to Accompany H.R. 10660). 84th Cong., 2d sess., 1956. S. Rep. 1965.

US Congress. Senate. *Report on the Condition of the South*, by Carl Schurz, 20. 39th Cong., 1st. sess., December 19, 1865.

US Congress. Senate. To Amend and Supplement the Federal-Aid Road Act Approved July 11, 1916, to Authorize Appropriations for Continuing the Construction of Highways; to Amend the Internal Revenue Code of 1954 to Provide Additional Revenue from the Taxes on Motor Fuel, Tires, and Trucks and Buses: Report (to Accompany H.R. 10660). 84th Cong., 2d sess., 1956. S. Rep. 2054.

Presidential Remarks

US President. *Excerpt on Highways* from *Final Report of the Commission on Intergovernmental Relations.* 84th Cong., 1st sess., June 28, 1955. H. Doc. 198, 211–20.

US President. *Message from the President of the United States Relative to a National Highway Program.* 84th Cong., 1st sess., February 22, 1955. H. Doc. 93.

Statutes, Codes, and Ordinances

Baltimore, Md., Ordinance 692 (May 15, 1911).

Birmingham, Ala., General Code § 35–859 (Separation of Races) (1944).

Conn. Gen. Stat. § 2–24b (2018).

Iowa Code Ann. § 2.56 (2019).

N.J. Rev. Stat. § 2C:48B-2 (2017).

Or. Rev. Stat. § 137.683 (2019).

Va. Code Ann. § 30–19.1:13 (2021).

Notes

Introduction: The Other Side of the Tracks

5 **only fifteen of its 169 municipalities:** U.S. Census Bureau, 2010 Decennial Census, summary file 2, PCT 5; Open Communities Alliance, *A Stead Habit of Segregation: The Origins and Continuing Harm of the Separate and Unequal Housing and Public Schools in Metropolitan Hartford, Connecticut* (2020), 7.

5 **many residents lack access:** Joseph De Avila, "Hartford Highlights a State's Divide," *Wall Street Journal*, September 30, 2012; Jacqueline Rabe Thomas, "Trinity College Students' Analysis Finds State Far From Promises Made to Desegregate Hartford Schools," *CT Mirror*, May 15, 2022; Emily DiSalvo, "Greater Hartford's Race and Economic Disparities 'More Pronounced,' Report Shows," *CT Insider*, March 16, 2023.

7 **freeway was routed through Sugar Hill:** Stanley G. Robertson, "L.A. Confidential: Will New Freeway Affect Us?" *L.A. Sentinel*, October 27, 1966.

7 **"This Nigger Voted":** *Effigy Strung Up by the Ku Klux Klan, Miami, Florida, 1940,* photograph, Georgia State University Library Digital Collection.

8 **"usually in cities each street":** W. E. B. Du Bois, *The Souls of Black Folk* (A. C. McClurg, 1903), 125.

9 **the freedom to move:** The passages on the historic relationship between Black people and mobility draw on the following books and articles: Elizabeth Stordeur Pryor, *Colored Travelers: Mobility and the Fight for Citizenship Before the Civil War* (University of North Carolina Press, 2016); Sally E. Hadden, *Slave Patrols: Law and Violence in Virginia and the Carolinas* (Harvard University Press, 2001); Tera Hunter, *To 'Joy My Freedom: Southern Black Women's Lives and Labors After the Civil War* (Harvard University Press, 1998); Leon F. Litwak, *Been in the Storm So Long: The Aftermath of Slavery* (Vintage Books, 1979); Justin S. Conroy, " 'Show Me Your Papers': Race and Street Encounters," *National Black Law Journal* 19, no. 2 (2007): 149; A. Leon Higginbotham Jr., *In the Matter of Color: Race and the American Legal Process* (Oxford University Press, 1978); Eric Foner, *Nothing but Freedom: Emancipation and Its Legacy* (Louisiana State University Press, 2007); Richard C. Wade, *Slavery in the Cities: The South 1820–1860* (Oxford University Press, 1967); Aaron Hall, "Slaves of the State: Infrastructure and Governance through Slavery in the Antebellum South," *Journal of American History* 106, no. 1 (2019): 19; William G. Thomas et al., "Reconstructing African American Mobility after Emancipation, 1865–1867," *Social Science History* 41, no. 4 (2017): 673.

10 **Black people were confined:** Pryor, *Colored Travelers*, 46.

11 **"the local 'niggertown' ":** Richard Rothstein, *The Color of Law: The Forgotten History of How Our Government Segregated America* (Liveright, 2017), 128.

11 **"a wonderfully versatile and self-contained society":** Coleman Young and Lonnie Wheeler, *Hard Stuff: The Autobiography of Coleman Young* (Viking, 1994), 143–44; Bill McGraw, "Bringing Detroit's Black Bottom Back to (Virtual) Life," *Detroit Free Press*, February 27, 2017; Beenish Ahmed, "Historical Marker Commemorates Demolished Black Bottom Neighborhood in Detroit," *Michigan Public*, August 9, 2021. The following passages about Black Bottom draw from these sources.

12 **it can never bring back all that was lost:** Johnny Miller, "Roads to Nowhere: How Infrastruc-
ture Built on American Inequality," *Guardian*, February 21, 2018; Warren C. Evans, "Opinion:
Demolition of I-375 Can Never Erase the Sins of the Past," *Detroit Free Press*, September 19, 2022;
Noelle Gray, "Detroit Marks Black Bottom Neighborhood Lost When I-375 Built," *Detroit News*,
August 9, 2021.

14 **Dr. Martin Luther King Jr. and Rev. Ralph Abernathy:** Jonathan Eig, *King: A Life* (Farrar,
Straus and Giroux, 2023).

15 **I-94 destroyed:** James Walsh, "Why Was I-94 Built Through St. Paul's Rondo Neighborhood?"
Star Tribune, December 18, 2020.

15 **thousands of protesters occupied I-94:** Mara H. Gottfried, "1,500 Protesters March from Capitol onto I-94 in St. Paul for about 1 Hour," *Twin Cities Pioneer Press*, May 31, 2020.

15 **Just four years earlier:** Merrit Kennedy, "Hundreds Protest After Minnesota Officer Found Not
Guilty in Philando Castile Death," National Public Radio, June 16, 2017; Roby Brock, "Protest in
Little Rock Turns Confrontational with I-630 Shut Down, Property Damage," Little Rock Public
Radio, May 31, 2020; Faith Woodard, "The Black History Lost in Little Rock After I-630's Devel-
opment," THV11, February 15, 2023; Katherine Burgess, "For 6 days, Memphis Protests Have
Remained Mostly Peaceful," *Memphis Commercial Appeal*, June 2, 2020; Raymond A. Mohl, "Citi-
zen Activism and Freeway Revolts in Memphis and Nashville: The Road to Litigation," *Journal of
Urban History* 40, no. 5 (2014): 870, 880.

15 **In Little Rock, Arkansas:** Brock, "Protest in Little Rock"; Woodard, "The Black History Lost."

15 **In Memphis, Tennessee:** Burgess, "For 6 days, Memphis Protests"; Mohl, "Citizen Activism,"
880.

15 **in Cincinnati, Ohio:** Sarah Walsh, "Protesters Continued March After Dark, Disruptions Escalated Downtown Friday Night," WCPO, May 29, 2020; Sharon Coolidge and Dan Horn, "Cincinnati Leaders to Apologize for Destruction of Black Neighborhood in 1950s," *Cincinnati Enquirer*,
June 13, 2023.

Chapter 1: Killing Two Birds with One Stone

18 **The law that would:** Passages discussing the history of the Federal-Aid Highway Act of 1956 draw
from the following books and articles: Kat Eschner, "Three Ways the Interstate System Changed
America," *Smithsonian Magazine*, June 29, 2017; Tom Lewis, *Divided Highways: Building the Interstate Highways, Transforming American Life* (Cornell University Press, 2013); Roger Biles, Raymond A. Mohl, and Mark H. Rose, "Revisiting the Urban Interstates: Politics, Policy, and Culture
Since World War II," *Journal of Urban History* 40, no. 5 (2014): 827; L. Roel Hammerschlag, "Legislating the Highway Act of 1956: Lessons for Climate Change Regulation," *Environs: Environmental
Law and Policy Journal* 31, no. 1 (2007): 59; Mark H. Rose, "Reframing American Highway Politics,
1956–1995," *Journal of Planning History* 2, no. 3 (2003): 212. I also draw from my own research and
work in Deborah N. Archer, "'White Men's Roads through Black Men's Homes': Advancing Racial
Equity through Highway Reconstruction," *Vanderbilt Law Review* 73, no. 5 (2020).

19 **"If this be so":** Plessy v. Ferguson, 163 U.S. 527 (1896).

19 **Jim Crow laws flourished:** In addition to specific laws passed during Jim Crow, the discussion
of Jim Crow laws in this chapter draws on C. Vann Woodward, *The Strange Career of Jim Crow*
(Oxford University Press, 1974); Higginbotham, *In the Matter of Color*; Elizabeth Guffey, "Know-
ing Their Space: Signs of Jim Crow in the Segregated South," *DesignIssues* 28, no. 2 (2012): 41;
Ronald L. F. Davis, "Racial Etiquette: The Racial Customs and Rules of Racial Behavior in Jim
Crow America," California State University, Northridge, accessed February 20, 2024.

19 **"unlawful for any amateur":** "Jim Crow Laws," National Park Service, Martin Luther King Jr.
National Historical Park, accessed February 23, 2024.

20 **"Separate but equal" dictated:** "Jim Crow Laws."

20 **nominally part of such laws:** E. H. Beardsley, "Goodbye to Jim Crow: The Desegregation of
Southern Hospitals, 1945–70," *Bulletin of the History of Medicine* 60, no. 3 (1986): 19.

21 **"the South [would] not abide"**: "The Southern Manifesto and Massive Resistance to Brown," NAACP Legal Defense Fund, accessed February 20, 2024.

21 **"the most serious blow"**: Katy June-Friesen, "Massive Resistance in a Small Town," *Humanities*, September/October 2013.

21 **"If we can organize"**: NAACP, "The Southern Manifesto."

21 **massive resistance to *Brown***: Stories of the resistance to Brown v. Board of Education draw from many sources, including: Derrick Bell, *Silent Covenants: Brown v. Board of Education and the Unfulfilled Hopes for Racial Reform* (Oxford University Press, 2005); Richard Kluger, *Simple Justice: The History of Brown v. Board of Education and Black America's Struggle for Equality* (Vintage Books, 2004); Charles Ogletree, *All Deliberate Speed: Reflections on the First Half-Century of Brown v. Board of Education* (W. W. Norton, 2004); Rawn James Jr., *Root and Branch: Charles Hamilton Houston, Thurgood Marshall, and the Struggle to End Segregation* (Bloomsbury Press, 2010); Jack Greenberg, *Crusaders in the Courts: How a Dedicated Band of Lawyers Fought for the Civil Rights Revolution* (Basic Books, 1994).

23 **the states would maintain control**: Discussions on the impact, benefits, and burdens of the interstate highway system draw from the following book and articles: Paul Mason Fotsch, *Watching the Traffic Go By: Transportation and Isolation in Urban America* (University of Texas Press, 2007); Archer, "Transportation Policy," 2125; Archer, "'White Men's Roads'": 1259; Raymond A. Mohl, "Planned Destruction: The Interstates and Central City Housing," in *From Tenements to the Taylor Homes: In Search of an Urban Housing Policy in Twentieth-Century America*, ed. John F. Bauman, Roger Biles, and Kristin M. Szylvian (Pennsylvania State University Press, 2000), 239; Raymond Mohl, "The Interstates and the Cities: The U.S. Department of Transportation and the Freeway Revolt, 1966–1973," *Journal of Policy History* 20, no. 2 (2008): 193–96; Kevin Douglas Kuswa, "Suburbification, Segregation, and the Consolidation of the Highway Machine," *Journal of Law in Society* 3, no. 1 (2002): 47; Joseph F. C. DiMento, "Stent (or Dagger?) in the Heart of Town: Urban Freeways in Syracuse, 1944–1966," *Journal of Planning History* 8, no. 2 (2009): 133–39; Rose, "Reframing American Highway Politics."

24 **more than 475,000 households**: *Beyond Traffic 2045*, prepared by the US Department of Transportation (Office of the Under Secretary for Policy, 2017), 95.

24 **the congressional debate**: Raymond A. Mohl, *The Interstate and the Cities: Highways, Housing, and the Freeway Revolt*, prepared for the Poverty and Race Research Action Council (2002), 29 (explaining that white people started to associate urban blight with poor Black communities beginning in the 1940s); *The Road to Civil Rights*, prepared by Richard F. Weingroff, Federal Highway Administration (2011), 232; "The Great Migration (1910–1970)," National Archives, reviewed June 28, 2021.

25 **The Manual encouraged**: *Underwriting Manual: Underwriting and Valuation Procedure Under Title II of the National Housing Act*, prepared by the Federal Housing Administration (Government Printing Office, 1938).

26 **"a high speed traffic artery"**: *Underwriting Manual.*

26 **"the divider between neighborhoods"**: Joseph Barnett, "Express Highway Planning in Metropolitan Areas," *Transactions of the American Society of Civil Engineers* 112, no. 1 (1947): 636.

26 **federal highway builders now hid**: Discussion of the link between highway development and urban renewal draws largely from Biles, Mohl, and Rose, "Revisiting the Urban Interstates," 829; Mohl, "Planned Destruction," 239; Raymond A. Mohl, "Race and Space in the Modern City: Interstate-95 and the Black Community in Miami," in *Urban Policy in Twentieth-Century America*, ed. Arnold R. Hirsch and Raymond A. Mohl (Rutgers University Press, 1993), 135; Robert . Bullard, introduction to *Highway Robbery: Transportation Racism and New Routes to Equity*, ed. Robert D. Bullard, Glenn S. Johnson, and Angel O. Torres (South End Press, 2004); Raymond A. Mohl, "Stop the Road: Freeway Revolts in American Cities," *Journal of Urban History* 30, no. 5 (2004): 677; Charles E. Connerly, "From Racial Zoning to Community Empowerment: The Interstate Highway System and the African American Community in Birmingham, Alabama," *Journal of Planning Education and Research* 22, no. 2 (2002): 101–4.

27 **"ninety percent of low-income housing":** Fotsch, *Watching the Traffic Go By*, 170.

27 **2,532 urban renewal projects:** Mindy Thompson Fullilove, "Eminent Domain and African Americans, What Is the Price of the Commons," *Perspectives on Eminent Domain Abuse*, Institute for Justice (2015), 5.

27 **five times more likely:** Fullilove, "Eminent Domain and African Americans," 2.

27 **James Baldwin gave an interview:** "A Conversation with James Baldwin," interview by Kenneth Clark, GBH Archives, June 24, 1963.

28 **Black people called it home:** The discussions about Berman v. Parker, 384 U.S. 26 (1954) and Southwest Washington, DC, are largely drawn from the various opinions in the case as it worked its way up to the United States Supreme Court and Amy Lavine, "Urban Renewal and the Story of Berman v. Parker," *Urban Lawyer* 42, no. 2 (2010): 423–75.

28 **half had outside toilets:** Berman, 348 U.S. at 30.

29 **"tak[e] from one businessman":** Berman, 348 U.S. at 33.

29 **"Miserable and disreputable housing":** Berman, 348 U.S. at 32–33.

30 **"just compensation":** Berman, 348 U.S. at 36.

30 **70 percent were white:** Chris Meyers Asch and George Derek Musgrove, *Chocolate City: A History of Race and Democracy in the Nation's Capital* (University of North Carolina Press, 2017); Quinlyn R. Spellmeyer, "Southwest DC: A Cycle of Urban Renewal and 'Revitalization,'" *Storymaps*, 2020.

30 **"the elimination of unsightly":** Rothstein, *The Color of Law*, 127.

31 **"occupied by the humblest citizens":** *Toll Roads and Free Roads*, H.R. Doc. No. 272, prepared by the Bureau of Public Roads (Government Printing Office, 1939); see also Richard F. Weingroff, "The Genie in the Bottle: The Interstate System and Urban Problem, 1939–1957," *Public Roads*, September/October 2000.

31 **Roosevelt warned:** *Interregional Highways: Message from the President of the United States Transmitting a Report of the National Interregional Highway Committee, Outlining and Recommending a National System of Interregional Highways*, H.R. Doc. No. 379 (1944).

31 **"employ its powers of eminent":** *Interregional Highways*, 88.

31 **Cleveland Today ... Tomorrow:** Cleveland (Ohio) City Planning Commission, *Cleveland Today ... Tomorrow: The General Plan of Cleveland* (Cleveland Public Library, 1950).

32 **"In most instances":** Thomas H. MacDonald, "The Case for Urban Expressways," *American City* 62 (June 1947): 92–93.

32 **displacing almost 7,000:** Robert A. Caro, *The Power Broker: Robert Moses and the Fall of New York* (Vintage Books, 1974), 1014.

32 **He built the Cross Bronx:** Caro, *The Power Broker*, 856.

33 **"discouragingly long and arduous":** Caro, *The Power Broker*, 318.

33 **"must go right through cities":** Statement of Robert Moses, City Construction Coordinator of New York City, in *Hearing Before the President's Advisory Committee on a National Highway Program* 48 (October 7, 1954).

33 **"this new highway program":** Robert Moses, "The New Super-Highways: Blessing or Blight?" *Harper's Magazine*, December 1956, 31.

33 **"white men's roads":** "White men's roads through black men's homes" was the mantra of a coalition led by Reginald M. Booker and Sammie Abbott in opposition to highway development in Washington, DC. See Harry Jaffe, "The Insane Highway Plan that Would Have Bulldozed DC's Most Charming Neighborhoods," *Washingtonian*, October 21, 2015.

Chapter 2: Substance over Form

37 **"land of rats and roaches":** Thomas J. Sugrue, *Sweet Land of Liberty: The Forgotten Struggle for Civil Rights in the North* (Random House, 2008), 201.

37 **"the most segregated city in America":** Martin Luther King Jr., *Why We Can't Wait* (Harper & Row, 1964).

37 **law requiring racial segregation:** Birmingham, Alabama, General Code, Sec. 35-859 (Separation of Races) (1944).

37 **ensuring that the residential segregation:** The following passages regarding efforts to protect residential segregation in Birmingham, Alabama, draw largely from the following books and articles: Helen Shores Lee, Barbara S. Shores, and Denise George, *The Gentle Giant of Dynamite Hill: The Untold Story of Arthur Shores and His Family's Fight for Civil Rights* (Zondervan, 2012); Connerly, *The Most Segregated City in America*; Connerly, "From Racial Zoning to Community Empowerment"; Walker Mason Beauchamp, "The Legacy of Racial Zoning in Birmingham, Alabama," *Cumberland Law Review* 48, no. 2 (2018): 359; and from conversations with the late Chervis Isom, a longtime resident of Birmingham, Alabama. Throughout this chapter, I also draw from my own research and work in Archer, "'White Men's Roads.'"

38 **"an ordinance for preserving peace":** Baltimore, Maryland, Ordinance 692 (May 15, 1911).

38 **Following Baltimore's lead:** Garrett Power, "Apartheid Baltimore Style: The Residential Segregation Ordinances of 1910–1913," *Maryland Law Review*, 42, no. 2 (1983): 310.

38 **"had several complaints":** Connerly, *The Most Segregated City in America*, 64.

38 **In 1917, it won the case:** Buchanan v. Warley: 245 U.S. 60 (1917).

39 **"the case presented":** Buchanan v. Warley: 245 U.S. 60 (1917), 78.

39 **"the federal constitution prohibits discrimination, not segregation":** "Wynn Explains Zoning Measure," *Birmingham News*, January 21, 1923, 25.

39 **the Birmingham City Commission drafted:** "Wynn Explains Zoning Measure."

40 **psychological value in passing the bill:** "Wynn Explains Zoning Measure."

40 **"without the necessary sanitary arrangements":** "Negroes Make Appeal to City Commission for Relief Against Segregation Law in Zoning Act," *Birmingham Reporter*, January 20, 1923, 1.

41 **published in the *Birmingham Reporter*:** "Mischievous, Harmful, and Useless Legislation," *Birmingham Reporter*, January 13, 1923, 4.

41 **less than 20 percent:** Connerly, *The Most Segregated City in America*, 53.

41 **"the fact that Negro citizens":** Emory Jackson, "Tip Off," *Birmingham World*, August 12, 1949.

42 **fifty bombings of Black homes and churches:** Susan Willoughby Anderson, "The Part on Trial: The Sixteenth Street Baptist Church Bombing, Civil Rights Memory and the Remaking of Birmingham," PhD diss., University of North Carolina at Chapel Hill, 2008, 91.

44 **press the city to enforce:** "Real Estate Dealers Told to Observe Zoning Lines," *Birmingham Post-Herald*, May 19, 1950, 13.

44 **"If you let the situation disintegrate":** Glenn T. Eskew, *But for Birmingham: The Local and National Movements in the Civil Rights Struggle* (University of North Carolina Press, 1997), 62.

45 **They meet in the heart of Birmingham:** Connerly, "From Racial Zoning to Community Empowerment."

45 **"explore all possible routes":** "College Hill Residents Ask Negro-White Dividing Line," *Birmingham Post-Herald*, February 12, 1957, 19.

45 **Its route followed:** Connerly, "From Racial Zoning to Community Empowerment," 104.

46 **Birmingham commissioned a feasibility study:** *Ensley-Pratt City Urban Renewal Study*, prepared by De Leuw, Cather and Company (1958).

46 **a buffer between Birmingham's west side:** Connerly, *The Most Segregated City in America*; Connerly, "From Racial Zoning to Community Empowerment."

46 **devastation left by a bomb blast:** "Public Is Given Preview of Freeway Plans; Wins Protests, Praise," *Birmingham News*, November 7, 1958, 37.

46 **lost almost 5,000 residents:** Connerly, *The Most Segregated City in America*.

47 **Atlanta adopted its first:** "Atlanta Race Riots," Atlanta University Center's Robert W. Woodruff Library, accessed February 21, 2024; City of Atlanta, *Ordinance Book* 11 (June 17, 1913): 391–93, cited in LeeAnn Bishop Lands, "A Reprehensible and Unfriendly Act: Homeowners, Renters, and the Bid for Residential Segregation in Atlanta, 1900–1917," *Journal of Planning History* 3, no. 2 (2004): 97; Ronald Bayor, "Roads to Racial Segregation: Atlanta in the Twentieth Century," *Journal of Urban History* 15, no. 1 (1988): 3.

47 **It was quickly struck down:** Carey v. City of Atlanta,: 84 S.E. 456 (Ga. 1915).

47 **"Courts are not blind":** Harden v. City of Atlanta, 93 S.E. 338, 403 (Ga. 1917).

47 **struck the law down:** Smith v. City of Atlanta, 132 S.E. 66 (Ga. 1926).

47 **which was to be called the Grand Boulevard:** "Parkway Separating Black and White Neighborhoods," *The Atlanta Constitution*, June 3, 1917, 1.

47 **That seed would:** *The Atlanta Zone Plan: Report Outlining a Tentative Zone Plan for Atlanta*, prepared by Robert Harvey Whitten (Atlanta City Planning Commission, 1922), 10 ("Servants quarters located on the same lot as the residence they serve will nevertheless be allowed in either district without distinction as to race"); Ronald H. Bayor, *Race and the Shaping of Twentieth-Century Atlanta* (University of North Carolina Press, 1996), 55; Archer, "'White Men's Roads,'" 1284–85.

48 **As Atlanta embarked on extensive highway construction:** The following passages on Atlanta's construction of its highways to facilitate racial segregation are largely drawn from Bayor, *Race and the Shaping of Twentieth-Century Atlanta*, 55 (1996); Archer, "'White Men's Roads,'" 1259; Bayor, "Roads to Racial Segregation," 3.

48 **the *Atlanta Daily World* published:** Lerone Bennet, Jr., "Southwest Citizens Group Discloses 'Barrier' Plans Endorsed by City Officials," *Atlanta Daily World*, October 14, 1952, 1.

48 **the Atlanta Bureau of Planning acknowledged:** Bayor, *Race and the Shaping of Twentieth-Century Atlanta*, 61.

49 **increased from 21,816 to 43,967:** Emma L. Thornbrough, "Segregation in Indiana during the Klan Era of the 1920's," *Mississippi Valley Historical Review* 47, no. 4 (March 1961): 595.

49 **"horse thieves and other felons.":** Kenneth T. Jackson, *The Ku Klux Klan in the City, 1915–1930* (Oxford University Press, 1967), 145.

49 **the Klan added to its political power:** Leonard J. Moore, *Citizen Klansmen: The KKK in Indiana, 1921*-1928 (University of North Carolina Press, 1997), 145.

49 **White People's Protective League:** Paul Mullins, "Racist Spite and Residential Segregation: Housing and the Color Line in Inter-War Indianapolis," *Archaeology and Material Culture* (blog), January 20, 2019. See also Ryan T. Schwier, "Historical Injustice in the Urban Environment: The Ecological Implications of Residential Segregation in Indianapolis," *Indianapolis Legal Archive*.

50 **February 1926 letter to the editor:** Omer Whiteman, letter to the editor, *Indianapolis News*, February 9, 1926, 6.

50 **reportedly bombed a home:** "Vandals Throw a Bomb," *Indianapolis Recorder*, July 23, 1927, 3.

50 **the only resolution to "the race problem":** Mullins, "Racist Spite"; Mrs. O. J. Deeds, letter to the editor, *Fiery Cross*, January 19, 1923, 2.

50 **"the immediate work of":** "$5,000 Fund to Fight Resident Bar," *Indianapolis Recorder*, March 20, 1926, 1.

50 **"Do you want a nigger for a neighbor?":** Thornbrough, "Segregation in Indiana," 598.

50 **When Dr. Lucien B. Meriwether:** "Fences Isolate Colored Owner," *Indianapolis Star*, July 16, 1920, 1.

51 **A May 1925 article:** "Klan Gives Its Backing to Duvall," *Indianapolis Times*, May 4, 1925, 1.

51 **All but one of them:** *Journal of the Common Council of the City of Indianapolis, Indiana, from January 1, 1926, to December 1, 1926* (1927), 78.

51 **Mayor Duvall signed the measure into law:** Thornbrough, "Segregation in Indiana," 599.

51 **"in the interest of public peace":** Indianapolis, Indiana, General Ordinance No. 15 (passed March 15, 1926), reprinted in *Journal of the Common Council* at 53.

51 **"That it shall be unlawful":** Indianapolis, Indiana, General Ordinance No. 15.

51 **Indianapolis state judge ruled:** "Judge Rules Segregation Law Void," *Indianapolis Recorder*, November 27, 1926, 1.

52 **striking it down:** Harmon v. Tyler, 273 U.S. 668 (1927).

52 **was in effect for only eight months:** "Judge Rules Segregation Law Void," *Indianapolis Recorder*, 1.

52 **"the Ordinance is the outcome":** "Local Segregation Act Void, U.S. Court," *Indianapolis Recorder*, March 19, 1927, 1.

52 **HOLC sought to systematize the property appraisal:** *Underwriting Manual: Underwriting and Valuation Procedure Under Title II of the National Housing Act*, prepared by the Federal Housing Administration (Government Printing Office, 1938), 935–37.

53 **among the primary factors in assessing mortgage risk:** Richard R. W. Brooks and Carol M. Rose, *Saving the Neighborhood: Racially Restrictive Covenants, Law, and Social Norms* (Harvard University Press, 2013), 109.

53 **a mere 2 percent:** "Race and the Power of Illusion," PBS, accessed February 24, 2024.

54 **Indiana Avenue provides a telling example:** The passages on Indianapolis, Indiana, in this chapter draw on conversations I have had with residents and advocates in Indianapolis, including Indianapolis community organizer Paula Brooks; residents Taylor Hughes, Thomas Ridley, Miz Pete, Kathi Ridley-Merriweather, Jennifer Baskerville-Burrows; Professors Susan Hyatt, the late Paul Mullins, and Jordan Ryan; leaders of the Rethink Coalition, including Brenda Hacker Freije and Charlie Richardson; A'Lelia Bundles, the great-great-granddaughter of Madam C. J. Walker; and Robert Edwards's grandson, Justin Garrett Moore. I also draw from the research of Professors Hyatt, Mullins, and Ryan, including Susan B. Hyatt, *The Neighborhood of Saturdays: Memories of a Multi-Ethnic Community on Indianapolis' South Side* (Dog Ear Publishing, 2012); Jordan Ryan and Paul Mullins, interview with Taylor Bennett, *All in Indiana*, WFYI Indianapolis, February 24, 2021; Mullins, "Racist Spite"; Paul Mullins, "In the Shadow of the Interstate: Living with Highways," *Archaeology and Material Culture* (blog), October 3, 2019.

54 **"every sort of Black expressive culture":** Ryan and Mullins, *All in Indiana*.

56 **But their request was rejected:** Mullins, "In the Shadow of the Interstate."

56 **residents organized a protest:** Mullins, "In the Shadow of the Interstate."

56 **soon that property was taken:** Hyatt, *The Neighborhood of Saturdays*, xiii–xiv.

57 **"The neighborhood is an old one":** Mullins, "In the Shadow of the Interstate."

57 **The highway was destroying her:** Mullins, "In the Shadow of the Interstate."

57 **"proximity to a highway":** Mullins, "In the Shadow of the Interstate."

57 **Paula Brooks, an Indianapolis community organizer:** This passage draws from conversations I had with Paula Brooks, a community organizer in Indianapolis, Indiana.

58 **the Edwards family:** The following passages draw from conversations I had with Justin Garret Moore, Robert Edwards's grandson.

60 **Before I-70:** Mullins, "In the Shadow of the Interstate," 5. Much of the following passages on Indianapolis draws from conversations with Professor Hyatt and her research.

61 **highway development and the broken promises:** Rothstein, *The Color of Law*, 131; Archer, "Transportation Policy" (2021), 2125; Archer, "'White Men's Roads,'" 1259; Mohl, "Stop the Road," 674; Paul Mason Fotsch, "Contesting Urban Freeway Stories: Racial Politics and the O.J. Chase," *Cultural Studies* 13, no. 1 (1999): 110; Katherine L. Bradbury, Anthony Downs, and Kenneth A. Small, *Urban Decline and the Future of American Cities* (Brookings Institution Press, 1982), 69–77; Anthony Downs, *Urban Problems and Prospects* (Rand McNally, 1976).

Chapter 3: It's Just a Highway

64 **"deconstruct the racism":** Stuti Mishra, "Buttigieg Says America's Highways Are Racist and Infrastructure Bill Will Help Fix It," *Independent*, November 9, 2021.

65 **Interstate 95 was built:** The discussion of Overtown and the impact that the construction of I-95 had on the Black community there draws on the following sources: Raymond A. Mohl, "Making the Second Ghetto in Metropolitan Miami, 1940–1960," *Journal of Urban History* 21, no. 3 (March 1995): 398; Mark H. Rose and Raymond A. Mohl, *Interstate: Highway Politics and Policy Since 1939* (University of Tennessee Press, 2012); Mohl, *Interstate and the Cities*, 121; Joseph F. Dimento et al., *Changing Lanes: Visions and Histories of Urban Freeways* (MIT Press, 2013): 154–55; Mohl, "Race

and Space," 100; Mohl, "Planned Destruction." Throughout this chapter, I also draw from my own research and work in Archer, "'White Men's Roads.'"

65 **"a complete slum clearance":** Mohl, "Making the Second Ghetto in Metropolitan Miami," 398.

66 *Miami Herald* **published:** "What About the Negroes Uprooted by the Expressway?" *Miami Herald*, March 4, 1957, 29.

66 **Most of them ended up:** Eric Tscheschlok, "Long Time Coming: Miami's Liberty City Riot in 1968," *Florida Historical Quarterly* 74, no. 4 (1996): 441–42.

66 **"With shocking ruthlessness":** Mohl, "Race and Space," 122.

67 **"seemed to have escaped":** Mohl, "Race and Space," 134.

67 **Overtown is now experiencing:** See Thomas W. Sanchez, Rich Stolz, and Jacinta S. Ma, *Moving to Equity: Addressing Inequitable Effects of Transportation Policies on Minorities* (Civil Rights Project at Harvard University, 2003), 20; Rose and Mohl, *Interstate: Highway Politics.*

67 **The demolition of Black neighborhoods:** Biles, Mohl, and Rose, "Revisiting the Urban Interstates," 850.

67 **Many displaced residents:** Fotsch, "Contesting Urban Freeway Stories," 120.

68 **so-called second ghettos:** Arnold R. Hirsch, *Making the Second Ghetto: Race and Housing in Chicago, 1940–1960* (University of Chicago Press, 2021).

69 **"nearly 100% effective":** Robert Spiegel, "A Penetrating Look at Negro Housing Here; Segregation Nearly 100% Effective," *Des Moines Tribune*, June 20, 1956, 1.

69 **After redlining was made illegal:** Robert Spiegel, "A Negro Family Moves In: Homes Put Up for Sale" *Des Moines Tribune*, June 25, 1956, 1, 6.

69 **"When I told people":** George Shane, "Negroes Hit High Prices for Homes," *Des Moines Register*, May 27, 1959, 13.

69 **2016 Dear Colleague Letter:** See Julián Castro, secretary of the Department of Housing and Urban Development, *Dear Colleague Letter: Regarding Mobility via Education and Socioeconomic Opportunity*, June 3, 2016.

69 **The increased traffic:** Maria Cecilia Pinto De Moura and David Reichmuth, *Inequitable Exposure to Air Pollution from Vehicles in the Northeast and Mid-Atlantic* (Union of Concerned Scientists, 2019). ("On average, communities of color in the Northeast and Mid-Atlantic breathe 66 percent more air pollution from vehicles than white residents. . . . Exposures for African American residents are 61 percent higher than for white residents.")

70 **eight out of every nine:** Jules Struck, "Forced to Live Here, Forced to Leave: The Twin Injustices of I-81 and the Demolition of the 15th Ward," *Syracuse.com*, July 13, 2022, https://www.syracuse .com/news/2022/07/forced-to-live-here-forced-to-leave-the-twin-injustices-of-i-81-and-the -demolition-of-the-15th-ward.html.

70 **30 percent of Black people:** Alana Semuels, "How to Decimate a City," *Atlantic*, November 20, 2015.

70 **"line of demarcation":** Daniel C. Vock, "A Road Runs Through It," *Governing*, July 2014, 52.

70 **I-81 to the Berlin Wall:** Angie Schmitt, "Building Highways Made Racial Segregation Worse. Can Removing Them Undo That Legacy?," *Streetsblog USA*, June 7, 2018.

71 **many of the people who lived:** Ehsan Alam, "Before It Was Cut in Half by I-94, St. Paul's Rondo Was a Thriving African-American Cultural Center," *MinnPost*, June 19, 2017.

72 **One in every eight:** "Rondo Neighborhood and I-94: Overview," Gale Family Library, Minnesota Historical Society, accessed February 21, 2024.

72 **the spirit of Rondo was gone:** Fotsch, *Watching the Traffic Go By*, 171–72.

72 **"As a community we":** Vikki Sanders and Remember Rondo Committee, "Profile of a Visionary: Interview with Roger Anderson," in *Remember Rondo: A Tradition of Excellence* (Bethel University, 1995), 26–27.

72 **the last house standing:** Colleen Powers, "Roots of Rondo Honors a Neighborhood, Looks to the Future," *Creative Exchange*, March 8, 2017.

72 **In Rondo, he felt safe:** Maury Glover, "How I-94 Ripped Apart the Rondo Neighborhood and One Group's Plan to Help Restore It," FOX 9, February 15. 2021.

72 **Khaliq remembers the police:** Laura Yuen, "Central Corridor: In the Shadow of Rondo," *MPR News*, April 29, 2010.

73 **"It broke my grandfather's heart":** Blake Makenzie, "Race and Housing Series: Rondo and I-94—A Conversation with Nick Khaliq," *Twin Cities Habitat for Humanity* (blog).

73 **"I especially remember":** Kimberly Zielinkski, ed., *Children of Rondo: Transcriptions of Rondo Oral History Interviews* (Hamline University, 2006), 26–27.

73 **"but that was in the early 1960s":** Sam Fulwood III, "When Home Disappears," Center for American Progress, April 7, 2016.

74 **James Wilson was finishing up:** The following passages draw from conversations I had with James Wilson.

Chapter 4: Berlin Walls

78 **Main Street in Buffalo, New York:** See Anna Blatto, *A City Divided: A Brief History of Segregation in Buffalo* (Partnership for the Public Good, 2018); "Brown University Diversity and Disparities" (Residential Segregation; accessed February 22, 2024); *The Racial Equity Dividend: Buffalo's Great Opportunity, Racial Equity Buffalo* (Buffalo Regional Institute, 2018).

78 **Eight Mile Road in Detroit, Michigan:** See "Most to Least Segregated Cities in 2020," Othering and Belonging Institute, University of California, Berkeley, accessed February 22, 2024; "Most to Least Segregated Metro Regions in 2020," Othering and Belonging Institute, University of California, Berkeley, accessed February 22, 2024; "City Snapshot: Detroit," Othering and Belonging Institute, University of California, Berkeley; Caroline Llanes, "Detroit Ranked as One of the Most Segregated Cities in the Country," Michigan Public Radio, June 21, 2021; Sarah Cwiek, "Protesters Highlight Detroit Area's Racial Divide on Eight Mile Road," Michigan Public Radio, June 17, 2020.

78 **Troost Avenue in racially segregated Kansas City:** See Elle Moxley, "How Kansas City's Complex Racial History Is Still Influencing Education Choices," KCUR, May 9, 2018; Sylvia Maria Gross, "Despite Whites Moving In and Blacks Moving Out, Kansas City Still Isn't Very Integrated," KCUR, November 20, 2015; Eric Salzman, "For Decades a Dividing Line, Troost Avenue in Kansas City, Mo., Sees New Hope," NBC News, October 11, 2018.

78 **"you have a division":** Chico Harlan, "In St. Louis, Delmar Boulevard Is the Line That Divides a City by Race and Perspective," *Washington Post*, August 22, 2014.

78 **home value of $78,000:** *For the Sake of All* (Washington University and Saint Louis University, 2014), 29.

78 **only 5 percent of residents:** Oscar Perry Abello, "Breaking Through and Breaking Down the Delmar Divide in St. Louis," *Next City*, August 19, 2019.

79 **The subtle and not-so-subtle uses:** For example, as part of a "segregationist compromise" in New Orleans, developers used "canals and dead-end streets" to "wall off" Pontchartrain Park, a Black neighborhood, from adjacent white neighborhoods. Vern Baxter and Maria Casati, "Building Black Suburbs in New Orleans," in *Remaking New Orleans: Beyond Exceptionalism and Authenticity*, ed. Thomas Jessen Adams and Matt Sakakeeny (Duke University Press, 2019), 212–15. In Yonkers, white residents used dead ends and chicken wire to physically prevent their Black neighbors from entering their community. Elsa Brenner, "If You're Thinking of Living In/Runyon Heights, Yonkers; 'Dead End' Signs Recall a Bitter Legacy," *New York Times*, November 17, 2002. And in Baltimore, one-way streets and dead ends make it difficult to travel from Black neighborhoods to white neighborhoods. Sarah B. Schindler, "Architectural Exclusion: Discrimination and Segregation through Physical Design of the Built Environment," *Yale Law Journal* 124, no. 6 (2015): 1970; Gary A. Tobin, *Divided Neighborhoods: Changing Patterns of Racial Segregation* (Sage Publications, 1987), 219.

80 **home of the Muscogee (Creek) and Cherokee Nations:** Muscogee (Creek) removal may be considered as beginning well before 1838 with the Treaty of Indian Springs in 1821 and 1825 or the Treaty of Washington in 1826. Others may cite the beginning of the removal as the federal Indian Removal Act of 1830.

80 **Black people began migrating:** "Boundary Line Set for Negroes," *Atlanta Constitution*, October 12, 1910, 1; Lands, "A Reprehensible and Unfriendly Act," 96; *The Atlanta Zone Plan*, 10; Bayor, "Roads to Racial Segregation."

80 **the city enacted a segregation ordinance:** Lands, "A Reprehensible and Unfriendly Act," 96; Bayor, "Roads to Racial Segregation," 4.

81 **second wave of racial zoning:** *The Atlanta Zone Plan*, 10; Bayor, "Roads to Racial Segregation," 4–5.

81 **"establishing colored residence":** Rothstein, *The Color of Law*, 39.

81 **attached residential segregation to anti-miscegenation:** Bayor, *Race and the Shaping of Twentieth-Century Atlanta*, 55.

82 **Black people comprised 35.7 percent:** Andy Ambrose, "Atlanta," *New Georgia Encyclopedia*, last modified June 8, 2022.

82 **with Black people no longer facing:** Bayor, "Roads to Racial Segregation," 7–11; Betsy Riley, "A Separate Peace: Collier Heights," *Atlanta Magazine*, April 30, 2010; Christopher Johnson, "The Epic of Collier Heights," *99% Invisible*, December 9, 2021.

82 **officials used the construction:** Bayor, "Roads to Racial Segregation," 8–18.

82 **the West Side Mutual Development Committee:** Bayor, "Roads to Racial Segregation," 11–12; Riley, "A Separate Peace."

83 **Through the West Side Mutual Development Committee:** Bayor, "Roads to Racial Segregation," 11.

83 **Under the agreement:** Bayor, "Roads to Racial Segregation," 11–12.

84 **white residents of Mozley Park:** Bayor, "Roads to Racial Segregation," 12; Ronald H. Bayor, "Racism as Public Policy in America's Cities in the Twentieth Century," in *Crossing Boundaries: The Exclusion and Inclusion of Minorities in Germany and the United States*, ed. Larry Eugene Jones (Berghahn Books, 2001), 73–74; Samuel L. Adams, "Blueprint for Segregation: A Survey of Atlanta Housing," *New South* 22, no. 2 (Spring 1967): 76.

84 **"Drive from downtown Atlanta":** Bayor, "Race and the Shaping of Twentieth Century America."

84 **"streets were terminated":** Bayor, "Roads to Racial Segregation," 16.

85 **Consider Willis Mill Road:** Bayor, "Racism as Public Policy," 74; Bayor, "Roads to Racial Segregation," 14.

85 **"a holocaust among the whites there":** Ivan Allen Jr., *Mayor: Notes on the Sixties* (Simon & Schuster, 1971), 71.

86 **Erecting the proposed barriers:** Paul Crater, "Atlanta's Berlin Wall," *Atlanta Magazine*, December 1, 2011.

86 **"the epitome of Southern womanhood":** Crater, "Atlanta's Berlin Wall," 20.

86 **The following day:** Crater, "Atlanta's Berlin Wall."

87 **blowback from the Black community:** Kevin Michael Kruse, *White Flight: Atlanta and the Making of Modern Conservativism* (Princeton University Press, 2007), 5.

87 **"Never do anything wrong":** Kruse, *White Flight*, 72.

87 **only fifteen white families:** Kruse, *White Flight*, 5.

87 **Memphis attracted similar notoriety:** Nicholas D. Krawec, "Constitutional Law—Racial Discrimination—Thirteenth Amendment," *Duquesne Law Review* 20, no. 1 (1981): 88.

87 **It all started years earlier:** "Justices Say Closing Off Street Is Not a Violation of Civil Rights," *New York Times*, April 21, 1983, 13.

88 **West Drive was also:** Memphis v. Greene, 451 U.S. 100, 104 (1981).

88 **On April 1, 1974, Black residents:** Memphis v. Greene, 119.

88 **The United States Supreme Court disagreed:** Memphis v. Greene, 144 (Marshall, J., dissenting).

89 **"The problem is less":** Memphis v. Greene, 147 (Marshall, J., dissenting).

89 **Justice Marshall grasped:** Memphis v. Greene, 147 (Marshall, J., dissenting).

89 **Elsewhere, white residents took:** Plaintiffs' Pre-Trial Memorandum at 2–5, Jennings v. Patterson, 488 F.2d 436 (5th Cir. 1974).

90 **The forty-foot section of the road:** Jennings, 488 F.2d at 438–39.

90   **Nearly two years later:** Jennings, 488 F.2d at 438–39.

90   **believed that they were entitled:** Jennings, 488 F.2d at 440.

91   **Six years later, in Nacogdoches County:** Evans v. Tubbe, 657 F.2d 661, 662 (5th Cir. Unit A Sept. 1981).

91   **According to Evans's lawsuit:** Evans v. Tubbe, 657 F.2d 661, 662 (5th Cir. Unit A Sept. 1981); United States District Court Docket, Evans v. Tubbe, No. TY-79-201-CA (E.D. Tex. June 29, 1982).

91   **In Georgia, in 1990:** Steele v. City of Port Wentworth, 2008 WL 717813, at *1, *10 (S.D. Ga. Mar. 17, 2008); Complaint—Class Action at 10, Steele 2008 WL 717813 (No. CV405–135); Plaintiffs' Memorandum in Opposition to Defendant's Motion for Summary Judgment at 8, Steele 2008 WL 717813 (No. CV405–135).

91   **the city facilitated Jeffers's efforts:** Complaint—Class Action at 10, Steele 2008 WL 717813 (No. CV405–135); Plaintiffs' Memorandum in Opposition to Defendant's Motion for Summary Judgment at 8, Steele 2008 WL 717813 (No. CV405–135).

91   **The Black residents ultimately settled:** Report and Recommendation of the Special Master on Petitioner's Motion for Partial Summary Judgment at 16–18, City of Port Wentworth v. Steele, No. CV09-2440-FR (Super. Ct. Chatham Cty. June 26, 2012); Order on Special Master's Report on Petitioner's Motion for Partial Summary Judgment, City of Port Wentworth v. Steele, No. CV09–2440-FR (Super. Ct. E. Jud. Cir. Ga. Jan. 29, 2013).

92   **A number of New York City avenues:** Reuben S. Rose-Redwood, "From Number to Name: Symbolic Capital, Places of Memory and the Politics of Street Renaming in New York City," *Social and Cultural Geography* 9, no. 4 (2008): 443–44.

93   **The naming or renaming:** Sweta Tiwari and Shrinidhi Ambinakudige, "Streetscapes and Stereotyping: Streets Named After Martin Luther King, Jr., and the Geographies of Racial Identity," *GeoJournal* 87, no. 1 (2022): 921–34.

93   **In a 2020 study:** Tiwari and Ambinakudige, "Streetscapes and Stereotyping."

93   **The 2020 study also:** See Derek H. Alderman, "Street Names as Memorial Arenas: The Reputational Politics of Commemorating Martin Luther King Jr. in a Georgia County," *Historical Geography* 30 (2002): 99.

93   **An attempt to name Ninth Street:** Tiwari and Ambinakudige, "Streetscapes and Stereotyping," 923.

93   **the Kansas City, Missouri, city council voted:** Margaret Stafford, "Group Seeks to Reverse Naming of Kansas City Street for King," Associated Press, April 26, 2019.

94   **"Many vendors would say":** Sam Roberts, "Metro Matters: Battle to Block the Re-naming of Fifth Avenue," *New York Times*, February 15, 1988, B1.

94   **renaming them based on demographics:** Adams, "Blueprint for Segregation," 73–80; Bayor, "Roads to Racial Segregation," 16.

95   **the city made it easy for white residents:** Bayor, "Roads to Racial Segregation," 16; Robert K. Nelson, LaDale Winling, Richard Marciano, and N. D. B. Connolly, *Atlanta, Georgia*, in *Mapping Inequality: Redlining in New Deal America* (University of Richmond, 2023).

95   **Much of the racialized renaming:** Adams, "Blueprint for Segregation," 80; Nelson, Winling, Marciano, and Connolly, *Atlanta, Georgia*.

96   **Today, within Atlanta's city center:** Ibid.

96   **A few blocks further east:** Ibid.

96   **On the west side:** Ibid.; Kruse, *White Flight*, 58.

97   **Louisville, Kentucky, has followed a similar practice:** Robert K. Nelson, LaDale Winling, Richard Marciano, and N. D. B. Connolly, *Louisville, Kentucky* in *Mapping Inequality: Redlining in New Deal America* (University of Richmond, 2023).

97   **Louisville's racial zoning ordinance:** George C. Wright, *Life Behind a Veil: Blacks in Louisville, Kentucky, 1865-1930* (Louisiana State University Press, 1985), 236.

97   **White residents were determined:** Wright, *Life Behind a Veil*.

97   **Amira Johnson learned:** Much of the following paragraphs regarding Sandridge, South Carolina, comes from conversations I had with various residents of the community and Title VI Com-

plaint, South Carolina State Conference of the NAACP v. Horry County et al. (US Department of Transportation, Office of Highway Administration, 2022).

98   **Sandridge was founded:** Title VI Complaint at 6, South Carolina State Conference of the NAACP v. Horry County et al. (US Department of Transportation, Office of Highway Administration, 2022).

100   **The town is near US-701:** Title VI Complaint at 6.

104   **In Norfolk, Virginia:** Kevin Lang Ringelstein, "Residential Segregation in Norfolk, Virginia: How the Federal Government Reinforced Racial Division in a Southern City, 1914–1959" (Master's diss., Old Dominion University, 2015), 17.

104   **A familiar story followed:** Ringelstein, "Residential Segregation in Norfolk," 18.

Chapter 5: Still at the Back of the Bus

107   **during a sweltering July heatwave:** "1919: The Race Riot," Chicago Historical Homicide Project, accessed February 24, 2024.

107   **increased from 44,000 in 1910:** Melissa Petruzzello, "Chicago Race Riot of 1919," *Encyclopaedia Britannica*.

108   **The Committee's work resulted in a report:** *The Negro in Chicago: A Study of Race Relations and a Race Riot*, prepared by the Chicago Commission on Race Relations (University of Chicago, 1922).

109   **nearly six million Americans:** "It's Not Just Transportation, It's Health Justice for Patients," *Health News*, University of California, Davis, April 6, 2022.

110   **over 23.5 million Americans:** *Access to Affordable and Nutritious Food: Measuring and Understanding Food Deserts and Their Consequences* (US Department of Agriculture, Economic Search Service, 2009), 35.

110   **one of the biggest challenges:** Caroline Ratcliffe et al., *Disrupting Food Insecurity: Steps Communities Can Take* (Urban Institute, 2019), 8–13.

110   **they are more likely to live in food deserts:** Courtnee Melton, *How Transportation Impacts Public Health* (The Sycamore Institute, 2017), 2.

110   **The 1980 Atlanta Comprehensive Plan:** Bayor, *Race and the Shaping of Twentieth-Century Atlanta*, 68.

110   **Moving Africans Rapidly Through Atlanta:** In 2018, a Google search asking what MARTA stands for would return this derogatory result in bold letters at the top of its results, reflecting Google users' racist commentary on MARTA's predominantly Black ridership. Google would remove the definition from its results. Becca J. G. Godwin, "Google Search Answered 'What Does MARTA Stand For' with Racist Joke," *Atlanta Journal-Constitution*, March 29, 2018.

111   **"90 percent a racial issue":** Kevin M. Kruse, "What Does a Traffic Jam in Atlanta Have to Do with Segregation? Quite a Lot," *New York Times Magazine*, August 14, 2019.

111   **Gwinnett County voted MARTA down:** Tyler Estep and Amanda C. Coyne, "Gwinnett's MARTA Referendum Has Failed," *Atlanta Journal-Constitution*, March 19, 2019.

111   **"will come up with twelve":** Kruse, "What Does a Traffic Jam in Atlanta."

111   **"The end result, we suspect":** "Supreme Court Decision in Montgomery Case Foretells the End of City Bus Services in Deep South Cities," *Columbus Ledger*, November 14, 1956, 4.

111   **"people in Cobb County":** Earl Black and Merle Black, *The Rise of Southern Republicans* (Belknap Press, 2002), 7.

112   **Consider the death of a seventeen-year-old:** Evelyn Nieves, "In the Wake of a Teen-Ager's Death, a Cloud of Racism, Then a Lawsuit," *New York Times*, December 19, 1996. See also Johnnie Cochran and David Fisher, *A Lawyer's Life* (Thomas Dunne Books, 2003), 237.

112   **Consider a recent episode from Dayton, Ohio:** The following passages discussing public transportation in Dayton, Ohio, and Beavercreek, Ohio, largely draw from documents related to the US Department of Transportation Federal Highway Administration's investigation, including *Beavercreek Investigative Report*, prepared by Lester Finkle, US Department of Transportation, Federal Highway Administration, July 20, 2012; Title VI Complaint, LEAD v. City of

Beavercreek (US Department of Transportation, Federal Highway Administration, 2011); Decision Letter, LEAD v. City of Beavercreek (US Department of Transportation, Federal Highway Administration, 2013); interviews with Lester Finkle, former Title VI program coordinator for the US Department of Justice Federal Highway Administration, Ellis Jacobs, attorney for Leaders for Equality and Action in Dayton (LEAD), and Ronnie Moreland, former president of LEAD; *Free to Ride: The Documentary* (Kirwan Institute for the Study of Race and Ethnicity, 2014).

113   **other community members also testified:** *Free to Ride.*

113   **more racially segregated:** Joseph Watras, "The Racial Desegregation of Dayton, Ohio, Public Schools, 1966–2008," *Ohio History* 117 (2010): 93–107.

113   **the legacy of redlining:** See Adam A. Millsap, "How the Gem City Lost Its Luster and How It Can Get It Back: A Case Study of Dayton, Ohio" (Mercatus Center at George Mason University, 2017).

114   **"We lost it all":** *Free to Ride.*

114   **"an accident waiting to happen":** *Free to Ride.*

114   **In a study commissioned by LEAD:** Decision Letter, LEAD v. City of Beavercreek (US Department of Transportation, Federal Highway Administration, 2013); Title VI Complaint, LEAD v. City of Beavercreek (US Department of Transportation, Federal Highway Administration, 2011).

114   **about 73 percent of riders:** *Beavercreek Investigative Report*, Finkle.

115   **The RTA's application:** Decision Letter, LEAD v. City of Beavercreek (US Department of Transportation, Federal Highway Administration, 2013); Title VI Complaint, LEAD v. City of Beavercreek (US Department of Transportation, Federal Highway Administration, 2011).

115   **Following pushback from Beavercreek officials:** *Beavercreek Investigative Report*, Finkle.

115   **the hearing took a dramatic turn:** *Beavercreek Investigative Report*, Finkle; *Free to Ride.*

116   **Following the hearing:** *Beavercreek Investigative Report*, Finkle.

116   **The city council reconvened:** *Beavercreek Investigative Report*, Finkle; *Free to Ride.*

116   **Some council members said:** *Free to Ride.*

117   **city council also raised nineteen new requirements:** Decision Letter, LEAD v. City of Beavercreek (US Department of Transportation, Federal Highway Administration, 2013); *Beavercreek Investigative Report*, Finkle.

117   **saw these conditions for what they were:** Ibid.

117   **"all the issues that have been at the Salem Mall":** *Free to Ride.*

118   **"nothing but thinly veiled discrimination":** *Free to Ride.*

118   **Following the vote:** *Beavercreek Investigative Report*, Finkle.

118   **LEAD filed an administrative complaint:** Title VI Complaint, LEAD v. City of Beavercreek (US Department of Transportation, Federal Highway Administration, 2011).

119   **goal of the FHWA's:** Decision Letter, LEAD v. City of Beavercreek (US Department of Transportation, Federal Highway Administration, 2013).

119   **Finkle and the investigation team visited Dayton:** *Beavercreek Investigative Report*, Finkle.

119   **FHWA issued a letter of noncompliance:** Decision Letter, LEAD v. City of Beavercreek (US Department of Transportation, Federal Highway Administration, 2013).

120   **Early that Sunday morning:** *Free to Ride.*

120   **a shift in government resources:** See Rothstein, *The Color of Law.*

120   **"the lion's share of transportation dollars":** Robert D. Bullard, "Addressing Urban Transportation Equity in the United States," *Fordham Urban Law Journal* 31, no. 5 (2003): 1186.

120   **Fixing America's Surface Transportation Act:** Fixing America's Surface Transportation (FAST) Act, Pub. L. No. 114–94, §§ 1101, 1104, 129 Stat. 1312, 1322–25, 1329–32 (2015).

120   **first long-term national:** See "Fixing America's Surface Transportation (FAST) Act: Highway Research, Technology Deployment, and Education," US Department of Transportation.

120   **It authorized $305 billion:** Fixing America's Surface Transportation (FAST) Act, Pub. L. No. 114–94, §§ 1101(a)(1), 129 Stat. 1312, 1322 (2015).

120   **That latter amount:** *APTA Primer on Transit Funding: The Fixing America's Surface Transportation Act and Other Related Laws, FY 2016 Through 2020,* prepared by John Neff (American Public Transportation Association, 2016), 14–16.

121 **only 31 percent of capital funds:** *APTA Primer on Transit Funding*, 14.

121 **Black people are more likely:** *Who Rides Public Transportation*, prepared by Hugh M. Clark (CJI Research Corporation and American Public Transportation Association, 2017), 22.

121 **"would enable poor, inner-city blacks":** Roberto Gutierrez et al., "Baltimore Metro: An Initiative and Outcome in Rapid Public Transportation" (Johns Hopkins University, 1990).

121 **"would not force a transit line":** Rothstein, *The Color of Law*.

121 **"beneath some of this opposition":** Gwinn Owens, "Down by the Station (But Not in Ruxton)," *Baltimore Sun*, May 14, 1998.

122 **"drug addicts, crooks, and thieves":** Owens, "Down by the Station."

122 **some of the longest commute times in the city:** Title VI Complaint, Baltimore Regional Initiative Developing Genuine Equality, Inc. v. Maryland, et al. (US Department of Transportation, Federal Highway Administration, 2015).

122 **As scholar Sheryll Cashin noted:** Sheryll Cashin, "How Larry Hogan Kept Blacks in Baltimore Segregated and Poor," *Politico*, July 18, 2020.

122 **For fourteen years:** Title VI Complaint, Baltimore Regional Initiative Developing Genuine Equality.

122 **they announced a pause:** Title VI Complaint, Baltimore Regional Initiative Developing Genuine Equality; Colin Campbell, "Five Years Later, Many Across Baltimore Bitterly Lament Gov. Hogan's Decision to Kill the Red Line Light Rail," *Baltimore Sun*, September 11, 2020.

122 **he did not cancel plans:** Title VI Complaint, Baltimore Regional Initiative Developing Genuine Equality.

123 **The Red Line had been designed:** Title VI Complaint, Baltimore Regional Initiative Developing Genuine Equality.

123 **"The Red Line would also have served":** Title VI Complaint, Baltimore Regional Initiative Developing Genuine Equality, 9–10.

125 **"to think of white and Asian people":** Joseph Goldstein and Ashley Southall, "I Got Tired of Hunting Black and Hispanic People," *New York Times*, June 17, 2020.

125 **the notably diverse Transit District 32:** Goldstein and Southall, "I Got Tired."

125 **Black and Latino people received nearly 73 percent:** Goldstein and Southall, "I Got Tired."

125 **Black riders received 22 percent:** *Safety for All*, prepared by Chris Van Eyken (Transit Center, July 2021), 21–23.

125 **63 percent of "use of force" incidents:** *The Science of Justice: Bay Area Rapid Transit Police Department National Justice Database City Report* (Center for Policing Equity, 2020), 3.

126 **In Detroit:** Detroit, Michigan, Code of Ordinances, Sec. 47-1-4 (Refusal to Pay Fare).

126 **By contrast:** Detroit, Michigan, Code of Ordinances, Sec. 46-1-32 (Schedule of Fines for Parking Violations).

126 **In New Orleans:** New Orleans, Louisiana, Code of Ordinances, Sec. 122-13 (Legal Fares and the Payment Thereof Required); Sec. 154–686 (Civil Nature of Parking and Stopping Violations); Sec. 154–699 (Schedule of Fines), Sec. 154–865 (Parking Time Limited on Certain Street).

126 **In Atlanta:** "MARTA Customer Code of Conduct" (Metropolitan Atlanta Rapid Transit Authority, 2013), 5–6; Atlanta, Georgia, Code of Ordinances, Sec. 150-133 (Overtime Parking).

126 **New York City recently:** Spectrum News Staff, "Alternate Side Parking Fines Set at $65 Citywide," *Spectrum News*, February 20, 2020; Sewell Chan, "Penalty for Fare Beating Rises to $100," *New York Times*, July 7, 2008.

127 **the citation can ultimately result in a misdemeanor:** "Prepare to Show Your Fare: New Compliance Policy Takes Effect Nov. 15," *SoundTransit* (blog), November 1, 2023.

127 **in Portland, fare evasion:** "Code of Conduct/Transit Exclusion Policy," MetroTransit, updated June 1, 2017.

127 **Oscar Grant was killed:** Dandhya Dirks et al., "'On Our Watch' Litigation Reveals New Details in Police Shooting of Oscar Grant," KQED, July 8, 2021.

Chapter 6: The White Man's Right of Way

129 **D. W. Griffith's *The Birth of a Nation*:** *The Birth of a Nation*, directed by D. W. Griffith (1915; Kino Classics, 2011), DVD.

130 **"require[ing] all colored people":** Brief for Plaintiff in Error at 29, Plessy v. Ferguson, 163 U.S. 537 (1896).

130 **"parade of horribles" that might result:** James W. Fox Jr., "Doctrinal Myths and the Management of Cognitive Dissonance: Race, Law, and the Supreme Court's Doctrinal Support of Jim Crow," *Stetson Law Review* 34, no. 2 (2005): 328.

130 **The court's majority brushed off:** Plessy, 163 U.S. at 550.

130 **sidewalks have always been contested:** See Anastasia Loukaitou-Sideris and Renia Ehrenfeucht, *Sidewalks: Conflict and Negotiation over Public Space* (MIT Press, 2009), 85.

130 **"The suggestion that social equality":** Plessy, 163 U.S. at 559 (Harlan, J., dissenting).

130 **During slavery, Black city residents:** See Loukaitou-Sideris and Ehrenfeucht, *Sidewalks*; Benjamin Houston, *The Nashville Way: Racial Etiquette and the Struggle for Social Justice in a Southern City* (University of Georgia Press, 2012); Richard C. Wade, *Slavery in the Cities: The South 1820–1860* (Oxford University Press, 1967).

131 **laws regulating Black urban residents':** Wade, *Slavery in the Cities*, 109.

131 **"a negro meeting or overtaking":** Richmond, Virginia, Ordinances, December 22, 1857, cited in Wade, *Slavery in the Cities*, 108.

131 **Any violation was punishable by whipping:** Wade, *Slavery in the Cities*, 107–9.

131 **relatively more freedom walking:** Loukaitou-Sideris and Ehrenfeucht, *Sidewalks*, 87–89.

131 **"the white man's right of way":** Bertram Wilbur Doyle, *The Etiquette of Race Relations in the South: A Study in Social Control* (University of Chicago Press, 1937), 168.

132 **"I can remember very close in my mind":** Charles Gratton, "Get Off the Sidewalk," *Remembering Jim Crow, American RadioWorks* (November 2001).

132 **"the appropriation of public space":** Jane Dailey, "Deference and Violence in the Postbellum Urban South: Manners and Massacres in Danville, Virginia," *Journal of Southern History* 63, no. 3 (August 1997): 558.

132 **The riot took place against a backdrop:** Charles Chilton Pearson, *The Readjuster Movement in Virginia* (Yale University Press, 1917); Brent Tartar, "The Readjuster Party," *Encyclopedia Virginia*, last modified September 22, 2023; Franklin Hughes, "William Mahone," Jim Crow Museum, Ferris State University, September 2017; see also Dailey, "Deference and Violence."

133 **"the injustice and humiliation":** Dailey, "Deference and Violence," 568–69.

133 **On November 3, 1883:** Dailey, "Deference and Violence," 575–76.

133 **Later that night:** Dailey, "Deference and Violence," 577–81.

134 **the legacy of Jim Crow:** See Angie Schmitt, *Right of Way: Race, Class, and the Silent Epidemic of Pedestrian Deaths in America* (Island Press, 2020), 4–29; David Zipper, "The High Cost of Bad Sidewalks," *Bloomberg*, June 16, 2020.

135 **Missing or neglected sidewalks:** Michael Pollack, "Sidewalk Government," *Michigan Law Review* 122: 7–9; Loukaito-Sideris and Ehrenfeucht, *Sidewalks*, 3–5.

135 **In many southern cities:** R. Devon Bise et al., "Sidewalks as Measures of Infrastructure Inequities," *Southeastern Geographer* 58, no. 1 (2018): 53.

135 **A group of scholars found:** Bise et al., "Sidewalks as Measures," 50.

135 **Trimble Bottom, a Black neighborhood in Nashville:** Rachel Martin, "Why Half of Nashville's Roads Still Don't Have Sidewalks," *Bloomberg*, January 6, 2017.

135 **Studies of sidewalks in New Orleans:** Kate Lowe, "Environmental Justice and Pedestrianism: Sidewalk Continuity, Race, and Poverty in New Orleans, Louisiana," *Transportation Research Record* 2598, no. 1 (January 1, 2016): 119.

136 **the federal government does little to oversee:** The Americans with Disabilities Act is one notable exception. Pollack, "Sidewalk Government," 22–24.

136 **socioeconomic disparities map directly:** Mozhgon Rajaee et al., "Socioeconomic and Racial Disparities of Sidewalk Quality in a Traditional Rust Belt City," *SSM—Population Health* (2021): 1–2; Pollack, "Sidewalk Government," 28.

136 **Dallas is one of many:** Dallas, Texas, City Code Sec. 43–63 (Repair of Defective Sidewalks or Driveways by Abutting Property Owners). Homeowners can turn to the city's Sidewalk Replacement Program to fix damage in a cost-sharing arrangement. The program is called the Sidewalk Replacement Program, and it is available to all single-family residences, including townhomes and condominiums. They split the approximately $2,000 cost 50/50. "Sidewalk Replacement Program," City of Dallas, accessed February 22, 2024.

136 **1,081 miles of broken and inadequate sidewalks:** *Dallas Sidewalk Master Plan: Final Report*, prepared by the City of Dallas Department of Public Works (2021), 7; Rod Scales, "Why Dallas Sidewalks Are in Such Bad Shape," *Dallas Morning News*, April 3, 2022.

137 **City of Memphis handed out citations:** Stacy Jacobson, "Who Pays to Repair Broken Memphis Sidewalks? You Do, City Says," WREG, September 26, 2022; Jacob Steimer, "Do You Live in One of Memphis' Blackest, Whitest or Most Segregated Neighborhoods? Read This Story to Find Out," *MLK50: Justice Through Journalism*, August 6, 2021.

137 **A related problem comes:** Laura Sandt, Tabitha Combs, and Jesse Cohn, *Pursuing Equity in Pedestrian and Bicycle Planning* (Pedestrian and Bicycle Information Center, March 2016), 8.

137 **over Boston's 1,600 miles:** Meghan E. Irons, "Sidewalks Tell of Two Bostons," *Boston Globe*, March 4, 2018.

137 **those living in poverty:** Schmitt, *Right of Way*, 35; Donna Glassbrenner, Gabrielle Herbert, Leah Reish, Caitlin Webb, and Tonja Lindsey, *Evaluating Disparities in Traffic Fatalities by Race, Ethnicity, and Income* (National Highway Traffic Safety Administration Report No. DOT HS 813 188, 2022).

137 **Black pedestrians' fatality rate:** Glassbrenner et al., *Evaluating Disparities*, 16; see also *An Analysis of Traffic Fatalities by Race and Ethnicity* (Governors Highway Safety Association, 2021), 13 (finding that Black pedestrians had a per capita fatality rate roughly 1.5 times that of white pedestrians between 2015 and 2019); Nathan J. Robinson, "The Silent Epidemic of Pedestrian Deaths in America," *Current Affairs*, May 9, 2022.

138 **American cities systematically deprioritized:** Schmitt, *Right of Way*, 28–29; Zipper, "High Cost of Bad Sidewalks."

138 **Such cities are concentrated in the American Southwest:** Ebony Venson, Abigail Grimminger, and Stephen Kenny, *Dangerous by Design 2022* (Smart Growth America, July 2022), 27, 30.

138 **rates of pedestrian injuries and deaths are on the rise:** *Pedestrian Traffic Fatalities by State: 2022 Preliminary Data* (Governors Highway Safety Administration, 2022), 3 (projecting that 7,508 pedestrians were killed in traffic crashes in 2022, the highest number in over forty years); Amanda Holpuch, "U.S. Pedestrian Deaths are at Highest Level in 41 Years," *New York Times*, June 27, 2023; Emily Badger, "Why Are So Many More Pedestrians Dying in the U.S.?" January 4, 2024, in *The Daily*, produced by Mooj Zadie and Clare Toeniskoetter, podcast; Emily Badger, Ben Blatt, and Josh Katz, "Why Are So Many American Pedestrians Dying at Night?" The Upshot (blog), *New York Times*, December 1, 2023; Ian Duncan, "Traffic Deaths Increased During the Pandemic. The Toll Fell More Heavily on Black Residents, Report Shows," *Washington Post*, June 22, 2021.

138 **drivers are less likely to slow down:** Courtney Coughenour et al., "Examining Racial Bias as a Potential Factor in Pedestrian Crashes," *Accident Analysis and Prevention* 98 (2017); Tara Goddard, Kimberly Barsamian Kahn, and Arlie Adkins, "Racial Bias in Driver Yielding Behavior at Crosswalks," *Transportation Research Part F: Traffic Psychology and Behaviour* 33 (August 2015).

139 **It does not even make:** Venson, Grimminger, and Kenny, *Dangerous by Design*, 27, 30.

139 **Its central street grid:** Douglas W. Rae, *City: Urbanism and Its End* (Yale University Press, 2003), 37.

139 **Greater New Haven was the deadliest:** Venson, Grimminger, and Kenny, *Dangerous by Design*, 26.

139 **local streets and collector roads:** *Citywide Active Transportation Plan*, prepared by Safe Routes for All New Haven (2022), 17.

139 **leaders mounted a campaign:** Lizabeth Cohen, *Saving America's Cities: Ed Logue and the Struggle to Renew Urban America in the Suburban Age* (Farrar, Straus and Giroux, 2019), 50.

139 **infamous "Oak Street Connector project":** Rae, *City*, 332–35; Mandi Isaacs Jackson, *Model City Blues: Urban Space and Organized Resistance in New Haven* (Temple University Press, 2010), 14–16.

139 **New Haven's urban renewal–era leaders:** Cohen, *Saving America's Cities*, 54; Rae, *City*, 223–30.

140 **"more than twice the sum":** Richard C. Lee, "Annual State of City Message to Board of Aldermen," February 4, 1957, Yale University Library, Manuscripts and Archives, City and Regional Planning Collection, Box 15, Folder 2, MS 1970.

140 **"a good system of streets":** Lee, "Annual State of City Message," 17.

140 **"I cannot impress too much":** Lee, "Annual State of City Message," 17.

141 **poorest per capita:** Rae, *City*, 254–59; Jackson, *Model City Blues*, 18–19; "Connecticut City Neighborhood Profiles," DataHaven, accessed February 23, 2024.

141 **Several of the city's biggest arterial roads:** *Whalley Avenue Corridor Study*, prepared by Parsons Brinckerhoff (South Central Regional Council of Governments, December 2010), 2–15; Laurie Roark, "Mixed Signals: The Future of Pedestrian Safety in New Haven," *Yale Herald*, February 7, 2020; Isaac Yu, "Where the Sidewalk Mends," *New Haven Independent*, May 14, 2021; Thomas Breen, "Whalley Walked in the Dark (and Some Light)," *New Haven Independent*, February 26, 2020; "City Seeks to Make Boulevard Safer," *New Haven Independent*, July 11, 2017.

141 **highest rates of pedestrian death:** Thomas Breen, "Fatalities Mount on Death Blvd.," *New Haven Independent*, January 6, 2021, https://www.newhavenindependent.org/article/ella_t_grasso_blvd; Mark Zaretsky, "New Haven's Most Accident-Prone Roads: UConn Data Shows the Hot Spots," *New Haven Register*, September 4, 2021.

142 **"In my perspective":** "Newhallville and Dixwell Neighborhood Community Index," DataHaven (August 2019), 43.

142 **After eleven-year-old resident Gabrielle Lee:** "Gabrielle Lee Buried," *New Haven Independent*, June 16, 2008; Roark, "Mixed Signals."

142 **The city has responded:** *City of New Haven Complete Streets Design Manual* (City of New Haven, 2010); *Citywide Active Transportation Plan*, 26.

142 **explicit reversals of the policies:** Emily DiSalvo, "How New Haven's Urban Renewal in the 1960s Continues to Influence the City," *Shorthand*.

143 **"giv[ing] tickets for jaywalking":** Laurie Roark, "Mixed Signals."

143 **the city's police department has failed:** Paul Bass, "Crash into a Kid? Still No Crime," *New Haven Independent*, August 24, 2018.

143 **The Infrastructure Investment and Jobs Act of 2021:** Sadie Bograd, "New Haven Gets Rolling on Pedestrian, Cycling and Transit Infrastructure," *Yale Daily News*, September 8, 2022; Jim Tankersley and Zolan Kanno-Youngs, "Biden Seeks to Use Infrastructure Plan to Address Racial Inequities," *New York Times*, April 1, 2021.

143 **the web of laws and regulations:** Hanna Love and Jennifer S. Vey, "To Build Safe Streets, We Need to Address Racism in Urban Design," *Brookings Institution*, August 28, 2019.

144 **"Walking while black":** Topher Sanders, Kate Rabinowitz, and Benjamin Conarck, "Walking While Black," *ProPublica*, November 16, 2017.

144 **Michael Brown and a friend were walking:** *Report Regarding the Criminal Investigation into the Shooting Death of Michael Brown by Ferguson, Missouri, Police Officer Darren Wilson* (US Department of Justice, March 4, 2015), 5–8 (hereafter cited as *Brown Report*).

144 **many roads either lack sidewalks:** Aubrey Byron, "In Much of Ferguson, Walking in the Street Remains the Only Option," *Strong Towns*, February 20, 2018.

145 **One of the main thoroughfares in Ferguson:** Byron, "In Much of Ferguson, Walking."

145 **West Florissant is not an anomaly:** Byron, "In Much of Ferguson, Walking."

145 **walking in the street in Ferguson is illegal:** US Department of Justice, *Brown Report*, 6.

146 **Shreveport, Louisiana, has a similar law:** Tracy Clemons, "Woman Files Suit Against City and Shreveport Police Officer," KSLA News 12, December 6, 2010; Maya Lau, "Echoes of Ferguson Visible in Shreveport," *Shreveport Times*, August 24, 2014; Marjorie R. Esman, "When 'Walking' Becomes a Criminal Act," *Louisiana Weekly*, September 8, 2014.

146 **Kelly filed suit:** Clemons, "Woman Files Suit Against City"; Lau, "Echoes of Ferguson Visible in Shreveport"; Esman, "When 'Walking' Becomes a Criminal Act."

146 **In 2015, fifty-eight-year old Cedrick Murphy:** "Cedrick Murphy Talks About Getting a Ticket for Riding His Wheelchair on the Street," *Shreveport Times*, April 25, 2015.

146 **Shreveport police have deployed the sidewalk law:** Lau, "Echoes of Ferguson."

147 **Enforcing laws against jaywalking:** James Q. Wilson and George L. Kelling, "Broken Windows," *Atlantic*, March 1982; Kit R. Roane, "Police Balk at Crackdown on Jaywalkers by Giuliani," *New York Times*, February 8, 1998; Danica Ceballos, "Is Jaywalking the New Stop-and-Frisk? De Blasio Pulls a Page from Giuliani's Playbook," *Observer*, January 20, 2014.

147 **90 percent of jaywalking tickets:** Gersh Kuntzman, "'Jaywalking While Black': Final 2019 Numbers Show Race-Based NYPD Crackdown Continues," *Streetsblog NYC*, January 27, 2020.

147 **Black people received 55 percent of jaywalking:** Sanders, Rabinowitz, and Conarck, "Walking While Black."

148 **89 percent of jaywalking arrestees:** Rebecca J. Rosen, "In Champaign-Urbana, Illinois, 89% of Those Arrested for Jaywalking Are Black," *Atlantic*, August 24, 2012.

148 **Black residents received 26 percent:** Gene Balk, "Seattle Police Writing Fewer Jaywalking Tickets, but High Rate Still Issued to Black Pedestrians," *Seattle Times*, July 20, 2017.

148 **Black residents of San Diego:** "Freedom to Walk Campaign," CalBike.

148 **over 25 percent of jaywalking tickets:** Lena Howland, "'Freedom to Walk': Why One California Lawmaker Wants to Decriminalize Jaywalking," ABC 10, March 6, 2021.

148 **median household income:** US Census Bureau, American Community Survey, 2022 American Community Survey 5-Year Estimates, table no. S1901; Gloria Guzman and Melissa Kollar, *U.S. Census Bureau, Income in the United States: 2022*, Report No. P60–279 (US Census Bureau, September 12, 2023), 1; Kirby G. Posey, *Household Income in States and Metropolitan Areas: 2022*, Report No. ACSBR-017 (US Census Bureau, December 2023), 3.

149 **home to 148,654 residents:** US Census Bureau, 2020 Decennial Census, table no. P1.

149 **Shel Silverstein described:** Shel Silverstein, "Where the Sidewalk Ends," in *Where the Sidewalk Ends* (Harper & Row, 1974).

149 **American suburbs:** Jose Perez, "Why Do Some Neighborhoods Have No Sidewalks?," *House Notebook*, February 28, 2021; Benjamin Ross, *Dead End: Suburban Sprawl and the Rebirth of American Urbanism* (Oxford University Press, 2014), 16.

150 **suburbs continue to this day to resist:** Eleanor Cummins, "The Surprising Politics of Sidewalks," *Popular Science*, April 10, 2018, https://www.popsci.com/politics-versus-sidewalks; Scott McFetridge, "Sidewalks Become a Battlefield for Some Suburbs," *Detroit News*, November 20, 2016.

150 **Loewen calls "defended neighborhoods":** James W. Loewen, *Sundown Towns: A Hidden Dimension of American Racism* (New Press, 2005), 254–55.

150 **Others are actively resisting:** Schmitt, *Right of Way*, 10, 25–26.

Chapter 7: The Limited Reach of Traditional Legal Tools

152 **Nashville, Tennessee:** The discussion of the construction of Interstate 40 through Nashville, Tennessee, draws in large part from the opinions and documents in the underlying litigation and Bobby L. Lovett, *The Civil Rights Movement in Tennessee: A Narrative History* (University of Tennessee Press, 2005); Mohl, "Citizen Activism," 870; Campbell Haynes, "One Mile North," *Belmont Law Review* 8, no. 1 (2020), 1; Houston, *The Nashville Way*, 205–6. Throughout this chapter, I also draw from my own research and work in Archer, "'White Men's Roads.'"

152 **filed a lawsuit against Tennessee:** Nashville I-40 Steering Comm. v. Ellington, 387 F2d 179, 184 (6th Cir. 1967).

152 **The challenged portion of the highway:** Lovett, *The Civil Rights Movement in Tennessee*, 122.

153 **"the result of detailed study":** Gilmore D. Clarke and Michael Rapuano, Report on the Inter-State Controlled-Access Highway System, Davidson County, Tennessee (September 30, 1955) (on file with Metropolitan Nashville Planning Commission), 1.

153 **were not happy with the outcome:** Hubert James Ford, "Interstate 40 Through North Nashville, Tennessee: A Case Study in Highway Location Decision Making" (unpublished master's thesis, University of Tennessee, 1970), 34–36.

153 **"the routing through the black community":** Ford, "Interstate 40 Through North Nashville," 43.

153 **"aim[ing]" the interstate system:** Houston, *The Nashville Way*, 205–6.

153 **When the Federal-Aid Highway Act:** Houston, *The Nashville Way*, 205–6.

154 **The required hearing for I-40:** Mohl, "Citizen Activism," 882; Haynes, "One Mile North," 22.

154 **"we can't give out":** Charles A. Zuzak et al., *Beyond the Ballot: Citizen Participation in Metropolitan Nashville* (University of Tennessee Press, 1971), 30–31.

155 **"the wisdom and not the legality":** Nashville I-40 Steering Committee, 387 F.2d at 181.

155 **although he agreed:** Petition for Writ of Certiorari at 13–14, Nashville I-40 Steering Committee v. Ellington, 390 U.S. 921 (1968) (No. 995).

156 **Steering Committee appealed:** Nashville I-40 Steering Committee, 387 F.2d at 183.

156 **the appeals court found that:** Nashville I-40 Steering Committee, 387 F.2d at 183.

157 **"I certify that":** Nashville I-40 Steering Committee, 387 F.2d at 185.

157 **"it would be virtually impossible":** Nashville I-40 Steering Committee, 387 F.2d at 185.

158 **"wretched, inhumane, illogical":** Houston, *The Nashville Way*, 188.

159 **"Once you sink that first stake":** Caro, *The Power Broker*, 850.

159 **The case of *Washington v. Davis*:** Washington v. Davis: 426 U.S. 229 (1976).

161 **The plaintiffs argued:** Davis v. Washington, 348 F. Supp. 15, 16 (D.D.C. 1972), rev'd, 512 F.2d 956 (D.C. Cir. 1975), rev'd, 469 U.S. 229 (1976).

164 **Title VI states:** 42 U.S.C. § 2000d.

165 **"most powerful civil rights statute":** Olatunde C. A. Johnson, "Lawyering That Has No Name: Title VI and the Meaning of Private Enforcement," *Stanford Law Review* 66, no. 6 (2014): 1294.

165 **"the sleeping giant":** Johnson, "Lawyering That Has No Name," 1294.

165 **courts have limited:** Regents of the Univ. of Cal. v. Bakke, 438 U.S. 265, 283–85, 287 (1978).

165 **The Supreme Court has ruled:** Alexander v. Sandoval, 532 U.S. 275, 293 (2001).

165 **Another case from Ohio:** Coal. of Concerned Citizens Against I-670 v. Damian, 608 F. Supp. 110 (S.D. Ohio 1984).

166 **"There is no dispute that":** Coal. of Concerned Citizens Against I-670 v. Damian.

166 **"defendants are not per se":** Coal. of Concerned Citizens Against I-670 v. Damian, 127.

166 **"it is true that all of the *reasonable*":** Coal. of Concerned Citizens Against I-670 v. Damian, 127.

166 **"freeway revolts":** Mohl, "Stop the Road."

167 **They were also successful in:** Biles, Mohl, and Rose, "Revisiting the Urban Interstates," 828.

167 **After over a decade of fighting back:** See Mohl, "Citizen Activism," 878. Only in 1981 did the Tennessee DOT "throw in the towel" and request that planned expressway funding—about $300 million—be transferred to other transportation needs in Memphis. Citizens to Preserve Overton Park v. Volpe became a landmark case in environmental and administrative law, setting important precedents still applied decades later.

167 **received federal aid:** See Federal-Aid Highway Act of 1962, Pub. L. No. 87–866, 76 Stat. 1145 (1962) (current version at 23 U.S.C. § 18 (2018)) (requiring states and localities to work together in developing a cooperative, comprehensive, and continuing urban transportation planning process).

167 **parks, historic districts:** See Federal-Aid Highway Act of 1966, Pub. L. No. 89–574, 72 Stat. 891 (1966) ("The Secretary shall use maximum effort to preserve Federal, State, and local government parklands and historic sites and the beauty and historic value of such lands and sites."); National Historic Preservation Act of 1966, Pub. L. No. 89–665, 80 Stat. 915 (1966) (establishing federal councils to help agencies act as stewards of natural resources).

167 **secure new housing:** See Federal-Aid Highway Act of 1962, Pub. L. No 87–866, 76 Stat. 1145 (1962) (requiring assurances from state highway departments of relocation of families displaced by clearance of rights of way for Federal-aid highways); Federal-Aid Highway Act of 1968, Pub.

L. No. 90–495, 82 Stat. 815 (1968) (requiring relocation payments and advisory assistance be provided to people, businesses, farmers, and nonprofit organizations displaced by Federal highway programs); Uniform Relocation Assistance and Land Acquisition Policies Act of 1970, Pub. L. No. 91–646, 84 Stat. 1894 (1970) (providing "for uniform and equitable treatment of persons displaced from their homes, businesses, or farms by Federal and federally assisted programs"). In addition, beginning in 1966, the newly formed US Department of Transportation—which itself was formed to help curb some of the destructive practices—issued rules and procedures designed to stop many of the worst practices of state highway departments.

167   **"It is time that Congress":** Mohl, "The Interstates and the Cities," 198.

167   **"federally assisted highways":** Mohl, "The Interstates and the Cities," 198.

169   **National Environmental Policy Act of 1969:** National Environmental Policy Act of 1969, 42 U.S.C. §§ 4321–4370h (2012).

169   **NEPA, sometimes referred to:** See Evan J. Ringquist and David H. Clark, "Local Risks, States' Rights, and Federal Mandates: Remedying Environmental Inequities in the U.S. Federal System," *Publius* 29, no. 2 (1999): 87–89 (discussing the reach of NEPA). A small sampling of actions covered under NEPA includes relocating military bases, building highways, preserving historic infrastructure, logging, erecting affordable housing units, and granting operating licenses to energy facilities. See *NEPA Success Stories: Celebrating 40 Years of Transparency and Open Government* (Environmental Law Institute, 2010), 9, 16, 25, 28. Twenty states have passed their own versions of NEPA, establishing environmental review processes for state government action. "States and Local Jurisdictions with NEPA-like Environmental Planning Requirements," Council on Environmental Quality, Executive Office of the President, accessed February 23, 2023.

169   **At the heart of the NEPA:** 42 U.S.C. § 4332(C) and § 4332(C)(iii). The NEPA regulations specify that an agency preparing an EIS must "rigorously explore and objectively evaluate all reasonable alternatives, and for alternatives which were eliminated from detailed study, briefly discuss the reasons for them having been eliminated." 40 C.F.R. § 1502.14(a).

169   **Congress's goal in requiring EISs:** Robertson v. Methow Valley Citizens Council, 490 U.S. 332, 349 (1989).

170   **"ecological, . . . aesthetic, historic":** 40 C.F.R. § 1508.8.

170   **"when an environmental impact":** 40 C.F.R. § 1508.14.

170   **"explicit consideration of":** *Guidance on Environmental Justice and NEPA* (Federal Highway Administration, US Department of Transportation, 2011).

170   **a federal district court decided the case:** 944 F. Supp. 2d 656 (W.D. Mich. 2013).

170   **"NEPA merely prohibits uninformed":** Methow Valley Citizens Council, 490 U.S. at 351.

171   **"the most successful environmental law":** Oliver A. Houck, "'Is That All?' A Review of *The National Environmental Policy Act: An Agenda for the Future*, by Lynton Keith Caldwell," *Duke Environmental Law and Policy Forum* 11, no. 1 (2000): 173.

171   **the Second Circuit determined:** Karlen v. Harris, 590 F.2d 39, 42–44 (2d Cir. 1978).

172   **"once an agency has":** Strycker's Bay Neighborhood Council v. Karlen, 444 U.S. 223 (1980).

172   **limit the racial justice impact of the Constitution:** For an excellent example, read Erwin Chemerinsky, *The Conservative Assault on the Constitution* (Simon & Schuster, 2011).

Chapter 8: The Goal Is Justice

176   **On a recent trip to Indianapolis, Indiana:** The passages on Indianapolis, Indiana, in this chapter draw on conversations I have had with residents and advocates in Indianapolis, including Indianapolis community organizer Paula Brooks; residents Taylor Hughes, Thomas Ridley, Miz Pete, Kathi Ridley-Merriweather, and Jennifer Baskerville-Burrows; Professors Susan Hyatt, Paul Mullins, and Jordan Ryan; leaders of the Rethink Coalition, including Brenda Hacker Freije and Charlie Richardson; A'Lelia Bundles, the great-great-granddaughter of Madam C. J. Walker; and Justin Garrett Moore. Throughout this chapter, I also draw from my own research and work in Archer, "'White Men's Roads.'"

177 **press release celebrating:** *Fact Sheet: The Bipartisan Infrastructure Deal* (The White House, 2021).

178 **1,300 homes and businesses:** Title VI Complaint, Air Alliance Houston et al. v. TxDOT (US Department of Transportation, Federal Highway Administration, 2021).

178 **"evaluat[e] reasonable opportunities":** Voluntary Resolution Agreement for the North Houston Highway Improvement Project (US Department of Transportation, Federal Highway Administration, March 3, 2023).

179 **"Shiloh today is just washing away":** Jared Kofsky, Maia Rosenfeld, and Steve Osunsami, "Black Alabamans Say Highway Project Caused Major Flooding, Threatening Their Community," ABC News, October 31, 2023.

180 **late historian Manning Marable:** Manning Marable, *How Capitalism Underdeveloped Black America*, 2 (italics added).

182 **A prime example is the "Preference Policy":** *Evaluating the N/NE Preference Policy*, prepared by Amie Thurber, Lisa Bates, and Susan Halverson (Portland State University, 2021), 2.

182 **The Preference Policy was born of protest:** *Evaluating the N/NE Preference Policy*, 2.

182 **the Policy "is an effort":** "Frequently Asked Questions, Preference Policy," City of Portland.

182 **focusing on "marginalized communities":** Andrew Theen, "Gentrification: Can Portland Give Displaced Residents a Path Back?" *Oregonian*, December 23, 2015.

183 **These addresses include:** *Evaluating the N/NE Preference Policy*, 3.

183 **Others expressed economic stress:** *Evaluating the N/NE Preference Policy*, 13–14.

183 **"The history of this neighborhood matters to me":** *Evaluating the N/NE Preference Policy*, 2, 7–9.

185 **how abolitionist lawyers used:** Daniel Farbman, Resistance Lawyering, 107 Calif. L. Rev. 1877 (2019).

185 **Until the Supreme Court hobbled:** Shelby County v. Holder: Although the Supreme Court did not strike down Section 5 of the Voting Rights Act, it did invalidate the coverage formula under Section 4b, leaving no jurisdictions subject to the preclearance requirement.

187 **These studies would force us to grapple:** See Archer, "'White Men's Roads,'" 1259; R. A. Lenhardt, "Race Audits," *Hastings Law Journal* 62, no. 6 (2011): 1527; Regional Hearing, New York, Before the United States Sentencing Commission (July 10, 2009) (statement of Rachel E. Barkow), 28.

188 **Iowa became the first state:** Iowa Code Ann. § 2.56 (2019).

188 **several states, including Connecticut:** Conn. Gen. Stat. § 2–24b (2018); Madeleine O'Neill, "Maryland Will Add Racial Impact Assessments to Key Pieces of Legislation," *USA Today*, February 1, 2021; N.J. Rev. Stat. § 2C:48B-2 (2017); Or. Rev. Stat. § 137.683 (2019); Va. Code Ann. § 30–19.1:13 (2021).

189 **REISs must do more:** See Archer, "'White Men's Roads,'" 1259; K. Sabeel Rahman and Jocelyn Simonson, "The Institutional Design of Community Control," *California Law Review* 108, no. 3 (2020): 104–5.

190 **displaced more than 17,000 residents:** *Total Value Report*, prepared by Arup for the Indianapolis Chamber of Commerce (ReThink Coalition, 2021).

191 **Rethink released a design study:** "Who We Are," ReThink Coalition, accessed February 23, 2024, https://www.rethink65-70.org/who-we-are.

192 **"more than just roads; it's a pathway":** "Help Us Propel Indy Forward," Propel Indy, accessed February 23, 2024, https://propelindy.com.

Photo Credits

Index